D1367104

THE
IMPERILED
ACADEMY

THE
IMPERILED
ACADEMY

EDITED BY HOWARD DICKMAN

Transaction Publishers
New Brunswick (USA) and London (UK)

Published by the Social Philosophy and Policy Center and by Transaction Publishers 1993

Library of Congress Cataloging-in-Publication Data

The imperiled academy / edited by Howard Dickman
        p.   cm. — (Studies in social philosophy & policy : no. 17)
    Includes bibliographical references and index.
    ISBN 1-56000-097-X (cloth) — ISBN 1-56000-675-7 (pbk.)
    1. Education, Higher—United States—Philosophy. 2. Education, Higher—Political aspects—United States. 3. Intercultural education—United States. 4. Education, Humanistic—United States. 5. Academic freedom—United States. 6. Political correctness—United States.
    I. Dickman, Howard. II. Series.

LA227.4.I48   1993
378.73—dc20   92-41461
                                                  CIP

Cover Design: Kent Lytle

Contents

Introduction

Howard Dickman

The decade of the 1960s was a tumultuous one for university campuses across the country. Much public scrutiny attended such dramatic events as building takeovers, bombings of ROTC buildings, and anti–Vietnam War protests. By the mid-1970s, however, the turmoil subsided, and amidst the seeming calm the media spotlight receded. Universities went about their business in the 1980s relatively immune from public scrutiny. With the dawning of the 1990s all this was to change. Major media outlets, including the *New York Times* and *Time,* suddenly discovered that disturbing trends were once again roiling the universities. With remarkable alacrity, media throughout the land took up the refrain of "political correctness" and began writing a plethora of articles on this new variant of intolerance and ideological orthodoxy sweeping the universities. From controversies over revamping the curriculum in the name of "multiculturalism" and "diversity," to affirmative action in student admissions and faculty appointments, to speech codes restricting freedom of expression and intellectual inquiry, universities have once again become political battlegrounds. Belatedly, the larger community beyond the ivory tower has come to realize that the campus movements spawned in the 1960s never really abated, but merely festered and gained strength during the years of apparent quiescence.

The essays in this volume analyze the cultural and intellectual disputes concerning relativism, multiculturalism, and radical feminism, which have attracted so much recent public concern. While many academics have argued that such concern is the deplorable result of misinformation disseminated by nonacademics concerning these controversies, the authors of these essays are exceptions to that characterization. Their dissent is made from within the academy and is informed by their experiences within it.

Those who remain "politically incorrect" represent a beleaguered minority on university faculties, and those with the courage to speak out in defense of the liberal values that the academy once enshrined are a mere handful. It is to these voices that we now turn, the voices of nine scholars who defend a vision of the liberal academy—the academy of political toleration, unbiased scholarship, unrestricted freedom of speech, and reward based on merit—as a way of salvaging our institutions of higher learning.

In the opening essay of this volume, "Leviathan U.," Daniel Bonevac explores an apparent tension between two recent trends at American universities: multiculturalism and political correctness. He notes that these trends ought to be mutually opposed; one seeks to promote pluralism and diversity, the other to limit the expression of views deemed insensitive or inappropriate. Yet the advocates of multiculturalism are commonly the very people who wish to enforce politically correct codes of speech and conduct, and who have enjoyed some measure of success. Bonevac contends that their success is the product of a "bait-and-switch" operation, in which an illiberal and highly political agenda hides behind appealing pluralistic rhetoric. A group of insurgent professors with a radical egalitarian ideology, he says, have found fertile ground for their ideas on American campuses, especially in departments that lack a unified goal. In the course of his essay, Bonevac examines several models for understanding multiculturalism. The most promising, he argues, is a mercantilist or protectionist model which treats multiculturalism, and its accompanying doctrine of political correctness, as ways of shielding radicals and their ideas from evaluation, criticism, and competition. Those opposed to such protectionism, Bonevac concludes, should expose the "bait-and-switch" tactics of the radicals and refuse to let them set the university's goals.

"Tradition and Change: The University Under Stress," Stanley Rothman's contribution to this collection, is an attempt to understand recent developments in American universities by relating changes in higher education to changes in the role of intellectuals and, more broadly, to changes in the character of Western culture. In order to achieve historical perspective, Rothman takes what he calls "a long step back": he traces the development of higher education from the earliest European universities, founded in the twelfth century, to the modern universities of Europe and America. The portrait he sketches is one of increasing inclusiveness, as universities originally designed for the education of a privileged nobility were gradually opened to members of the middle and lower classes. A key point in Rothman's overview is his observation that universities have had a long history of turning out classically educated students who lacked skills or preparation for pursuing careers—students who made ideal converts to radical political or ideological causes. In nineteenth-century America, dominated by a liberal capitalist ideology, there were few causes to be joined, little influence to be exercised. The attitude toward intellectuals was one of ambivalence: impractical academics were often afforded little respect, while scientific experts—who offered technological innovations in agriculture and industry—were held in high esteem. The breakthrough for academic intellectuals came, Rothman notes, during the New Deal, when they began to exercise an important influence on policy decisions, and accelerated during the 1960s and early 1970s, amid the political upheavals over civil rights and the war in Vietnam. Disaffected university students and faculty had found their cause and were able to seize the opportunity to change their institutions and society at large. Rothman traces their efforts, from the 1960s to the present, to remedy perceived injustices by reforming university curricula and admissions practices, instituting ethnic and women's studies programs, and imposing codes to restrict offensive speech.

Like Rothman, Seymour Martin Lipset is concerned to understand the origins of current trends in the academic world. In "The Sources of Political Correctness on American Campuses," he points out that political correctness is not a new phenomenon—that in America's early church-affiliated schools, professors were hired and fired on the basis of their adherence to official doctrines. Lipset views recent events as expressions of the same kind of moralism, involving a belief in the perfectibility of humanity, in the obligation to avoid sin, and in the righteousness of moral crusades. In our century, the academic world has leaned toward the left, yet Lipset finds some statistical evidence that changes in the leanings of faculty and students tend to run in cycles. Thus, while the anti-war and civil-rights struggles of the 1960s and early 1970s radicalized campuses, faculty and students became somewhat less liberal in the late 1970s and early 1980s—until, in the late 1980s, the trend reversed itself again. In the future, as those who were students in the late 70s and early 80s establish themselves more firmly in the academic world, we are likely to see yet another shift. Lipset also looks at evidence that radicals have been most numerous among professors in the humanities and qualitative social sciences, and explores how they have joined forces with activist minorities among students in seeking to delegitimize and marginalize conservatives (and even moderates) as politically incorrect.

Eric Mack's contribution to this volume examines the theoretical foundations of the multiculturalist and political-correctness movements. In "The Limits of Diversity: The New Counter-Enlightenment and Isaiah Berlin's Liberal Pluralism," Mack draws parallels between the view of diversity held by today's multiculturalists and pluralists, and the views of historian of ideas Isaiah Berlin. The modern doctrine of diversity, Mack contends, involves the rejection of the belief in objective facts and values, and of universally binding epistemological and moral norms. It proposes that different cultures and different ways of thinking and evaluating are incommensurable, and that rational dialogue among representatives of different cultures is impossible. The virtue of Berlin, Mack argues, is that he recognizes the limits and dangers of such a radical view. Berlin seeks to find a way of rejecting monism—the belief, which he sees lying at the heart of the Western tradition, that there is one true end or value which all people and cultures ought to serve. Yet he seeks to reject it without embracing a radical version of diversity that has untenable logical implications. Mack places Berlin's views in the context of the intellectual conflict between the French Enlightenment of the eighteenth century, a movement which embraced monism, and the (predominantly German) Counter-Enlightenment of the eighteenth and early nineteenth centuries, a movement which rejected monism and embraced diversity. Mack explores Berlin's position on the dangers of the Counter-Enlightenment view of diversity: the political dangers of authoritarianism and aggressive nationalism, and the intellectual dangers of relativism and nihilism. He concludes with a look at Berlin's recent efforts to reappropriate central themes of the monist tradition in order to strengthen the underpinnings of liberalism and tolerance.

The next two essays of this collection turn from the multiculturalists' theories to focus on some of the specific practices they advocate. Lino A. Graglia's "Racial Preferences in Admission to Institutions of Higher Education" looks at the question of affirmative action. Since the late 1960s, Graglia notes, law and public policy have moved from prohibiting to requiring racial discrimination: "affirmative action" is a euphemism for the use of racial preferences in making decisions about employment in and admissions to institutions of higher education. He contends that the central intractable fact that has given rise to demands for affirmative action in higher education is that blacks as a group perform much less well than whites as a group on tests of academic aptitude and achievement. The admission of blacks to selective educational institutions requires, therefore, that ordinary admissions standards be altered or discarded. As a result, he says, the implementation of affirmative-action

programs has been characterized by denial and a lack of candor. ?
over, the admission of significantly underqualified students based on
their race is a prescription for frustration, resentment, and racial animosity. It is the primary cause of increased racial tensions on campuses
and the source of demands for black studies programs, multiculturalism,
and "hate speech" codes. Graglia considers the standard justifications
for affirmative action—that it is required as compensation for unfair
disadvantage or as a means of increasing student-body diversity—and
finds them wanting. He challenges the compensation rationale's insistence that whites are opposed to black progress, and the diversity
rationale's insistence that there are fundamental differences between
blacks and whites. Neither contention is supportable, he concludes, and
both undermine efforts to achieve racial equality and racial harmony.

While Graglia focuses on affirmative-action policies, he notes that
they lead to demands for the institution of codes regulating offensive
speech. In "Bad Faith: The Politicization of the University *In Loco
Parentis,*" Alan Charles Kors undertakes a critique of such codes, and of
the anti-harassment policies and programs of "diversity education" that
often accompany them. The policies are part of a politicization of
American universities that goes beyond transformation of the curriculum to affect many other aspects of life on campus. A revolution of the
past few years, Kors contends, has created a vast array of ideologically
partisan and often coercive agencies, codes, and programs that have
transformed student life. The generation of the 1960s once tore down
the role of the university *in loco parentis* (standing in the place of
parents) in order to achieve its own freedoms. Kors argues that now, in
a remarkable act of bad faith, the same generation has reconstructed and
enlarged that role, in order to impose its own political agenda upon
undergraduates. A similar attempt by conservative or religious groups to
impose *their* values on students would be greeted with outrage, yet under
the guise of diversity and sensitivity the multiculturalists have managed
to achieve some notable successes. In light of this, Kors maintains that
those who favor a critical education should view with alarm the rise of
partisan indoctrination through codes and programs initiated by campus
offices of student life.

"Liberal Intolerance," Joseph Hamburger's essay, is an attempt to
understand the theory that lies behind efforts to set boundaries on
acceptable speech on campus and to shape university curricula. In view
of liberalism's history of opposition to intolerance, Hamburger finds it
ironic that liberals in academia today are often in favor of formal and
informal sanctions against those expressing views that deviate from what
is deemed acceptable. He suggests that the "persecutory spirit" on

modern campuses derives from the liberals' conviction that the elimination of inequalities based on race, class, and sex is the most pressing problem facing our society, and that the urgency of the problem warrants the use of powerful institutions (like the university) to solve it. Moreover, Hamburger argues that liberal theory is not as unequivocally opposed to intolerance as is usually thought. To illustrate his point, he examines John Stuart Mill's classic defense of tolerance in *On Liberty*, which underpinned the liberals' view of toleration for over a century. He finds within it support for a certain kind of intolerance, an intolerance to be backed not by legal sanctions but by the force of condemnation in public opinion. What Mill envisioned, Hamburger contends, was not merely relying on the force of public opinion to maintain an atmosphere of civility conducive to open debate; rather, he intended to bring that force to bear against dispositions and character traits that were deemed moral flaws, even when they issued in no harmful action. Hamburger suggests a parallel between Mill's advocacy of these kinds of sanctions, and the atmosphere that prevails on campuses today: an atmosphere of formal and informal pressures that serve to stifle debate and to intimidate those who would challenge or reject orthodox views. In such an atmosphere, the university's mission of fostering open inquiry and discussion is endangered.

A concern with the proper role and mission of the university is also a central theme of Jerry L. Martin's contribution to this volume, "The University as Agent of Social Transformation: The Postmodern Argument Considered." Martin believes that a significant body of opinion in the academic world holds that the mission of higher education should be, not the pursuit of "objective" truth, but the fundamental transformation of society. He contrasts this transformationist view with the less radical view of traditional reformers who wanted to use knowledge, especially from the social sciences, to aid social progress. This traditional project, he notes, was based on the search for truth and, hence, in principle, was open to intellectual debate. The transformationist view, in contrast, is based on the postmodern idea that objective truth is an illusion fostered by the dominant classes. It maintains that all ideas are merely perspectives which represent the interests of the groups (defined primarily by race, class, and gender) that hold them, and that they are used by dominant groups to exercise power over marginalized ones. Since it is wrong for some groups to dominate others, the transformationist view holds that the university should be changed so that what is taught advances the interests of those who have been marginalized. Since this goal is more valid than the pursuit of an illusory truth, it justifies the practices of restricting speech and basing academic decisions on political standards. Martin contends that the transformationist arguments fail on several grounds: he claims that their use of the metaphor of ideas as perspectives actually supports an objectivist account of knowledge rather than a relativist one; that their arguments about the relation of interests to group identity rest on equivocation and inadequate definition and are not empirically confirmed; and that their position fails to take account of ways in which values such as freedom and equality may conflict. He concludes that the transformationist view fails, on both ethical and epistemological grounds, to make its own political commitments immune from criticism.

The final essay, " 'The Enemy Is Us': Objectivity and Its Philosophical Detractors" by Fred Sommers, echoes Martin's concern that the idea of objective truth is under attack in today's academic world. Sommers points out that one's view of the possibility of gaining objective knowledge determines one's view of what to teach and, more broadly, of the proper role of teachers and of universities. Many contemporary intellectuals seem unaware of the need to defend objectivity from its critics. Indeed, Sommers argues that reputable philosophers of the analytic school are unwittingly aiding in the assault: critics of objectivity are drawing on the work of analytic philosophers to support their arguments against a realist theory of truth. Sommers compares these critics to the ancient Greek Sophists, who challenged Plato's efforts to distinguish knowledge from opinion and reality from appearance, and he examines the arguments of modern "neosophists" who draw on the analytic school to mount a similar challenge. After rejecting the arguments of the neosophists, Sommers sketches a realist conception of truth that relies on the idea of "truth-making facts"—aspects of reality or existence that make true claims true. He argues that a correct account of the nature and role of facts, and of the relationship of facts to existence, has eluded analytic philosophers, and that their failure to discover such an account is what has led to their rejection of truth realism and, ultimately, to modern academics' assault on objectivity.

Leviathan U.

Daniel Bonevac

I want to offer some models for understanding two recent campus phenomena: multiculturalism and political correctness. These should be in opposition; one advocates pluralism and diversity, while the other tries to stamp them out. But, as everyone familiar with the issues knows, the terms are in that sense misleading. The multiculturalists have in many cases been precisely those who have enforced politically correct thought, speech, and behavior. How have these two movements come to be allied? And why have they been so successful?

Multiculturalism and various forms of repression, grouped together under the banner "political correctness," have been very successful indeed. A recent survey showed 54 percent of colleges and universities reporting newly enacted multiculturalism requirements. Hundreds of campuses have enacted speech codes, ranging from very narrowly focused bans on hate speech to broad assaults on insensitivity. A political-correctness hotline established in the fall of 1991 by the *American Spectator* received hundreds of complaints from students, faculty, and administrators who believed themselves to have suffered at the hands of the campus thought-police; the journal found seventeen complaints serious and well-documented enough to investigate for possible legal action.

American institutions of higher education are dedicated to the free exchange of ideas and have successfully resisted previous attempts to subjugate that freedom to politics. The world has, moreover, been witnessing, in Tiananmen Square, Eastern Europe, and the former Soviet Union, dramatic displays of the importance and power of freedom. All the more ironic, then, that repression should be not only surviving but blooming on American campuses today.

I. Multiculturalism

Multiculturalism began in Britain, spread to Canada, and then invaded the U.S.: first at Stanford, with the reshaping of Western Civilization into Cultures, Ideas, and Values; then at Michigan, in the form of a required course on American ethnic cultures; and now at a majority of American colleges and universities in some form or other.

Multiculturalism seems liberal in its goals. Many definitions of it make it sound innocuous and obviously desirable. At the University of Texas at Austin, for example, the Faculty Senate and University Council Committees on Multicultural Education defined multicultural education as "an approach to teaching and learning that acknowledges the need for people to exist interdependently in a culturally pluralistic world, and accordingly, seeks to foster understanding of the differences and similarities of diverse groups and various cultures in the United States and throughout the world." Who could oppose that?

The definition reflects a view of multiculturalism to be found in writings of many of the earliest British multiculturalists. It reflects, for example, the concern of the U.K. Department of Education and Science in a policy paper released fifteen years ago: "Our society is a multicultural, multiracial one and the curriculum should reflect a sympathetic understanding of the different cultures and races that now make up our society. . . ."[1] The department reaffirmed its conception in a 1981 report:

> [T]he curriculum in all schools should reflect the fact that Britain is both multiracial and culturally diverse. . . . [T]he intention of multicultural education is simply to provide all children with a balanced education which reflects the nature of our society. . . . [A]ll heads should be prepared to develop a multicultural approach toward the curriculum.[2]

Despite the last sentence's foreshadowing of the intolerance that has become political correctness, and the evaluative, even ideological flavor of the phrase "sympathetic understanding," there is no doubt that many multiculturalists have, from the beginning, been what Diane Ravitch has called *pluralistic*.[3] Pluralistic multiculturalists seek to enrich our common culture, to make it more inclusive and less parochial by incorporating elements of other cultures. In the words of one of the most influential pluralists, "to advocate multicultural education is not to deny the need for a common public culture, but only to argue that the common culture could be less rigid and biased."[4] Thus, multiculturalists argue that Hindi students, for example, should not be forced to eat beef at lunch, or that Muslim girls should not be forced to wear gym uniforms that they find embarrassing and immoral. Again, who could disagree?

If this were all there were to multiculturalism, it would be hard to explain how it could lead to thought control or inspire much controversy. From the beginning, however, there have been other strains of multiculturalism. Ravitch has contrasted pluralism with *particularism,* which rejects the notion of a common culture altogether. This has influenced Afrocentric school curricula developed and implemented in cities such as Pittsburgh and Washington. According to particularists, American society and culture do not, and should not, approximate a "melting pot" producing one culture out of many. In such a blend, they maintain, the bland, white majority and its culture overwhelm minorities and their cultures. Inevitably, minorities occupy subservient social positions; minority cultures play minor roles in the culture as a whole, if they manage to survive at all. Pluralists might respond that we should seek to change our recipe, preserving the melting-pot image, or that we should seek a smorgasbord, allowing each culture to preserve its own identity while allowing people to choose among the offerings of many cultures. Particularists, in contrast, see the smorgasbord idea as deceptive. The majority culture is bound to dominate the available offerings; it will be hard to find a place for minority cultures on the table. Moreover, people cannot transcend their own cultural bounds easily. Perhaps they cannot transcend them at all. In either case, the image of people happily picking tidbits from various cultural platters is a mirage. From the particularist perspective, education must recognize that students are culture-bound and teach them, not an oppressive or illusory common culture, but their own culture—as it is or as academicians reconstruct it.

In higher education, particularism became a significant force in the late 1960s. Majors in black studies, women's studies, and other ethnic-studies fields typically owe their existence to it. But particularism has little to do with the debate currently taking place on campus. Multiculturalists in colleges and universities have not been seeking to make various ethnic-studies programs more available, or to give students additional degree or course options. They have consistently sought to impose requirements on *all* students. Far from rejecting the idea of a common culture, they seek to impose one quite different from that currently reflected in the curriculum. The melting pot is competing, not with a smorgasbord or a series of ethnic restaurants, but with a stew of different composition. In part, the campus multiculturalists want to reshape the stew to emphasize minority cultures and downplay the majority culture. Their favored culture, like that of the pluralists, includes more works by minorities and from non-Western cultures. But it is organized for political ends. *Illiberal* multiculturalists, as I shall call them, seek to overthrow the cultural oppression they see as inherent in the melting-pot conception. They choose works to be included in the curriculum as means to this end. The end, it is worth stressing, is inevitably political: specifically, left-wing, egalitarian, and revolutionary. Consequently, the curriculum envisioned for all students is filled with left-wing, egalitarian, and revolutionary courses and texts. The illiberal curriculum reflects diversity without difference.

The illiberal strain has been reflected in the literature on multiculturalism for at least a decade. Various authors have explicitly called for the political reorientation of the curriculum. J. Katz wants multicultural education to "promote analytical and evaluative abilities to confront issues such as participatory democracy, racism, and sexism, and the parity of power; [and to] develop skills for values clarification including the study of the manifest and latent transmission of values. . . ."[5] R. Hatcher and J. Shallice argue that "the fight against racism is primarily a political one, which takes place in every region of social life, including on the terrain of education. The success of anti-racism in education will depend on how it is inserted into that wider political struggle."[6] They differentiate their brand of multiculturalism from pluralism, stressing that it "prioritises the demand for equality rather than integration or the recognition of cultural diversity." Illiberal multiculturalists attack pluralism, maintaining that "it must become more radical. Multicultural education must be politicized and made more power-sensitive. . . ."[7] At a recent conference, Wahneema Lubiano advocated "strong multiculturalism," which is not "about the liberal tolerance of difference, but about the contestation of differences"; Stanley Aronowitz spoke of multiculturalism as, not "a struggle for balance and fairness, but for democracy and anti-authoritarianism."[8]

Illiberal multiculturalism lies behind much of the campus activism that leads to course requirements, sensitivity training sessions, speech codes, and, ultimately, attacks on politically incorrect students and faculty. Its echoes were heard in the debate over the Stanford curriculum. Dinesh D'Souza quotes two Stanford activists: "We're not saying we need to study Tibetan philosophy. We're arguing that we need to understand what made our society what it is."[9] "Forget Confucius. We are trying to prepare ourselves for the multicultural challenge we will face in the future."[10] When one considers that Confucianism and Buddhism are central to the world-views of much of Asia's population, and that Asian Americans constitute the fastest-growing ethnic groups in the United States, one cannot help being amazed. The objective, plainly, is not inclusion or enrichment but political change.

II. The Insurgency Model

This leads to a way to understand multiculturalism and political correctness that I call the *insurgency* model. It dates at least from Roger Kimball's *Tenured Radicals*. According to this model, a sizable group of radicals is trying to take over American higher education. Students during the 1960s, they went on to academic careers and now occupy positions of power in colleges and universities, where they use their power to promote radical political goals.

Radical faculty and administrators see the curriculum primarily as a political weapon. Education transmits, not just information, but values and culture to the young. It passes culture from one generation to the next. Those who want to revolutionize culture sensibly look to education as the easiest route to accomplishing their goals. Changing the minds of those already acculturated is much harder than forming politically correct minds from the start.

From this perspective, multiculturalism emerges as a classic bait-and-switch operation. The insurgents are illiberal multiculturalists, seeking to redirect the curriculum to serve their political goals. Open advocacy of such redirection offers little hope even within the academy, since tenured radicals, although numerous, are outnumbered by liberals who remain committed to the political independence of the university. The insurgents thus masquerade as pluralists. They argue for pluralism—a goal highly congenial to liberals—while seeking, in practice, its elimination.

This explains the affinity of multiculturalism and political correctness. In its illiberal form, multiculturalism seeks to turn the campus into an education camp, where the young can be trained to see the world correctly by a curriculum containing large doses of propaganda. Those who do not take well to the training must be re-educated, punished, or exiled. Thus, we find purported advocates of an innocuous pluralism using totalitarian methods: scheduling faculty and students for "sensitivity training sessions"; using grades and salary increases to reward whoever hews to the party line and to punish whoever dissents; initiating hate campaigns; driving out or dismissing dissenters who dare to go public with their objections; and defending course requirements for students as really increasing their freedom. Like the uncooperative in Rousseau, the students must "be forced to be free."[11]

The insurgents parade under many banners; they are Marxists, neo-Marxists, new historicists, deconstructionists, critical theorists, feminists, and other progressives who espouse no overall, unified theory.

These divisions are not a sham. When the radicals attain power, they devote almost as much energy to squabbling among themselves as to seizing control of the academy. Nevertheless, the divisions should not be taken too seriously. There is a core around which the insurgents tend to rally.

The ideology is by now familiar. It is bipolar, dividing the world into two kinds of people and two kinds of cultures: oppressors and oppressed. Western culture, capitalism, and Western political systems require, produce, and enforce inequalities and are thereby responsible for most, if not all, oppression. Therefore, we need a radical transformation of the social, political, and economic order that will overthrow Western institutions.

This radically egalitarian ideology is powerful partly because it is simple. It can be cast in a form reminiscent of Buddhism's Four Noble Truths:

1. There is oppression.
2. Enforcing inequality leads to oppression.
3. One can stop oppression by preventing the enforcement of inequality.
4. One can prevent the enforcement of inequality by overthrowing Western institutions.

The term 'enforcing inequality' is mine, but I think it captures the central idea.[12] Inequality is inevitable, but, from the insurgents' perspective, unfortunate. Those with more—more talent, money, good looks, energy, or whatever—deserve no reward for this accident of nature; those with less are just as deserving.[13] Institutions enforce inequality when they reward the fortunate and penalize the unfortunate. The university, for example, enforces inequality by rewarding academic excellence. Capitalism enforces inequality both by allowing people to gather wealth—by exploiting the masses or selling their wage-labor, in the insurgents' terms, or by providing what other people want, in mine—and by allowing them to use that wealth. Western political systems enforce inequality by investing executive, legislative, and judicial institutions with considerable power. In the eyes of the insurgents, all of these are illegitimate, elitist, and oppressive. Hence, the insurgents are hostile to grading, academic standards, capitalism, and standard democratic procedures.

I have put the radicals' ideology in the form of four simple propositions to make two points. First, the ideology is quasi-religious. Its adherents pursue it with a kind of fervor usually reserved for religious battles. Second, the ideology is extremely general. Inequalities and decisions based on them pervade public and private life. All such decisions become subject to political scrutiny. The ideology's simplicity personalizes the political while its generality politicizes the personal.

Radical egalitarianism appeals very effectively to some graduate and undergraduate students for other reasons as well. Students find themselves near the bottom of the complex power hierarchies that institutions of higher education have become. They sometimes find themselves overwhelmed by the demands the institution makes on them. Education is a difficult task for student and teacher alike.[14] The insurgents tell students that they should not be on the bottom of the power hierarchies, that the demands made upon them are unjust and oppressive, and that they need not worry about fulfilling them. Learning in the traditional form, they say, is just another form of oppression. I have seen the reaction in some of my own students who have converted to this ideology. Why study the arguments of Aristotle, Descartes, or Kant? At best, they rationalize oppression. Students quickly use the insurgents' ideology as an excuse for laziness.

Crucial to this ideology is the idea that drawing distinctions among people and behaviors, rewarding some and punishing others, is illegitimate. In grading my students, for example, I think I am rewarding excellence and punishing incompetence. Not so, say the insurgents; I am using my power to oppress, to force conformity to some model of behavior that I find politically useful. My grading, in their view, is a political act. The economic argument is similar. I think I am rewarding excellence by buying one brand of beer or one make of car over another. According to the insurgents, however, my purchase is essentially a political act, and ought to be made—if it should be made at all—on political grounds. The insurgents thus have no qualms about grading, buying, investing, and, in general, deciding on political grounds. Students often know that they must follow the politically correct line in their papers or suffer a reduced grade. And university investment policies are often subject to political criticism.

There are two fundamental issues here. First, are there any criteria of excellence in any of these areas that are independent of politics? Second, if there are, should we use them to assign rewards and penalties? Should we, that is, enforce inequality?

Before addressing these issues, let me note two points. (1) A positive answer to both questions does not automatically support Western institutions. It may be that universities routinely reward the wrong kinds of students, that capitalism rewards the wrong kinds of productivity and innovation, and that democratic procedures elect the wrong people. Stances on these criticisms divide liberals from conservatives. But they are not the insurgents' criticisms. The insurgents claim, not that the wrong inequalities are being enforced, but that the enforcement of inequalities is itself oppressive. (2) The questions are logically independent. Obviously one could maintain that there are independent criteria of excellence but that they should not be enforced. Conversely, one could maintain that standards should be enforced even though they are political, subjective, or in some other sense constructed. Such a view might sound peculiar, but it is not logically incoherent. The alternative to the enforcement of even arbitrary standards might be worse.

Nevertheless, inspired by Frantz Fanon, Jacques Derrida, and others, the insurgents have sought to use a negative answer to the first question to argue for a negative answer to the second. That is, they have argued that inequalities should not be enforced because they are not independent of politics. They see policies that enforce inequalities as forcing people into arbitrary and unjustifiable molds rather than as reflecting realities. The insurgents' move relies on the plausible-sounding principle that what is not objective or independent should not be enforced. The principle, despite appearances, is false. My tastes may be merely my own, but that does not mean that I should not act on them—even if my action confers benefits on some people and withholds them from others.[15] Even if the principle is granted, however, the argument rests on the assertion that no criteria of excellence are independent. That claim is strong and difficult to justify.

This is why the insurgents' ideology is almost always reductive. To establish the claim that all criteria are in some way tainted, it must show that what purport to be independent standards are really something else. The current strategy for doing this updates but essentially follows that of the sophist Thrasymachus in Plato's *Republic,* who insists that justice is the advantage of the stronger.[16] To switch to the Nietzschean phrase, everything turns out to manifest a will to power.[17] Specifically, everything manifests power relations among people defining themselves and their relations in terms of race, class, and gender. Sometimes, advocates of multiculturalism are clear about the reductive character of their stand. Frank Lentricchia, for example, contends that "[n]othing passes through a mind that doesn't have its origin in sexual, economic and racial differentiae."[18] Stated baldly, this claim is so implausible that most illiberal multiculturalists hide it. Their view emerges, however, through their emphasis on issues of race, class, and gender, which would otherwise be only a few among many kinds of differences that might merit academic, moral, and political attention. The point becomes especially clear when illiberal multiculturalists seek to differentiate themselves from their pluralistic colleagues:

The interminable debate about multi-cultural education is a debate, fundamentally, about the values which will inform the working of society itself. The superficial [that is, pluralistic] multi-culturalism of Canada, Britain and the Netherlands not only fails to address the basic problem of class exploitation (of which racism is but a part); it also actively assists class exploitation by putting stress on what are in fact superficial differences between people. Multi-culturalism in its present form is little more than a masking ideology with which an artful and ruthless capitalism protects itself.[19]

More explicitly still:

For education to become truly liberating, it must push against the forces of oppression, be they centred on class, race, gender or all three.[20]

The focus on oppression is itself remarkable. Few social thinkers have believed that all one needs "to become truly liberating" and achieve utopia is to stop oppression. But the lack of any positive vision or program is only one strange feature of this view. There are many kinds of oppression, after all; people have been oppressed because of differences in strength, intelligence, appearance, form of government, religious conviction, political affiliation, and many other things. They are now being oppressed for opposing multiculturalism. Yet illiberal multiculturalists assume that all "forces of oppression" are "centred on class, race, gender or all three." Thus, we see course proposals like that for English 306, Rhetoric and Composition, at the University of Texas at Austin.[21] The English department proposed centering the required freshman composition course on Paula Rothenberg's *Racism and Sexism,* which consists almost exclusively of left-wing, anti-Western, anti-American diatribes and is rife with factual errors and conceptual confusions. But what have neutrality, accuracy, and clarity to do with liberation?

III. The Luddite Model

The insurgency model goes a long way toward explaining the affinity of multiculturalism and thought control. It comes as no surprise, from this model's vantage point, that serious social scientists such as Stephan Thernstrom and Reynolds Farley have been attacked for teaching the facts about ethnic relations, that Stanley Fish has blasted the National Association of Scholars as "racist, sexist, and homophobic" for defending traditional academic standards, that the entire Minnesota Scandanavian Studies department has been accused of sexual harassment, in some cases on evidence no stronger than assigning "patriarchal reading lists," that Alan Gribben has been hounded from the University of Texas for voting against an English M.A. concentration in Ethnic and Third World Literature and then fighting the proposed English 306, and that a dean at SUNY Binghamton has announced a "purge" of faculty insufficiently committed to diversity. The central tenet of the insurgency model is correct: leftists *are* trying to take over many American institutions of higher education.

What the insurgency model cannot explain, however, is their widespread success. There are not enough tenured radicals to bring about the changes we have been witnessing. In particular, not enough administrators are themselves insurgents. Moreover, the insurgents have not been able to force administrators to conform to their wishes. They do not command wide support within the universities; faculty at Washington, Texas, and elsewhere have voted multicultural requirements down by margins of about two to one, and students rarely favor additional requirements. Nor do the insurgents command wide support among alumni and other contributors, thus affecting administrative supply lines. Their successes at Stanford and Duke have led to drops in alumni funding. The government, increasingly an important source of funds for universities, has sometimes applied pressure in the name of diversity, but the bulk of government funding supports scientific research and has so far been largely immune from political interference. The insurgents sometimes succeed through extortion, threatening administrators with bad publicity if they resist. By now it should be clear, however, that giving in can also lead to bad publicity. Moreover, the administrators have hired, and continue to hire, the radicals who threaten them. Most administrators have encouraged or tolerated the hiring of the insurgents and then have actively supported them, passively accommodated them, or quietly encouraged faculty opposition without being willing to take a stand themselves. Why?

Robert L. Bartley has offered a second model for understanding current developments on campus, which I call the Luddite model.[22] The idea is that many of those who enlist in the multicultural cause, support it from the outside, or acquiesce to its demands are Luddites, opposed to social and intellectual changes stemming from technological innovation. This model diametrically opposes the multiculturalists' view that social and demographic changes argue *for* their program and that their opponents are Luddites, racists, sexists, classists, and homophobes, horrified at the prospect of universities of color. But it has some solid intellectual and sociological support.

The ideology of race, class, and gender espoused by illiberal multiculturalists can be traced back through Derrida and Fanon to Heidegger, Nietzsche, and Marx. There is ample evidence of Luddism in the works of the latter three. Marx devoted his life to railing against the Industrial Revolution, seeking to overturn it and the changes it caused. He spoke longingly of the pre-industrial era:

> The bourgeoisie, wherever it has got the upper hand, has put an end to all feudal, partriarchal, idyllic relations. It has pitilessly torn asunder the motley feudal ties that bound man to his "natural superiors," and has left remaining no other nexus between man and man than naked self-interest, than callous "cash payment."[23]

Marx left us with the image, after the state has withered away, of a life in which we hunt in the morning, fish in the afternoon, and criticize at night. He attacked other socialists as nostalgic for an earlier era, but, despite his occasional and, through Stalin, very influential support of technological development, his work rests in part upon a pastoral vision. Nietzsche frequently condemned rationality and science, looking forward to the modern era with a mixture of excitement and terror.[24] And Heidegger's essay on technology reveals his hostility to the social changes brought about by scientific advance.[25] Indeed, Heidegger's longing for the pastoral Black Forest life of his childhood bears more than an accidental similarity to the pastoral ideal of Nazism.

Nietzsche, Fanon, Derrida, and their followers extend the hostility to science and technology to a hostility to truth itself. Each considers truth captive to power. Fanon, for example, subjugates truth explicitly to politics:

> In every age, among the people, truth is the property of the national cause. No absolute verity, no discourse on the purity of the soul, can shake this position. . . . Truth is that which hurries the breakup of the colonialist regime; it is that which promotes the emergence of the nation; it is all that protects the natives, and ruins the foreigners. In this colonialist context there is no truthful behavior: and the good is quite simply that which is evil for "them."[26]

As the final sentence indicates, moral categories too become subject to politics. The hostility to truth and science extends to contemporary illiberals; many adopt the attitude expressed by Stanley Fish in what he has called "the most unfortunate sentence I ever wrote":

[My fiction] relieves me of the obligation to be right (a standard that simply drops out) and demands only that I be interesting (a standard that can be met without any reference at all to an illusory objectivity).[27]

Attitudes such as this, or Fish's later view that truth and "the obligation to be right" are relative to an interpretive community, work to "demystify" science, to suggest that science is "one more human activity, rather than a place at which human beings encounter a 'hard,' nonhuman reality"; that "modes of social knowledge such as theology, science, and magic are different, not inferior or superior"; and, correspondingly, that "we must resist the temptation to think that the redescriptions of reality by contemporary physical or biological science are somehow closer to 'the things themselves,' less 'mind-dependent,' than the redescriptions of history offered by contemporary culture criticism."[28] Feminists have been especially eager to conclude that science and objectivity itself are perniciously masculine ideas.[29] The Luddite model thus readily explains the illiberals' attack on independent criteria and social systems employing them.

It also explains the sociology of campus multiculturalism. Broadly speaking, support for illiberal multiculturalism is inversely proportional to the scientific nature of the disciplines. Multicultural initiatives tend to win wide support in education and humanities departments while suffering overwhelming rejection in science, engineering, and business departments. Even within the humanities, fields that see themselves as in some sense scientific, such as philosophy, are less fertile ground for multiculturalists than fields such as English, ethnic studies, foreign languages, and the arts. The Luddite model explains why: there are fewer Luddites among professors of physics or electrical engineering than among professors of literature or sculpture.

Looking at this another way, support for illiberal multiculturalism is inversely proportional to salaries. Across the disciplines, those who earn the lowest salaries in the universities are most likely to feel resentful, threatened, and even obsolescent. The poorest departments are thus fertile recruiting grounds for Luddism. This table lists departments according to average full professor salaries in public universities for 1991–1992:[30]

Field	Average Salary, Professor, 1991–92
Accounting	62,262
Engineering	60,028
Computer and information science	59,466
Economics	57,682

Business administration	57,168
Area and ethnic studies	55,444
Physics	55,088
Chemistry	53,452
Mathematics	53,438
Psychology	53,207
Geology	53,168
Anthropology	53,304
Political science and government	53,069
Philosophy and religion	52,590
Sociology	51,692
Foreign languages	51,637
History	51,432
Life sciences	51,051
Communications	51,019
Education	50,666
Multi-interdisciplinary studies	50,465
Letters (English)	50,198
Curriculum and instruction	49,380
All fields	52,819

(I have used figures for full professors both because they are more influential in their institutions than their junior colleagues and because comparing salaries across a single rank minimizes additional factors. For example, average faculty age and rank varies with field; fields with younger practioners tend, other things being equal, to have lower salaries than fields with older practioners.) The table is striking; those fields near the top of the salary hierarchy have been unaffected by illiberal multiculturalism, while those near the bottom are rife with it. Only one field below the mean for all fields—life sciences—has suffered few effects from political correctness. Only one field more than 1 percent above the mean for all fields—area and ethnic studies—has a strong streak of illiberalism. High salaries in that field are a story in themselves, a product of multiculturalism, affirmative action, and politics.[31]

The table suggests that degree of scientific procedure, salaries, and immunity to political correctness tend to go together. Disciplines significantly above the mean in salaries tend to be scientific and quantitative, in their methods and aims, at least; disciplines significantly below the mean are "soft." The former seem resistant to politicization, while the latter are increasingly radical. There are many ways to try to account for this correlation. Scientific disciplines often have practical payoffs which lead to higher salaries; indeed, the most practical fields tend to have the highest salaries. Scientific disciplines also have strong empirical constraints that work against politicization. The Luddite model is committed to no particular explanation of the correlation except to say that the more scientific a discipline is, the less likely it is to be politicized.

As it stands, however, the Luddite model falters precisely where the insurgency model does: it fails to explain the success of illiberalism. It easily explains why English, foreign language, and a few other departments would find illiberal multiculturalism congenial. But it does nothing to explain why entire colleges and universities would succumb, or why administrators would behave so accommodatingly. The sciences are typically much more powerful than the softest humanities departments, partly because of their vastly greater ability to generate research funding. And practical fields such as business and engineering tend to generate far greater alumni and other outside revenue than departments of English or schools of education. It is hard to imagine many administrators holding or implementing anti-scientific ideas.

The Luddite model can be advanced in a different form, one that arguably explains the pervasiveness of political correctness more successfully. Multiculturalists are fond of pointing to demographic shifts, some of which are real and some of which are overblown.[32] They accuse their opponents of fearing the transformation of the university's ethnic, racial, and sexual composition. In fact, however, any such fear would border on the paranoid; for universities, despite aggressive—and in many cases arguably illegal—affirmative-action efforts, have not succeeded in bringing large numbers of minorities into either student bodies or faculties.[33] For much of the past decade, the number of blacks enrolled in institutions of higher education has been declining. Similarly, the number of blacks receiving Ph.D.s has been dropping. Differences in high-school performance and test scores suggest that, if it were not for affirmative-action programs, our elite higher-education institutions would be almost completely white and Asian.

Multiculturalists thus misrepresent the consequences of greater ethnic diversity and increased communication and travel. Groups now in positions of power are unlikely to be overwhelmed by others. If current standards of excellence remain in place, those groups will remain solidly in power for decades to come. The result, given demographic changes and an economy increasingly geared to information exchange, will probably be greater inequalities in educational level and economic success. Groups achieving educational success will reap larger rewards; those failing educationally will fall further behind economically. Illiberal multiculturalists, from this perspective, are Luddites in that they fear competition—specifically, competition in education and the information-based economy that rewards it. This explains the hostility to criteria for judging competition and to social systems that reward success and penalize failure in competition. It also explains much of the content of the illiberals' ideology, including its emphasis on groups and on racial, ethnic, class, and gender differences. It explains the illiberals' success to a greater extent as well, because far more administrators are committed to equality, specifically, to a group-based equality, than to an anti-scientific attitude or to radical political programs.

IV. The Mercantilist Model

This brings me to the final model I shall discuss, the mercantilist model. The central idea is that multiculturalism is a form of mercantilism; it is an attempt to avoid competition, to seek public subsidy of private gain. The illiberals, and those who support them, are academic protectionists. In economists' terms, they are engaging in rent-seeking behavior—they seek reward without effort.[34] All agents engaging in economic activity try to maximize returns on their effort; competition prevents rewards from extending very far beyond what efforts merit, however, for anyone attaining substantial rewards without effort is an easy mark for a competitor. Illiberal multiculturalists, for this reason, try to eliminate competition.

This explains why multicultural initiatives are invariably attempts to require something—usually, to require students to take courses. The multiculturalists fear that they cannot compete in the universities' perennial competition for students, faculty positions, and money. So, they advocate protectionism. They seek to protect themselves from competition for resources by forcing students into their courses and thereby forcing the universities to subsidize them with increased faculty positions and other forms of funding. The proper metaphor for the contemporary university, according to this model, is not Lenin or Luddism but Leviathan—the monster created through the activities of individuals that nevertheless has unlimited power to trample individual interests.[35]

There is no consensus on the proper role of a modern university. Institutions of higher education increasingly serve different constituencies in entirely different ways. They function as research institutions, performing grant and contract work for the federal government and private corporations. They act as agencies of economic development for states and local communities. They act as guilds, apprenticing graduate students to train them in the ways of academic and other professions. They act as schools, teaching some undergraduate students general knowledge preparing them for citizenship, and others quite specific knowledge preparing them for particular careers. There is no organizing principle that relates these functions, indicating their proper roles in a unified whole.

This lack of purpose and principle makes universities susceptible to the transformations we have been witnessing, and, specifically, to the plague of political correctness. The situation is analogous to that of the society in general. As James Buchanan has described it:

> With no overriding principle that dictates how an economy is to be organized, the political structure is open to exploitation by the pressures of well-organized interests. The special-interest, rent-seeking, churning state finds fertile ground for growth in this environment. And, depending on the relative strength of organized interests, we observe quite arbitrary, politicized interferences with markets.[36]

Apply this analysis to the university, and the following portrait emerges. There is no principle around which universities are organized; there is no principle that commands consensus about what goals the university should adopt or how it should strive to attain them. Few administrators have the vision, intellectual power, or courage to articulate and champion any particular set of goals. This leaves the university open to manipulation by well-organized special interests who can exert political pressure. Small wonder, then, that illiberals advocate what they call "the democratization of the university"; to a large extent, it has already happened.[37]

The result? First, competition for resources within the university becomes more intense and more highly politicized. In the absence of any agreed-upon criteria for allocating funds, quests for funding and decisions determining their fate become increasingly and more openly political. The changes that have taken place in Congress since the 1974 reforms have also taken place in academia. The smoke-filled room has yielded to the pork barrel.

Second, groups within the university engage in more rent-seeking behavior, advocating policies that benefit them by claiming a public interest in what produces their own private profit. Thus, departments seek requirements, such as multiculturalism requirements, that channel students into their courses and funds into their budgets. Faculty with similar interests within and across departments seek to establish research centers, special programs, and the like with independent claims to funding. Interdisciplinary programs especially receive emphasis, for they more easily establish independence from existing departmental structures. No surprise that they constitute "a wasteland where wolves run free," in Camille Paglia's words; they were designed to be.[38]

Third, administration consumes more and more of the university's total resources. As decisions about policy and funding become more highly politicized, political activity becomes more rewarding; in many places, it has already become more rewarding than intellectual achievement. Faculty members with great power but very short vitae and deans with minimal publication records are commonplace. Most of the funds colleges and universities have collected over the past twenty years from increased tuition payments have gone to support administration, not to enhance classroom teaching.[39]

Fourth, free choices are increasingly restricted for arbitrary and political reasons. Students find their curricula increasingly mapped out for them. Moreover, the basis for the map is not intellectual but political and in many respects arbitrary, since no one political group gains so much dominance that it can simply impose its own agenda. Similarly, faculty find themselves increasingly meeting political as well as intellectual demands in their teaching, research, and administrative duties. They find themselves pressured to put women and people of color on their reading lists; to teach courses that have a multicultural component or in some way promote diversity; to pursue research that is politically correct, forsaking certain controversial topics and linguistic practices; to spout politically correct opinions, voting with the politically correct groups on various issues; and to make admissions, hiring, and promotion decisions on political as well as intellectual criteria.

There remain, of course, institutional barriers to wholesale and blatant politicization of such decisions in most fields and universities. But the illiberals have manufactured ways of overcoming them. In many fields, they have either taken over editorial boards of existing journals or created their own journals. Most articles appearing in such journals seem to involve applying an egalitarian, race/class/gender formula to a problem, social phenomenon, or literary text. Anyone assailing the quality of the articles or the journals in which they appear faces charges of racism, sexism, and obsolescence. The articles themselves, moreover, praise each other extravagantly, enabling virtually anyone to compile an impressive list of positive citations of his or her own work.[40] Faculty in politicized areas thus find it easy to build curricula vitae that seem, at first glance, at least, solid by traditional academic standards. This not only makes it difficult for universities to fight politicization; it actively encourages it. Faculty who might otherwise be skeptical of contemporary egalitarianism find it a quick and easy route to academic success.

These consequences of the mercantilist model pervade contemporary academia. That alone provides strong support for the model as a way of understanding multiculturalism and political correctness. Consider the following surprisingly frank but all-too-typical demand:

> Women and minorities . . . want power. They want: more positions, a larger share of tenured positions, more important roles in departmental politics, more courses and more say in curriculum decisions, more significance in professional organizations and journals, better publishing opportunities, more influence on critical theory.[41]

The mercantilist model explains why people feel no obligation to *earn* these things.

Moreover, like the other models, it explains the illiberals' ideology. The absence of any independent criteria of judgment is simply a fact within the university. It is a fact, furthermore, that must be maintained if the political manipulation of the institution is to continue. Not only do we lack consensus on the basic mission of the university; we have generated large constituencies that require a lack of consensus for their survival and success. They have strong motives for opposing any encompassing vision—in their terms, for promoting the university's "democratization." Hence the strife that often follows a radical takeover of an institution; too many groups have a stake in keeping the decision-making process political (with a small 'p'). Any organizing principle, however congenial politically (with a big 'p'), would hinder groups from winning subsidies for their own private gain. The groups that profit from the Leviathan university, therefore, are bound to deny the availability of any independent criteria of judgment, and to deny the fairness of their application if there were any such criteria.

The mercantilist model, finally, explains a common but puzzling feature of many multiculturalist proposals. Most often, the proposals require courses with specific multicultural content—courses that focus on American minority groups or Third World cultures. The proposals thus contradict the pluralistic arguments advanced to support them.

At the University of Texas at Austin, for example, the University Council's Ad Hoc Committee on Multicultural Education, in a fifty-four page report, articulated only one argument in favor of multiculturalism. The committee noted that the world is becoming more interdependent, that U.S. society is becoming more complex, and concluded simply: "The time is now."[42] That the committee apparently thought this would persuade the faculty to adopt multiculturalism in any form, much less the six-hour university-wide requirement it proposed, is itself astounding. To the extent that it is an argument, however, it is a pluralistic argument relying on the increasing interaction of cultures.

The committee's proposal, however, was not only not pluralistic; it isolated minority and non-Western cultures in separate courses. It was an intellectual form of segregation. Despite its definition of multiculturalism as "an approach to teaching and learning that acknowledges the need for people to exist interdependently in a culturally pluralistic world," the committee proposed requiring of every undergraduate at least one U.S. multicultural course—"consisting of the study of at least one minority or non-dominant culture within the United States"—and at least one international multicultural course—"consisting of the study of at least one non-Western or third-world culture."[43] These definitions, unlike the general one, are illiberal. They are laden with ideology, and bad ideology, at that. The first assumes that some cultures dominate others; the second rests on a division between East and West that applies much better to Rudyard Kipling's era than to our own. Leaving that aside, however, the definitions rely on distinctions—between dominant and nondominant, and Western and non-Western cultures—that, according to the committee's own pluralistic argument, are breaking down. Indeed they are; they have been for some time. In junior high and high school, for example, I read Ralph Ellison, Countee Cullen, Langston Hughes, Martin Luther King, and Malcolm X as important American writers, not as representatives of a discrete and insular subculture.

If the pluralistic arguments for multiculturalism have any validity, then curricular revisions should further the breakdown of these distinctions. Yet the University of Texas multicultural proposal is typical in trying to reinforce them. The mercantilist model explains this incoherence. Merely encouraging faculty to include works by women, minorities, and Third World authors when they are important and intellectually worthwhile does nothing to justify new programs or new faculty lines. It does nothing to give any particular factions special power in hiring and promotion decisions. In short, it does nothing to strengthen any particular group within the Leviathan university.

V. Strategies

Each model I have discussed, I believe, reveals something important about the continuing crisis in higher education. The insurgency model is right to point to the tenured radicals trying to subvert the university for their own political ends. The Luddite model is right to point to an anti-scientific attitude that ends up attacking the notion of truth itself and promoting politics as an alternative. And the mercantilist model is right to point to the power politics bred by the lack of any overall purpose at Leviathan U. There is no real conflict between these models;

indeed, the mercantilist model encompasses the others. Some factions are likely to be driven by radical, egalitarian politics, a hostility toward quantitative methods, or a fear of increased inequality and social friction. Other factions may be motivated by a desire for power, advancement, or money. While the radical and Luddite groups may be too small to effect large-scale changes on their own, other groups, for their own selfish reasons, have motives to cooperate with them and help them achieve their goals.

But the models are better seen as complementary rather than as subsumed within the mercantilist model. That model, by itself, cannot explain the near-religious fervor of many campus illiberals. Nor does it explain why the academic protectionism it predicts would take a highly political direction. The insurgency model does explain these things. The models work together, then, to explain the success of the regimen of political correctness. The insurgency model explains the genesis and passion of the movement. The Luddite model explains why, in some areas of academia, the radical insurgents have found fertile ground for their influence to grow. And the mercantilist model explains how the movement has not only succeeded but itself become institutionalized.

Conservatives, despite some notable victories, have often been ineffectual as an interest group within the Leviathan university. Liberals have too often stayed on the sidelines or even aided the radicals, abiding by the old dictum that there should be no enemies on the left. Conservatives, moreover, tend to play by the rules, while the radicals feel no such constraints. Finally, the conservatives are at a natural disadvantage in the Leviathan university, for their goal is the good of the whole, not the good of their own group. The Leviathan university promotes rent-seeking, while the conservatives seek, not rent, but restrictions on rent-seeking.

How, then, can one fight the hegemony of the politically correct? The insurgency model suggests classic counterinsurgency measures: identifying and reinforcing important lines of communication and supply, eliminating public support for the insurgents, and pinpointing search-and-destroy missions. In the university setting, this means: (1) identifying courses and requirements to be defended—Freshman Composition, for example—and defending them from corruption at the hands of the insurgents; (2) identifying power centers—faculty governing bodies, committees, administrative posts—and trying to secure them; (3) maintaining communications by preserving the neutrality of the campus newspaper and faculty documents; (4) arguing against the insurgents' positions, on campus (to an audience of students, faculty, and administrators) and off (to an audience of alumni, concerned citizens, and politicians); (5) exposing incidents of political correctness to the media; and (6) using admissions, hiring, promotion, and budgetary decisions to shrink the hotbeds of revolutionary activity. Following these strategies entails much more political involvement, committee work, and the like than most conservatives would prefer. But I am convinced that such involvement is necessary.

The mercantilist model suggests additional strategies. James Madison and the other authors of *The Federalist Papers* were aware of the dangers that factions posed to just government. They sought to contain the power of factions through both procedural checks and balances and substantive rights. The moral for the universities is twofold. We must attend to procedural safeguards—rights of grievance, privacy, and due process—to prevent any one faction or set of factions from gaining control of centers of power. And we must seek to protect individual rights and freedoms—of thought, speech, and association, for example—from the encroachment of Leviathan U. Again, this requires considerable involvement in campus political affairs.

The mercantilist model presents those who care about excellence with a dilemma. The decentralization of power within the contemporary university suggests two conflicting strategies. One might seek further decentralization, preserving faculty and student liberty as much as possible by fighting almost all requirements. If the problem is protectionism, then the best strategy might be to fight for free trade. The illiberals, in curriculum requirements, speech codes, and practices governing student life on campus, try to substitute their judgment for the students' judgment. Conservatives, in contrast, can readily win student support by fighting to let students make choices for themselves. The radicals, many of whom came of age politically during the 1960s or early 1970s, cannot argue effectively against student power. Alternatively, one might seek greater centralization. The Leviathan university arises from a lack of vision about what the university is and what it should do. The most important thing those who care about higher education can do, then, is seek to articulate a compelling and encompassing picture of what the university ought to be. A university with a clearly defined mission would be far less vulnerable to radical attack than the contemporary university has turned out to be.

These strategies, of course, come into conflict. One promotes a cafeteria-style "multiversity" in which students can largely go their own ways; the other promotes a university with a well-defined mission. Which strategy holds the most promise surely depends on the institution in question. Large state universities, for example, probably cannot achieve a unified sense of purpose, even with a strong leader; a libertarian, free-trade approach may be the only realistic option. Even in such institutions, however, it may be possible to follow John Silber's tactic of creating within the larger institution a program that does have a strong sense of mission.[44] A small college or university, in contrast, may be able to maintain a well-defined purpose and defend it against the inevitable illiberal assault.

By far the most important strategy for defending higher education, in any kind of institution, is to expose the bait-and-switch technique of the illiberals. I began this essay by asking how multiculturalism and political correctness have come to be allied and to succeed. Their success has depended on their alliance. The theses to which the radicals are committed, once uncovered and understood, are preposterous. Only because illiberals who seek to politicize the curriculum have been able to masquerade as pluralists have administrators and liberal colleagues acceded to their demands. To fight illiberalism, therefore, one must expose the masquerade. One must show how preposterous the underlying ideas are. One must bring the bait-and-switch operation to light, both within and outside the universities.

This is partly an intellectual task. One must be able to explain the difference between pluralism and illiberalism and demonstrate the problematic character of the latter. Partly for this reason, and partly because there are good arguments for pluralism, one must try to implement a true, pluralistic multiculturalism that puts the lie to reductionistic and ultimately patronizing claims about non-Western cultures. But exposing the bait-and-switch is largely an exercise in public relations or, more accurately, public education. Students need to understand what they are likely to face in certain kinds of courses and from certain kinds of professors. Administrators need to know what is going on under a pluralistic banner. Alumni, parents, and legislators need to know what their dollars are supporting. Faculty in business, engineering, and the natural sciences need to know what is happening on the other side of the campus. Informed, many will become valuable allies.

It is vital, therefore, to insist on truth in advertising, insisting that colleagues represent the contents of their courses fairly, describe their policies publicly and accurately, and, above all, defend the pluralistic-sounding moral pronouncements they make. It is vital to come to the defense of colleagues persecuted for thinking or expressing politically incorrect thoughts. It is vital, too, to involve the public through direct contacts and the media. Political correctness, however powerful on campus, cannot stand the light of day. The public knows repression and outright silliness when it sees it; one anecdote is worth a thousand words on hegemony and interpretive communities.

Alexis de Tocqueville said that he knew "no country in which there is so little true independence of mind and freedom of discussion as in America."[45] Tocqueville observed that, while almost anyone could say almost anything, in principle, no one wanted or dared to say anything but what would meet with a listener's approval. He might as well have been speaking of the contemporary university. The best response is to encourage, not a "diversity without difference," but a true diversity of mind.[46]

NOTES

1. *Education in Schools: A Consultative Document,* U.K. Department of Education and Science, 1977.
2. The Rampton Report, *West Indian Children in Our Schools,* U.K. Department of Education and Science, 1981.
3. Diane Ravitch, "Multiculturalism: E Pluribus Plures," *American Scholar,* vol. 59 (1990), pp. 337–54; reprinted in Daniel Bonevac, ed., *Today's Moral Issues* (Mountain View: Mayfield, 1992), pp. 163–74.
4. Bhikhu Parekh, "The Concept of Multicultural Education," in Sohan Modgil, Gajendra K. Verma, Kanka Mallick, and Celia Modgil, eds., *Multicultural Education: The Interminable Debate* (London: Falmer Press, 1986), p. 29; reprinted in Bonevac, ed., *Today's Moral Issues.*
5. J. Katz, "Multicultural Education: Games Educators Play," *Multiracial Education,* vol. 10, no. 2 (1982), pp. 11–18.
6. R. Hatcher and J. Shallice, "The Politics of Anti-Racist Education," *Multiracial Education,* vol. 12, no. 1 (1983), pp. 3–21.
7. Brian Bullivant, "Towards Radical Multiculturalism: Resolving Tensions in Curriculum and Educational Planning," in Modgil et al., eds., *Multicultural Education,* p. 45.
8. Heather MacDonald, "Underdog and Pony Show: The Left Convenes at Hunter College," *The New Criterion,* June 1992, p. 88.
9. Dinesh D'Souza, *Illiberal Education: The Politics of Race and Sex on Campus* (New York: Free Press, 1991), p. 74; originally cited in Carolyn Mooney, "Sweeping Curricular Change Is Under Way at Stanford," *Chronicle of Higher Education,* December 14, 1988, p. A11.
10. D'Souza, *Illiberal Education,* p. 74.
11. Jean-Jacques Rousseau, *On the Social Contract,* trans. Donald A. Cress, in *The Basic Political Writings of Jean-Jacques Rousseau* (Indianapolis: Hackett, 1987); reprinted in Bonevac, ed., *Today's Moral Issues,* p. 241.
12. Various terms convey the same basic idea. Many authors speak of hierarchies, distinctions, or divisions rather than inequalities and their enforcement.
13. For a philosophical defense of at least a moderate form of this position, see William K. Frankena, "Some Beliefs about Justice," in Joel Feinberg and Hyman Gross, eds., *Justice* (Encino: Dickenson, 1977), p. 51.
14. See Lino Graglia's essay on affirmative action in this volume. Students admitted under preferential-admissions programs typically face greater diffi-

culties than other students. They have more reason to become resentful, therefore, and radical egalitarianism provides a correspondingly more pervasive response.

15. This is why the crime of "lookism" is absurd; people associate for many subjective, complicated, and poorly understood reasons. There is a more general principle involved as well. Some philosophers have maintained a version of the principle of sufficient reason, insisting that one should act in a certain way only if there are compelling reasons for so acting. The medieval logician John Buridan refuted the principle with an example of a donkey equidistant from two equally attractive bales of hay. The donkey has no reason to go to one bale instead of the other, so Buridan pointed out, if it subscribes to the principle of sufficient reason, it will starve.

16. Plato, *Republic*, 338c.

17. Compare Friedrich Nietzsche, *Joyful Wisdom*, trans. Thomas Common (New York: Frederick Ungar Publishing Co., 1960), p. 49: "We exercise our power over others by doing them good or by doing them ill—that is all we care for!"; and *The Will to Power*, trans. Walter Kaufmann and R. J. Hollingdale (New York: Vintage Books, 1967), aphorism 855: "What determines rank, sets off rank, is only quanta of power, and nothing else." For a discussion of the affinities between the insurgents and Nietzsche, see Allan Bloom, "Western Civ—and Me," *Commentary*, vol. 90 (1990), pp. 15–21; reprinted in Bloom, *Giants and Dwarfs* (New York: Simon and Schuster, 1991), and in Bonevac, ed., *Today's Moral Issues*, pp. 154–62. Nietzsche stressed race as well as power; in *Joyful Wisdom*, he wrote favorably of the maxim "The race is all, the individual is nothing" (p. 32).

18. Quoted in Scott Heller, "A Constellation of Recently Hired Professors Illuminates the English Department at Duke," *Chronicle of Higher Education*, May 27, 1987, pp. A12–A14.

19. Christopher Bagley, "Multiculturalism, Class, and Ideology: A European-Canadian Comparison," in Modgil et al., eds., *Multicultural Education*, pp. 56–57.

20. Mike Cole, "Teaching and Learning about Racism: A Critique of Multicultural Education in Britain," in Modgil et al., eds., *Multicultural Education*, p. 142.

21. The first digit of course numbers at the University of Texas at Austin indicates the number of credit hours; the last two digits indicate the level of the course. For the radicals' account of the English 306 struggle, see Sara Diamond, "Readin', Writin', and Repressin'," *Z*, February 1991. For an accurate account, see Peter Collier, "Incorrect English: The Case of Alan Gribben," *Heterodoxy*, vol. 1, no. 2 (May 1992), pp. 8–10.

22. See Robert L. Bartley, "Is America on the Way Down?" *Commentary*, March 1992, p. 26: "So too with intellectual elites, who find their skills fading in relevance and their positions endangered. Perhaps political correctness in the academy is best seen as a brand of Luddism."

23. Karl Marx and Friedrich Engels, *Manifesto of the Communist Party* (New York: International Publishers, 1932); reprinted in Bonevac, ed., *Today's Moral Issues*, p. 406.

24. In *Joyful Wisdom*, for example, we find: "In comparison with the ignoble nature the higher nature is *more irrational*:—for the noble, magnanimous, and self-sacrificing person succumbs in fact to his impulses, and in his best

moments his reason *lapses* altogether" (p. 37); "the most critical of all questions would then come into the foreground: whether science is in a position to *furnish* goals for human action, after it has proved that it can take them away and annihilate them. . . ." (p. 44); "Perhaps science is yet best known by its capacity for depriving man of enjoyment, and making him colder, more statuesque, and more Stoical. But it might also turn out to be the *great pain-bringer!*" (p. 49).

25. Martin Heidegger, *The Question Concerning Technology and Other Essays* (New York: Harper Colophon, 1977).
26. Frantz Fanon, *The Wretched of the Earth* (New York: Grove Press, 1963); excerpted in Daniel Bonevac, William Boon, and Stephen Phillips, eds., *Beyond the Western Tradition* (Mountain View: Mayfield, 1992), p. 51.
27. Stanley Fish, "Interpreting 'Interpreting the *Variorum,*' " in *Is There a Text in This Class?* (Cambridge: Harvard University Press, 1980), p. 180; renounced in the essay's foreword on p. 174. Despite Fish's renunciation of this sentence, similar sentiments appear elsewhere in his writings:

   . . . I must give up the claims implicitly made in the first part of this essay. There I argue that a bad (because spatial) model has suppressed what was really happening, but by my own declared principles the notion "really happening" is just one more interpretation. ("Interpreting the *Variorum,*" in *Is There a Text in This Class?*)

28. Richard Rorty, *Contingency, Irony, and Solidarity* (Cambridge: Cambridge University Press, 1989), p. 4; John Stanfield, "The Ethnocentric Basis of Social Science Knowledge Production," *Review of Research in Education,* quoted in Ravitch, "Multiculturalism: E Pluribus Plures," p. 345; Rorty, *Contingency, Irony, and Solidarity,* p. 16.
29. See Margarita Levin, "Caring New World: Feminism and Science," *American Scholar,* vol. 57 (Winter 1988), pp. 100–106.
30. *Chronicle of Higher Education,* June 10, 1992, p. A12.
31. See Mwangi S. Kimenyi, "Rent-Seeking in the Academy: The Political Economy of Specialty Programs," *Academic Questions,* vol. 5 (Spring 1992), pp. 41–54.
32. See Terrance Dunford, "Higher Education Confronts the 'New Demographics,' " *Academic Questions,* vol. 5 (Winter 1991–92), pp. 9–15.
33. Universities are unwilling to give many details about their affirmative-action programs. For a discussion of such programs, see Vincent Sarich, "The Institutionalization of Racism at the University of California at Berkeley," *Academic Questions,* vol. 4 (Winter 1990–91), pp. 72–81; and Lino Graglia's essay in this volume.
34. Adam Smith, *The Wealth of Nations* (Chicago: University of Chicago Press, 1976), pp. 69 and 162; see also Gordon Tullock, "The Welfare Costs of Tariffs, Monopolies, and Theft," *Western Economic Journal,* vol. 5 (1967), pp. 224–32; J. M. Buchanan, R. D. Tollison, and G. Tullock, eds., *Toward a Theory of the Rent-Seeking Society* (College Station: Texas A&M University Press, 1980); R. B. Ekelund and R. D. Tollison, *Mercantilism as a Rent-Seeking Society* (College Station: Texas A&M University Press, 1981); and Charles K. Rowley, ed., *Democracy and Public Choice* (Oxford: Basil Blackwell, 1987).
35. Thomas Hobbes, *Leviathan* (Oxford: Clarendon Press, 1909).

36. James Buchanan, "Socialism Is Dead; Leviathan Lives," *Wall Street Journal*, July 18, 1990, p. A8; reprinted in Bonevac, ed., *Today's Moral Issues*, p. 479.
37. Note the names of two left-wing organizations created to counter the National Association of Scholars: the Union of Democratic Intellectuals, and Teachers for a Democratic Culture.
38. Camille Paglia, "Junk Bonds and Corporate Raiders: Academe in the Hour of the Wolf," *Arion*, Spring 1991, pp. 139–212.
39. See Thomas Sowell, "The Scandal of College Tuition," *Commentary*, August 1992.
40. For examples, see Levin, "Caring New World," p. 106.
41. Carey Kaplan and Ellen Cronan Rose, *The Canon and the Common Reader* (Knoxville: University of Tennessee Press, 1990).
42. *Documents and Minutes of the General Faculty*, University of Texas at Austin, pp. 19434–35.
43. *Ibid.*, pp. 19426–27.
44. At the University of Texas at Austin, Silber established an honors program, Plan II, with a demanding and highly structured curriculum. It has succeeded in attracting top-notch students and involving the university's best teachers. Its recent history, however, illustrates the danger of creating a program with well-defined goals within a large university that lacks them. Radicals have taken over some required humanities courses, while science and mathematics courses have withered.
45. Alexis de Tocqueville, *Democracy in America*, translated by Henry Reeve (New York: J. and H. G. Langley, 1841); reprinted in Bonevac, ed., *Today's Moral Issues*, p. 29.
46. I am grateful to Ellen Frankel Paul and Alan Gribben, and to the other contributors to this volume, for their comments on an earlier draft of this essay.

Tradition and Change:
The University Under Stress

Stanley Rothman

Introduction

The American university is in a state of crisis. Indeed, the crisis may be a terminal illness. While higher education faces very concrete problems, it seems clear that, in part at least, these problems and the manner in which they are being confronted reflect broad shifts in the culture of American society. As the result of such shifts, new values have emerged which conflict sharply with those for which the university had come to stand.

If I am correct, the traditional university faces much greater difficulties than those outlined in such recent books as Allan Bloom's *The Closing of the American Mind* (1987), Page Smith's *Killing the Spirit* (1990), and Roger Kimball's *Tenured Radicals* (1990), which argue that American higher education has gone seriously awry, and may not even be salvageable. Indeed, I am even more skeptical than critics like Irving Kristol, who have come to believe that our hopes should be placed, if anywhere, with various think tanks. The university, Kristol argues, is hopeless.[1]

What is happening in American higher education? Is the situation as I suggest, or are traditional American institutions of higher education still, as Henry Rosovsky argues in *The University: An Owner's Manual* (1990), the best in the world, and on an upward trajectory?[2]

The answer to these questions requires a historical overview not only of the development of the university, but also of the changing character of the intellectual stratum which staffs it. Since the American university is European in origin, a discussion of the American scene must begin there. This essay, then, will place the events of the past thirty years in a broad historical perspective, relating higher education to the role of intellectuals in general, and relating both to the nature and character of Western culture.

Briefly, it is my argument that the peculiar nature of the European intelligentsia and the European university (including their American offshoots) has its origins in a particular civilization which encouraged the emergence of individualism, self-determination, and a rational world-view. It is my further argument that this civilization is now in a state of decline, as are some of its highest achievements, among which is the modern university. The decline, in the United States, stems in part from the nature of the culture itself, from the character of the intellectual class produced by it, and from certain additional features of American life which are peculiar to it.

In order to understand the present, then, we must take a long step back.

I. On European Civilization, Higher Education, and Intellectuals[3]

The first universities developed in Europe in the twelfth century. By 1600, Western Europe boasted 108 institutions of higher learning, many of which had obtained special privileges from existing regimes because of their close association with the Catholic Church. Their ties with the Catholic Church assured considerable influence and freedom from state interference.

In most European countries, universities came to educate the sons of nobility and gentry, though some poorer youths did attend. Scholarly standards often were low. For those who desired it, education for earning a livelihood in, say, medicine or the law, could be acquired after college by serving as an apprentice. For most students, however, the university served to confirm or confer status rather than as a direct source of social mobility.[4]

Only by the late nineteenth century did the dominance of universities by upper-class youth begin to wane. Children of the middle and lower-middle classes began to enter them in larger numbers, though attendance was still small. French, Russian, Italian, and many other university systems retained a classical model of education, emphasizing, with some few exceptions, study of Greek, Latin, "philosophy," and history.

It was partly for this reason that universities in these countries tended to produce an intellectual *lumpenproletariat* available for mobilization in radical causes. Such training provided little in the way of contributions to social and economic growth or to preparation for a career. Middle-class and lower-middle-class students graduated from universities without having acquired skills which were relevant to the marketplace.

In England, too, opportunities for higher education were quite limited in the nineteenth century. However, although Oxford and Cambridge remained the ideal models of English gentility, other universities—first the University of London (1826) and then, later in the century, various provincial "redbrick" universities—delivered a more practical education. These universities, along with systems of apprenticeship, provided opportunities for ambitious young men to obtain the kind of training which would help them succeed in what was, until the end of the century at least, still a relatively dynamic economy. In England, as in the rest of Europe, universities were controlled either by the Church or by the state. With few exceptions, no network of privately supported secular institutions of higher learning developed.

In the meantime a secular intelligentsia had developed in Western Europe.[5] Though not originally centered in the universities, it was eventually to dominate them. From the beginnings this intelligentsia differed from that of other great civilizations in its commitment to rationality and empirical understanding of the world. Max Weber outlined the reasons for this development (and its consequences) in a number of essays.[6]

Weber argued that the rationalization of the West, of which the growth of an intellectual stratum is both consequence and source, lay in its Christian tradition. Contrary to popular understanding, it was his view that this rationalization was initiated by the Roman Catholic Church. Calvinism only provided an additional push on the road to the development of a bourgeois, industrial society.

First, Christianity is a prophetic religion producing a conscience ("superego") of peculiar intensity. Second, Christianity emphasizes an individual rather than a communal relationship with God (as with Judaism, for example). Third, Christian religious-cultural imperatives stress general, universal moral rules, based on natural law. Fourth, as compared to other world religions, God is conceived as standing apart from nature, and his workings can be comprehended through reason. Finally, great emphasis is placed upon repressing the passions in the service of "inner worldly asceticism," that is, fulfilling one's obligations through activity in this world.[7]

The result of the Christian (especially Protestant, and particularly Calvinist) tradition was the internalization of a powerful set of comɹands that encouraged the emergence of a highly developed capacity for understanding and manipulating the environment in ways that were unprecedented in their instrumental power.[8] The cultural sources of ideology (in the sense of a cultural system) were inscribed in the realm of the "justified" and "righteous" self. Thus, aggressive (power) and erotic drives were transformed (through sublimation) into the kind of rationality which permitted the creation of modern industrial society, and the modern, rights-based, liberal-democratic political order. The need for power was remade as the need for achievement.

The uniqueness of much European, and later, American, culture lay in the creation of large numbers of individuals whose religious-cultural ethic made possible, first, a historically unprecedented kind of personal autonomy, and second, a sustained, practical self-discipline to achieve goals in this world. These created the basis for the development of science, modern democratic orders, and industrial society. In short, both liberalism and modern industrial capitalism sprang out of a common religious-cultural matrix, which encouraged the development of a relatively strong sense of what we call "self." The matrix was created by the Roman Catholic Church's synthesis of Judaism and classical thought, to which was added the heightened individualism and self-discipline encouraged especially by Calvinist Christianity.

The cultural balance thus created was dependent on a specifically religious world-view and, later, on a secular world-view which, albeit unconsciously, sprang from religious sources; for these provided the matrix that gave life meaning. They constituted the ideological base to which events in life referred. It is crucial to my argument to remember that this kind of cultural balance has never been a particularly stable one, as is evidenced by the fragility of democratic orders even in those nations of Western Europe which were responsible for democracy's birth.

It was out of this matrix that Western intellectuals emerged— intellectuals who, in the broadest sense, were to be responsible for the development of unique Western political institutions and secular science. It is no accident, then—to use a Marxist turn of language—that the modern university developed only in Europe and that the Catholic Church played so large a role in its creation. It is also no accident that modern rational systems of law draw their inspiration from the canon law of the Church.[9]

Eventually, of course, this matrix was also to produce the contemporary "disenchanted" world. As Max Weber noted in his *Sociology of Religion:*

The salvation sought by the intellectual is always based on inner need, and hence it is at once more remote from life, more theoretical and more systematic than salvation from external distress, the quest for which is characteristic of nonprivileged classes. The intellectual seeks in various ways, the casuistry of which extends into infinity, to endow his life with a pervasive meaning, and thus to find unity with himself, with his fellow men, and with the cosmos. It is the intellectual who transforms the concept of the world into the problem of meaning. As intellectualism suppresses belief in magic, the world's processes become disenchanted, lose their magical significance, and henceforth simply "are" and "happen" but no longer signify anything. As a consequence, there is a growing demand that the world and the total pattern of life be subject to an order that is significant and meaningful.

The conflict of this requirement of meaningfulness with the empirical realities of the world and its institutions, and with the possibilities of conducting one's life in the empirical world, are responsible for the intellectual's characteristic flights from the world. This may be an escape into absolute loneliness, or in its more modern form, e.g., in the case of Rousseau, to a nature unspoiled by human institutions. Again, it may be a world-fleeing romanticism like the flight to the people, untouched by social conventions, characteristic of the Russian *Narodnitschestvo*. It may be more contemplative, or more actively ascetic; it may primarily seek individual salvation or collective revolutionary transformation of the world in the direction of a more ethical status.[10]

The emergence of liberal capitalism produced both relative affluence (which could support a large stratum of intellectuals), and an ideology which supported—even insisted upon—a free market in ideas as well as in economic activity.[11] By the middle of the nineteenth century, with the growth of printing and the concentration of populations in cities, intellectuals in Europe had become an important force. The rapid expansion of university systems under the impetus of technical specialization, professionalization, and capitalist affluence had reduced the dependence of intellectuals upon private patronage. Moreover, their relative independence and their relative size as a group, as well as their separation from the direct exercise of power, had helped develop in the stratum—in some countries, at least—a degree of self-consciousness.

To be sure, their influence and role varied from country to country. In nineteenth-century Germany and England, intellectuals tended to be either part of the establishment or relatively moderate reformers. In France, and later in Russia, they tended to stand outside the dominant structure of power and to be far more radically critical of it. Despite the obvious cultural and economic differences, in both France and Russia intellectual ferment resulted from sharp social and class divisions that led, in both cases, to intense conflict.[12] There were, moreover, some important similarities; in both countries, for example, the educational system played an important role. Open to young people who sought upward mobility, the systems were oriented to the training of humanists who could not be absorbed by the economy, and both systems produced, at different times, a relatively large number of "intellectuals" who could not find employment which they regarded as suitable to their talents and training. In continental Europe, then, universities were often highly politicized, and students played important if not central roles in radical movements. The same phenomenon took place in a number of non-Western universities when they were created, based on Western models, in the nineteenth century.[13]

II. American Intellectuals

An intellectual stratum did not begin to emerge in the United States until the early to middle eighteenth century. As one might expect, its members took their leading ideas and character from the nation which had been primarily responsible for the American settlement, but with important differences. The intellectual statesmen and writers who comprised the founding generation resembled most closely in style and activity the reformist Whig gentry of late-eighteenth-century England. They were practical, sober men of ideas, whose intellectual activity was largely determined by the fact that, politically, at least, they were a governing class. Essentially, they wished to institutionalize in America a liberal Whig world-view derived from, but different from, the English tradition out of which they sprang. The American articulation of the nascent liberal creed was a recodification of Calvinist-derived "natural rights" and English politics, which worked itself out in the necessities of a new place, without a king, peasantry, or aristocracy.[14]

Thus, those descendants of the Calvinists who founded America were not only participants in a particular ethos; they were also, almost by necessity, intellectuals, and they lived in a time and place that was conducive to granting intellectuals power. As early as the 1830s, however, they were already being driven from political life. Despite the support he received from some intellectuals, Andrew Jackson self-consciously regarded himself as the very antithesis of a "man of ideas." He and his supporters were, in their eyes, practical, relatively unlettered men carrying out practical, pragmatic policies, and not mere "scribblers." His Whig Party opponents very quickly went him one better. By 1840, the Whigs were offering their own version of the man of the people in William Henry Harrison, emphasizing his popular origins and style as against the "effete" Martin Van Buren. The pattern was to continue well into the twentieth century, as Whig, Democratic, and Republican politicians exhibited relative disdain for what later were to be called "eggheads" in favor of "virile" and practical leaders.[15]

Nor was lack of interest in "scribblers" and their ideas confined to politicians. It was characteristic of the society as a whole, something Alexis de Tocqueville noted in *Democracy in America:*

> America has hitherto produced very few writers of distinction; it possesses no great historians and not a single eminent poet. The inhabitants of that country look upon literature with a kind of disapprobation. . . . The spirit of the Americans is averse to general ideas; it does not seek theoretical discoveries. Neither politics nor manufactures direct them to such speculations, and although new laws are perpetually enacted in the United States, no great writers there have . . . inquired into the general principles of legislation.[16]

Americans' lack of deference to intellectuals and lack of interest in social theory was remarked upon by other European visitors, and bemoaned by native-born, self-confessed intellectuals. They undoubtedly exaggerated somewhat. After all, the Transcendentalists and other groups were not without influence in American life. Nevertheless, compared to their European counterparts, the influence of American intellectuals was indeed marginal.

America's social and cultural dynamic was responsible for its failure, for so long, to develop an intellectual class with direct or indirect political influence. It was from a secularized version of Calvinism that liberal-capitalist ideology emerged in England and was transported to America. The ideology was advanced in other European societies by intellectuals, at least partly because they believed that England's stability, prosperity, and power derived from it.[17] In England and the rest of Europe, however, liberal capitalism developed in the midst of societies emerging from feudalism—societies which contained aristocracies, peasants, and long historical traditions. The entrepreneurs who brought capitalism into being were therefore engaged, from the first, in a conflict with a certain kind of traditional culture and class structure. They were conscious of themselves as a class, and particularly so because a new, class-conscious working class emerged (supported by intellectuals) to challenge them.

In Europe liberal capitalism was part of a complex whole; in America it was everything. Little wonder, then, that creative intellectuals played so small a role in America, and faded from the scene after the break with England. In a society lacking fundamental ideological conflict, potentially critical intellectuals lacked an environment to nurture them; there was no class to fight. By the 1830s, the business of America was business, and the god of America was hard practical work. So strong was the power of this American ethos—bolstered by an ever-expanding economy—that throughout the nineteenth century it rapidly integrated groups migrating to the country from other cultural and social backgrounds.

Theoretically, the Catholic Church, which, in Europe, was quite hostile to liberal capitalism, could have provided an alternative view.[18] Indeed, some more sensitive Catholic clerics were anxious to protect their growing immigrant flocks from the insidious influence of a liberal, individualistic, bourgeois culture which, as they correctly perceived, was Protestant at base.

They failed, of course. In part this was because the migration to the United States consisted primarily of lower-class workers and peasants (and very few intellectuals), but in larger measure it had to do with the assimilating power of the American environment itself. Catholics in the United States rapidly absorbed the American ethos, avoiding conflict with Rome—except for the "Americanist heresy" at the turn of the century—by ignoring the intellectual issues.[19]

Little wonder that for so long many intellectuals felt alienated, and often sought solace in Europe. Those who became involved in American politics—for example, as "Mugwumps" (political independents) or Progressives—did not transcend the basic ideological framework of their society. If they opposed slavery as abolitionists before the Civil War, or imperialism toward the end of the century, or the philistinism of the new entrepreneurial classes, they did so in the name of liberalism, and their reform efforts were largely directed toward ending corruption in government, living up to America's ideals, or preventing America's unique institutions from being eroded by social changes which they felt might undermine the promise of the founders of the Republic. Even the "Muckrakers," who, for a short time, exercised some influence, were, on the whole, only "liberal" reformers. As Richard Hofstadter pointed out, they were "moderate men who intended to propose no radical remedies." In fact, for the most part their sentiments were rooted in Protestant notions of sin and redemption: "their appeal was . . . to mass sentiments of responsibility, indignation and guilt. Hardly anyone intended that these sentiments should result in action drastic enough to transform American society."[20]

By the mid-nineteenth century, political parties in every European country were based on explicit ideological assumptions, calling upon intellectuals to provide them with systematic rationales. In the United

States, on the other hand, political parties, reflecting this culture, were practical organizations designed to achieve certain ends for certain groups. They were run by practical men, largely lawyers, who were not above getting their hands dirty. Intellectuals did play an important role from time to time (certainly Abraham Lincoln, Theodore Roosevelt, and Woodrow Wilson can be called intellectuals without stretching the definition too far), but, for the most part, when they did get involved, as in the case of the Mugwumps, their efforts were less than successful.[21]

By the end of the nineteenth century, America was rapidly industrializing, and a powerful new capitalist urban society was emerging. In addition, education and communication networks were expanding, as was a European-derived "high culture"; and Americans, at least on the east coast, were much more aware of the European scene and the intellectual ferment present there. Further, the continuing mass immigration from Europe now included those who had absorbed alternative ideological perspectives (primarily socialism and anarchism) in their mother countries. Many Swedish, Jewish, Finnish, and Italian migrants, who arrived in the United States in the latter part of the nineteenth and early twentieth centuries, came from countries in which a socialist or anarchist tradition had already been established.

On the whole, the influence of these groups was not very great, and the second generation, if not the first, gave up their radicalism for the "American way." In New York and other cities, however, many Jewish immigrants retained their early commitments and provided, along with some academic intellectuals, the nucleus of groups which urged a basic critique of American society.[22]

Something else was happening, too. Americans might not have admired intellectuals very much, but their faith in men of science ("experts") was growing. After all, these were people who could improve agricultural techniques, contribute to industrial expansion through techniques of "scientific management," and even find pragmatic solutions to social problems. Thus, governments increasingly turned to experts in a variety of areas for practical help, and contributed to the expansion of the university system for practical purposes as well as because of the pressure of populist ideas. On the state level, Robert M. La Follette was willing to rely upon a "brain trust" and to turn to the University of Wisconsin for expert advice. On the national level, Theodore Roosevelt and Woodrow Wilson did the same.

The willingness to rely on experts continued and even expanded during the 1920s, despite the conservatism of the period. It grew even more rapidly during the New Deal, as the government bureaucracy increased in size, and as federal and state governments turned to academic experts for advice on economic and social issues. In the newer social sciences—sociology, psychology, and political science—these experts were oriented toward social planning and were persuaded that government should seek social solutions to social problems, because such problems were a function of the organization of society rather than of individual failures or of the divine scheme of things. This perspective was an extension of the contradictory individualism of the liberal view of human nature, which had emphasized, from the time of John Locke, that human beings naturally pursued their own self interest, but also that each person came into the world as a "tabula rasa" upon which the environment wrote. Later, liberals would argue far more strongly than had Locke that individuals could be raised to recognize that their own interests coincided with the general welfare.

In the early nineteenth century, reformers concentrated on changing the environment to improve the individual. This perspective, as David Rothman argues, motivated those who created the first prison-reform movement.[23] By the late nineteenth century, however, progressive thought was changing again. The new enlightened view held that, since men's and women's attitudes were largely determined by the social environment in which they developed, one could more readily help large numbers of individuals by a careful examination and reform of society's irrationalities and weaknesses.

The New Deal probably provided some sort of breakthrough for "experts," but during World War II and its aftermath the stream turned into a river. Large numbers of academics were called to Washington during the war. In the postwar period a growing professional population took over an even larger number of tasks which had once been left to the individual, the family, the churches, and private philanthropy.

By the late 1950s and early 1960s, social policy in the United States was largely being made in consultation with trained professionals whose ideas had been formed in universities. Not all such professionals were intellectuals, but they were at least consumers, once or twice removed, of assumptions about the nature of reality created by cosmopolitan intellectuals in the university and elsewhere.[24]

Not only was government relying upon experts. A new generation of university-educated businessmen was turning to them for advice, and/or endowing foundations (run by professionals) as their contribution to solving society's problems. Of course, they assumed that such solutions would support the framework of a liberal-capitalist—although increasingly welfare-oriented—political and social order. Some of the businessmen and their professional staffs were even reading books by intellectuals, which told them that they were "other-directed" or "organization

men," or which counseled a kind of education for their children characterized by "democratic," rather than "authoritarian" methods, and
designed to promote "self-realization," rather than merely hard work.[25]
The contrast, even with the 1920s, could not have been sharper. In
former decades the key concepts for those in business had been organization and self-discipline, ideas easily traced back at least to Benjamin
Franklin.

In the meantime, the academic and intellectual communities had been
undergoing a transformation which stemmed partly from a growth in
size, and partly from the infusion of new ideas and new blood. By the
1920s, a substantial radical movement had developed among intellectuals in Eastern urban areas, as well as a more broadly based critique of
America's "narrow-minded, small-town," Calvinist cultural base. This
is clearly evident, for example, in the work of Sinclair Lewis, or in
Sherwood Anderson's *Winesburg, Ohio*.

The depression of the 1930s focused the critique even more sharply,
although it was increasingly directed against capitalism itself. And while
at least some of the criticism of America still derived from that traditional gentry mentality which had provided the cadres for the
Mugwumps and progressivism, these groups were now joined by newer
Jewish immigrants from Russia and Eastern Europe who had begun to
play a key role in the intellectual life of large urban centers such as New
York, Los Angeles, San Francisco, and even Washington.

Only a relatively small group of intellectuals actually joined the
Communist Party in the 1930s, but many more became at least closet
socialists. Such people gradually came to play a more important role in
the expanding number of intellectual magazines, such as *The Nation* and
The New Republic, in book publishing, and on the research staffs of
national magazines, as well as in the arts and the movie industry.[26]

By the 1950s, university-trained intellectuals were rapidly moving into
positions in major media outlets including television, as well as into
other cultural spheres, and their influence over other middle-class
Americans was growing. Both their numbers and their intellectual
sophistication were substantially increased by the new influx of largely
Jewish intellectuals from Europe, fleeing Nazi oppression.[27]

In the 1920s and 1930s, the thinking and writing of intellectuals did not
seem to matter very much, for they were still largely ignored by most
Americans, who, whether or not they lived in small towns, retained
much of a small-town mentality. In the 1950s, the influence of the
intellectual stratum was masked by the cold war and the advent of
McCarthyism. Both of these events, plus American affluence, tended to
mute direct criticism of American society.

In retrospect, however, the influence of the new strategic elites—those groups clustered around the dissemination of ideas—was clearly growing. McCarthyism represented (as did Nixon and those around him) the very hostile reaction of an older America to the new liberal cosmopolitanism. And both McCarthy and Nixon demonstrated that the ability of older ideas to muster troops was much weaker than the conventional wisdom would have us believe.

McCarthy was unable to build up a strong base of support, and the effects of what he did soon dissipated. Indeed, the consequences of the "Red scare" of the 1950s were far smaller than those of the "Red scare" of the 1920s, largely because the forces of the new liberal cosmopolitanism were much stronger in the universities, in the bureaucracy, in the courts, and among the general population. There is at least some evidence that, on many campuses, being a supporter of McCarthy was more likely to have a negative impact on one's career than being an opponent.[28] It is true that up to one hundred academics (almost entirely at less prestigious schools) lost their jobs. However, during the post–World War I "Red scares," literally thousands were arrested, although only a few were convicted of any crimes. More significantly, hundreds of aliens were deported, and "leftists" in the academic community were hounded.[29]

The 1960s was the decisive decade. Supported by conflicts resulting from the civil-rights movement and the war in Vietnam, those who had been on the left in the 1930s (and their children) helped spark a new radical movement which now received at least the passive support of large numbers of middle-class Americans, especially those attached to universities. The movement was both political and cultural, and the two aspects fused during the mid-1960s, only to split apart shortly after the end of the decade. But during the mid-1960s most traditional American institutions came under attack. Radicals like Jerry Rubin and Abbie Hoffman, and many others, viewed "Amerika" as a sick society because of its bureaucratic, imperialist, capitalist structure, and the rigid, puritanical values which had been created by it and which supported it. It had to be remade, and the way to remake it was to destroy its cultural institutions, erect a "counterculture," and replace its official, heartless, calculating politics with a transformed, humane (if rarely well-defined) social system. Unlike traditional leftist solutions, which focused on seizing the means of production in a workers' revolution, the New Left would encourage human growth instead of merely solving problems. It was an attack as much on traditional conceptions of personality as it was on a system of economic or political organization.

By no means did all intellectuals, professionals, or liberal politicians who sympathized with the explosion of the 1960s, or who benefited from it, accept the argument in its extreme form, but many resonated with it. Thus, at the height of the period, George McGovern could endorse Charles Reich's *The Greening of America* in the most glowing terms, and Senator Jacob Javits could attend parties (and hobnob knowingly) with leading counterculture figures. Hosts of activist groups ranging from "people's lawyers" to environmentalists, supported by the analyses of academics and the media, used both the courts and the media to produce—from the point of view of conservatives—significant changes in American society. These included a substantial escalation of government regulation of business activity, special aid to favored minority groups, and the removal of inhibitions against the free consumption and expression of new experiences and life styles. It was by no means a question of intellectuals, as a stratum, pitted against other segments of the population, but of a total ambience accepted by large segments of both the intellectual and professional communities as well as by many members of other strategic elites, including "enlightened" businessmen. Initially, the cultural and social views of these elites were far more "progressive" than those of members of the working or lower middle class.

The importance of intellectuals had been established, and it continued into the 1980s and beyond. While intellectuals as a group remained liberal or radical, a small band of ex-liberal (now labeled neoconservative) critics joined the even smaller number of traditional conservative academic intellectuals in mounting an attack on the new conventional wisdom. Many members of this group came to exert considerable influence in the media and in Republican administrations.[30]

Perhaps more significantly, social and political shifts in the Soviet Union, Eastern Europe, and even China during the late 1980s made it increasingly difficult for left-wing American and European intellectuals to convince others that Marxist categories could provide an adequate basis for a critique of capitalist institutions. With few exceptions, Communist countries were turning to capitalist-type mechanisms to revive stagnant economies, and in Russia, at least, openly admitting the crimes of the Stalinist and even Leninist epochs.[31] In 1989, the Chinese regime did crack down on students and others calling for even more "democracy." However, nothing indicates how far Western intellectuals had moved since the 1960s better than the fact that many who had supported Mao Tse-tung and the Cultural Revolution of the 1960s, now reacted with horror and dismay to such attacks upon liberalization.

On the other hand, as we shall see, many intellectuals have switched from a former Marxist stand to a new "multiculturalism," which they consider to be closely tied to what has come to be called "post-modernity."

III. Higher Education in the United States

At its founding, the American system of higher education was patterned after the British.[32] The ideal was that of small, relatively elite colleges and universities located in the country or in small towns. Most of the best of these, including Harvard, Yale, and Princeton, were founded by religious denominations. However, by the beginning of the nineteenth century they were losing their denominational cast, opening themselves to young men (and occasionally women) from a variety of backgrounds. They were also quite successful in replacing church support with funds from secular sources, including growing amounts of money contributed by alumni.

By the end of the nineteenth century most nonpublic American colleges and universities, while they retained a loose religious identification, were supported by secular private philanthropy. They were, and remained until very recently, purely private institutions, supported by a philanthropic impulse unknown anywhere else in the world. They developed their own particular form of governance, consisting of a board of trustees, in whom ultimate authority was vested, and a strong president who was responsible for the practical running of the institution.[33]

As with most European countries, higher education in America was first limited to the well to do, but by the mid-nineteenth century this had begun to change. The creation of liberal-arts state universities and state land-grant colleges devoted to improving agriculture, as well as new private universities, eventually revolutionized the American system of higher education. To some extent, public institutions modeled themselves on the pattern of leading private institutions, though, in the Midwest and West especially, they were more likely to emphasize education in practical matters than were the elite private colleges and universities of the East.

After the Civil War, the United States developed a lead in providing higher education for the masses, a lead which it still holds. Between 1870 and 1945, university enrollment in the United States doubled every fifteen years. The growth of higher education, however, really came into its own after World War II, when both the "GI Bill of Rights" for veterans and an explosion of funds expended by the states and the federal government contributed to a massive expansion of the university population. Today about half of the relevant age population enrolls in institutions of higher learning, staffed by over 500,000 college faculty.

In 1899–1900, 382 doctorates were granted in the United States. The number granted in 1976–1977 was 33,000, and the total number of Americans holding such degrees was close to 600,000. By 1982, approximately 750,000 Americans held doctoral degrees. In 1940, approximately 3.4 million Americans over twenty-five years of age had completed four or more years of college, less than 5 percent of the relevant age group. By 1973, the number was well over 11 million, and by 1982 it had reached 24 million, or almost 18 percent of the population.[34]

This growth was accompanied by massive changes in the system of higher education. First, most private universities lost their religious cast and became purely secular institutions. Second, while some religious and elite private colleges and universities retained something of a traditional curriculum, most state and private institutions gradually replaced it, in the late nineteenth and early twentieth centuries, with a system of elective courses emphasizing the newly emerging social sciences. Harvard University, under President Charles Eliot, actually took the lead in this movement.

America developed a pluralistic system of higher education. There were colleges which allowed one to obtain a degree in almost any craft, from accounting and engineering to home economics and physical education. Thus, the United States boasted a hierarchy of colleges and universities, from the elite schools which confirmed the status of the rich, but which were often followed by graduate school for professional training, to technical schools which granted degrees in various "practical subjects."

At the same time, the structure of power in the university began to change. The presidency declined in power to be replaced by departments, as faculty fought for an institutionalized notion of academic freedom and a tenure system, both of which protected them from arbitrary dismissal. Today, with exceptions, university presidents are far less strong than they once were, and boards of trustees, whether private or public, usually accept the authority of the professoriate in academic matters.[35] On the other hand, new constituencies, including students, have been gaining in power at the partial expense of academic staff.

The professoriate

For most of American history, college professors constituted only a segment of the intellectual community. The intellectual stratum largely consisted of persons who made their living as journalists and writers, primarily in a few cities where they could support themselves by publishing journals and engaging in some teaching. It also consisted partly of academics who supported themselves by teaching but turned most of their attention to the outside world.

The influence of the academic segment of the intellectual community grew steadily during the twentieth century and reached a new peak, first during the New Deal and then during World War II. There were outcroppings of radicalism at Harvard and other elite institutions in the 1930s, and many unaffiliated New York intellectuals joined the Communist Party or developed close relations with it. However, university faculties in particular were, until the 1950s, relatively conservative, or at least not very different from the electorate as a whole, as their voting records demonstrate. In the 1944 presidential election, for example, they voted only 3 percent more Democratic than did the general public.[36]

The end of the war produced a significant shift in the character of the professoriate. For one thing, as America became increasingly "modern and professionalized," the so-called "free" (unaffiliated) intellectual began to disappear. That is, the intellectual and academic communities in the United States tended to become one and the same.

At the same time the nature of the academic community began to change even as it grew in size. Traditionally, the academy had been populated largely by middle-class and upper-middle-class Protestants. The rapid expansion of college faculties which started in the early 1950s, the GI Bill, the decline of prejudice and quotas, and the insistence upon merit as defined by grades and tests, permitted the entry into the profession of scholars of lower-middle-class and working-class backgrounds who saw the academy as a source of social mobility. They could become intellectuals, and at the same time earn a living. Americans of Jewish background were especially helped by the shift. They chose the academic profession in large numbers.

C. Wright Mills had warned in *White Collar*[37] that this new cadre of intellectuals would, given their dependence on the system, be quite conservative. Nothing could have been further from the truth. Intellectuals of Jewish background remained on the left. They also probably converted at least some of their colleagues. In 1952, academics were 12 percent more Democratic, and in 1972, they gave George McGovern 18 percent more votes than did the general public.

The trend was even more pronounced at elite schools and in the social sciences and humanities than it was at nonelite schools or in technical fields. In the Ladd-Lipset study of the professoriate, some 76 percent of social scientists voted for McGovern, while 64 percent classified themselves as either "liberal" or "very liberal." Various attitudinal measures used in the study indicate that this self-description is not inaccurate. Further, the most liberal social scientists were those at the top of the pecking order in terms of both publication and reputation. The same study demonstrates that academics of Jewish background were well to the left of their Christian colleagues. They also published more than other academics, and were far more likely to be teaching in elite institutions than in those of the second rank or lower.[38]

The liberalism of the profession was by now self-reinforcing. "Liberal" or "radical" students chose to major in the social sciences much more frequently than did conservative students. They were further socialized into these modes of thinking by their training, and it is reasonable to expect that they tended to favor the hiring of those who thought as they did about the nature of social issues. Nielsen's study of philanthropic foundations demonstrates that, by the 1960s, a similar outlook was shared by the directors and staffs of these organizations, especially those concerned with public-policy issues.[39]

The academic community has become increasingly liberal and cosmopolitan, even as its influence has grown. Whereas in the 1960s universities still contained a remnant of the old Protestant professoriate who, along with "neoconservative" Jews, managed to block more radical changes, this group has been eroded by age and retirement. Thus, the faculty today is likely to be more to the left than it was twenty-five years ago. Increasingly, those with power are those who were more or less active in the New Left of the 1960s. While Marxism is not in fashion at the moment, cultural and social critiques of American society are. A substantial segment of the faculty supports a liberal cosmopolitan ideology which consists of three elements.[40]

The first element can be characterized by the term "expressive individualism," coined by Bellah et al. in their book *Habits of the Heart*.[41] It refers to the free expression and satisfaction of individual desires in the pursuit of the good life. The core of this concept is the priority given to free, unfettered expression of impulses, assumed to be good in and of themselves. Expressive individualism is characterized by a shift in the concept of the individual from a "being" as a part of a great chain of being, to a "self." Historically, it marks a shift from the traditional Christian restraint of impulse to its free expression, and the rejection of the traditional for the new and avant-garde.

A second strand, "collectivist liberalism" (or welfare-state liberalism), emerged from the Depression Era.[42] This often has been considered the major domain of contemporary ideology. Collectivist liberalism rests on the belief that the central government ought to ameliorate the economic inequalities of the capitalist system. It is in opposition to the traditional "rugged individualist" view that economic well-being stems from individual effort and personal achievement. Collectivist liberals support the expansion of the welfare state, favor more government-induced economic equality, support government regulation of business "in the public interest," and hold that those who are economically unsuccessful are not ultimately responsible for improving their own condition. They strive for relative equality of outcomes for all groups.[43]

A third strand of contemporary ideology, "system alienation," emerged during the "crisis" of the 1960s. It might be summarized by actor Paul Newman's sardonic description of Hollywood's inversion of patriotism during the 1960s: "Screw God Bless America." System alienation rests on the belief, expressed in its pure form by the New Left, that the social order of bourgeois-liberal society is inherently dehumanizing and repressive, and that its structures of authority are inherently suspect. The feelings of system alienation are closely tied to a critique of American capitalism. The feelings of general alienation and beliefs about the welfare state, however, are separate ideological dimensions. One can be patriotic and also a believer in the welfare state, as were many New Deal liberals before the Vietnam War.

We do know, despite some early findings to the contrary, that the world-view of college students is affected by the education they receive. Thus, academics have exercised considerable influence over an ever-larger number of Americans.[44]

The influence of academics, moreover, is no longer limited to the classroom. They are called upon as consultants to government, and the media now turn to them far more than they once did for independent expert opinion on various issues. They can write for a variety of "intellectual" journals of opinion, some of which have a fairly extensive readership among various leadership groups, and they are welcome on the op-ed pages of the *New York Times* and the *Washington Post.* Indeed, they are even interviewed on television, and their books are often reviewed in the *New York Times.*

The relationship between the national media and the academic community has been reciprocal. If journalists now turn to academic and other intellectuals, the intellectual community has fully embraced the media. Academic styles have changed as the professoriate competes for media attention. At one point a good book was supposed to make its way in the profession by itself; now some academic authors make efforts to be interviewed on talk shows and to attract reviews by large-circulation journals. Scientific bodies hold press conferences to obtain attention, and some academics, at least, make every effort to appear in op-ed pages, both for prestige and to get their ideas out to a larger audience.

As a result, the structure of influence within the academic profession itself has changed. In the past, professional success was determined by publication in peer-reviewed journals. Today, these may easily be by-passed, and both promotions and grants can depend upon media cover-age. Indeed, such coverage can sometimes be as important as profes-sional reviews, at least in the social sciences and humanities. And, insofar as journalists' taste and ideology determine what will be covered or reviewed, and how it will be covered or reviewed, journalists influ-ence the structure and content of academic writing. Such influence has reinforced the liberal cosmopolitanism of the academic profession.

The role of the academic profession began to shift in other ways in the 1950s. Many in the profession had, for some time, regarded research and writing as more important than teaching. Meanwhile, the growing public importance of social science and increased possibilities of academic mobility made concentration on research and writing an even more attractive option. Given increasing competition by universities for high-visibility scholars, publication was much more likely than teaching to translate into higher salaries and fringe benefits, including travel.

As late as the 1940s, academics in many schools (especially the smaller liberal-arts colleges) still viewed their profession as primarily that of teacher. Further, their ties to their college or university were such that they saw it as a community in which they played the role of surrogate parents, helping their young charges both to learn and to develop moral character.[45]

By the 1950s this had changed, and the pace of change escalated in the early 1960s. Research and publication in one's field became a major source of social mobility for academics, and to that they directed their energies. No longer was the school a community of teachers and stu-dents; rather, it had become a place (even at liberal-arts colleges) in which, for the best members of the faculty, academic publication and prestige in one's field were the primary goals. Needless to say, the sense of community which had once characterized American colleges and universities began to erode. The erosion continues today.[46]

The students

Except for the periods of the American Revolution and Civil War, American college and university students had, historically, been re-markably apolitical. While they complained or even rioted about poor food and other problems, these complaints were never elevated to the level of political-ideological rebellion. Student behavior reflected the lack of ideological conflict in the society, including the lack of ideological parties. (In Europe such parties on the right and the left often organized student affiliates in the universities.) It also reflected the nature of the American population, the character of the university, and the structure of the economy. Most upper-middle-class students at elite institutions continued to rely on the college or university as a means of confirming status, but generations of the children of immigrants used higher education as a means of social mobility in a dynamic economy, and as a way of becoming more American. Their ability to do so was partly a function of the manner in which universities developed in the society. As against most European countries, American colleges did not model themselves on the traditional elite schools. Thus, the system which developed ranged from elite schools to agricultural colleges, business schools, and even colleges of physical education, all of which provided college degrees.

If students engaged in any rebellion it was against the old country ways of their parents. As with intellectuals, they accepted the parameters of the system as given. Even the European student upheavals of the 1930s echoed only faintly in the United States. Left-wing student organizations were formed at New York's heavily Jewish City Colleges and, in very small numbers, at some elite schools, but they remained marginal.

During the first half of the twentieth century most residential colleges and universities continued their "parental" role. They enforced rules regarding personal activity (especially regarding sex and alcohol) and provided college-wide functions, including organized sports, to keep students busy in their "spare time." Teachers may have been somewhat authoritarian, but student and teacher did relate as surrogate parent and child.

The pattern was beginning to change by the late 1950s and early 1960s, though some of the old familiar landmarks were still present. Core curricula had all but disappeared, though at many institutions weakened sets of requirements remained in force. The acceptance of the "gentlemen's C" at many elite institutions was no longer so widespread, in part because the GI Bill and increasing government and private scholarships had brought to the elite universities a new breed of hard-working lower-middle-class and even working-class students.[47]

These students could now enter elite universities not only because of newly available funds, but also because admissions standards had changed. Once a bastion of Protestant sensibility (some Jews were admitted, but Jewish candidates, and others, encountered quotas), elite universities were now admitting students on "objective bases," relying heavily on grades, and scores of standardized tests, rather than estimates of character. The private, elite, pace-setting universities had not become meritocracies, but they were moving in that direction.

Other changes had taken place too. As pointed out earlier, many academics had become more interested in their professional fields than in their roles as teachers and mentors. While in some ways the focus on research and writing may have contributed to better teaching from a purely academic perspective, the old personal nexus between student and teacher had been weakened. The *in loco parentis* function of universities had diminished as parietal and other rules (including compulsory college-wide meetings, a remnant of the old required chapels) had been eliminated. State and many private universities grew rapidly in size from 5,000 to 10,000 to 30,000 students. Inevitably, universities of that size were rather impersonal institutions.

Perhaps most important, the new "liberal cosmopolitan" orientation had more or less triumphed, supporting alternate life styles. Partly as the result of this and other changes in the broader political world, many large universities (such as the University of California at Berkeley) developed a substantial core of young people hanging around on their fringes. These young people were often perpetual graduate students, taking a course or two and eking out an existence at now-and-then jobs and/or through welfare checks or parental support. Adopting expressive individualism as a life style, they joined the counterculture and refused to commit themselves to the workaday world.

From the 1960s to the 1990s

In the early 1960s, American universities were in what seemed to be an excellent position. The McCarthyism of the 1950s had been overcome, and although it had injured some faculty in lesser institutions, its impact had not been widespread or lasting. In any event, universities were garnering increasing funds from both the federal government and private sources. Teachers were secure in their tenured positions. The prestige of intellectuals was at an all-time high, and student bodies at ever-growing institutions seemed to be improving every year as merit and scholarship became key values on a large number of campuses.

Liberal commentators on education were quite pleased with what they had created. They gloried in the size of the university, and they were proud of its public impact. While they recognized that the change had resulted in some losses, these were far outpaced by the advantages which had accrued.

Speaking for and typifying these attitudes, Clark Kerr, President of the University of California at Berkeley, published, in 1963, a book entitled *The Uses of the University*.[48]

In it he enthusiastically described the power and size of Berkeley. The University

> had operating expenditures from all sources of nearly half a billion dollars, with almost another 100 million for construction; a total employment of over 40,000 people, more than IBM and in a far greater variety of endeavors; operations in over a hundred locations, counting campuses, experiment stations, agricultural and urban extension centers, and projects abroad involving more than fifty countries; nearly 10,000 courses in its catalogues; some form of contact with nearly every industry, nearly every level of government, nearly every person in its region. Vast amounts of expensive equipment were serviced and maintained. Over 4,000 babies were born in its hospitals. It is the world's largest purveyor of white mice. It will soon have the world's largest primate colony. It will soon have 100,000 students—30,000 of them at the graduate level; yet much less than one-third of its expenditures are directly related to teaching. It already has nearly 200,000 students in extension courses—including one out of every three lawyers and one out of every six doctors in the state. (pp. 7–8)

Kerr was not unaware that these achievements had been purchased at the price of a community of a certain kind, but that did not particularly disturb him:

> [T]here is less sense of community than in a village but also less sense of confinement. There is less sense of purpose than within the town but there are more ways to excel. . . . As against the village and the town the "city" is more like the totality of civilization as it has evolved and more an integral part of it; and movement to and from the surrounding society has been greatly accelerated. As in a city, there are many separate endeavors under a single rule of law. (p. 41)

Then the picture changed. Universities exploded in the middle and late 1960s. The proximate causes of the explosions were the civil-rights revolution and, a little later, the Vietnam War. The first was important because of the increasing identification of students with the "downtrodden," who, they claimed, were ignored by the society. The second was important because it was a war which students believed to be unjust, yet for which they might be drafted.

However, it is hard to conceive that the issues which led to the rise of the New Left would have been important even twenty-five years earlier. Without denying the importance of these events, it is, I believe, legitimate to argue that the rebellion was, at least in part, a rebellion against America's liberal Protestant culture—its collective superego—

facilitated by the changes that Kerr and others like him had produced in the university.

In any event the student radicals and their intellectual supporters on the faculty and in the community at large attacked the war, racism, and (later in the decade) sexism and the pollution of the environment. All the evil in America was, they insisted, ultimately a function of repressive capitalism.[49]

Drawing upon ideas developed by Charles Reich, Herbert Marcuse, and others, the radicals wanted to put expressive individualism (including the freedom to experiment with drugs and sex, and to be supported by the system) and some sort of "participatory" socialism in capitalism's place. At the same time, they claimed that they desired a society which fully incorporated black people, other minorities, and women.

At the university, they attacked the remnants of the traditional restraints upon student behavior, demanded the admission and support of more minority students, and violently opposed any university connections with the government and an "unjust war," including ROTCs on campus, military or CIA recruiting, and research on defense contracts.[50]

These demands and others were generally met, though often only after student sit-ins or demonstrations. Parietal rules were eliminated, as were, in some universities, the remnants of course distribution requirements. Speakers of a really conservative stripe were not invited to campuses or were sometimes disinvited to avoid possible conflict. A good many universities and colleges eliminated any connections with America's military, from research grants to the ROTC. Universities worked hard to bring in more black students, and to hire more black faculty, even if, in the former case, it meant taking some poorly qualified candidates.

Beyond this, students did gain a new voice in university decision making. Grade inflation, which began, it was argued, to protect students from the draft, became a permanent fixture, and spread widely—partly because, one suspects, faculty had become somewhat afraid of alienating students who were now, at an increasing number of institutions, publicly evaluating the performance of their teachers. In general, the distance between faculty and students was reduced; teachers and students dressed more informally; in some classes, instructors could be called by their first names. In many classes, more effort was expended on helping students effectively express their feelings than on conveying knowledge.

With the end of the Vietnam War, college campuses became quiet again. However, except at a few institutions, old understandings did not return. Important segments of the new perspective had been institutionalized. The ROTC may have been restored in some places but parietal rules were not. Indeed, the ground was being paved for a further assault on tradition by 1960s activists who had chosen education as a career and were moving upward in the academic system.

During the 1970s and 1980s, black and women's studies departments proliferated. Elite and other institutions competed intensively for black faculty. The evidence indicates that given equally qualified candidates, many colleges and universities preferred to hire the minority and/or female candidate before a white male. At a jobs panel at the 1989 convention of the American Sociological Association, it was openly admitted that this was so, and ads for teaching positions now all but state that this is the case. For example, the following advertisement for a job at the University of North Carolina at Wilmington appeared in the Job Information list of the Modern Language Association (English edition, October 1990, p. 24):

> We are seeking three generalists with a demonstrated interest in . . .
> We are particularly interested in minority candidates.

The same was true for student admissions. After the disastrous experience of the late 1960s, when black students from the ghetto were admitted despite their very low SAT scores, elite schools became somewhat more selective. However, they continued to admit African-American candidates who would not have qualified under normal circumstances. Even so, many colleges and universities simply could not meet the unwritten or written goals they had set for themselves under federal guidelines. To give the impression that such goals (which often came close to becoming quotas) had been met, some colleges and universities went out of their way to recruit high-scoring Asian students. They could then report that minorities were being admitted in ever-larger numbers.[51]

Black teachers presented an even more serious problem than did black students. A very small number of African Americans were obtaining Ph.D.s. Many of those obtained were in education. Very few were in the other social sciences, and almost none were in the sciences. In 1986, African Americans garnered only slightly more than 1 percent of Ph.D.s in the physical sciences. Asian Americans, on the other hand, received 7 percent of doctorates granted in the sciences.[52]

Any criticism of affirmative action was considered taboo at many universities and colleges, as were criticisms of black and women's studies programs. In these programs and elsewhere, the theoretical bases of the curriculum were being redefined. European philosophy and literature (sometimes even science) came under attack as providing a racist, male-dominated picture of the world. In addition, it was alleged, various marginal groups, such as blacks and Native Americans, were being left out of discussions of world and American history, as were women.

At the same time, many male and female homosexuals "came out of the closet." On some campuses they were well organized and aggressive. Reluctance to accept the proposition that homosexual life styles were merely legitimate alternate life styles, equal in every way to heterosexual life styles, was now regarded as evidence of homophobia. Speakers (such as religious fundamentalists) who did not hold "positive" views on the subject were rarely invited to campuses, and, when they came, were often prevented from speaking.

Toward the end of the 1980s, it became an offense to act in any way which might hurt the feelings of any group defined as a minority. This sometimes went to fairly ludicrous lengths as college administrations attempted to redefine the terms used to describe such groups. For example, according to a guide handed out to students by the Smith College Office of Student Affairs, there are no disabled people, only "the differently abled." In the same document, students are warned against "lookism," that is, evaluating people in terms of their appearance.

New programs were instituted which were designed to increase the proportion of minority students and faculty on campuses (especially elite campuses) and, it was asserted, to make them more comfortable. This involved setting new minimum quotas for black and Hispanic students at Berkeley, or goals for black students and faculty at Wellesley and Duke, or goals for numbers of "minority" students and faculty at Smith. As noted earlier, "goals" sometimes became quotas, although this was officially denied.[53]

These programs were partly a response to the fact that the proportion of black students on many elite college campuses had declined since the late 1960s or at least had not grown. Justifications were also found in the argument that students had to learn to live with culturally diverse groups, since they would have to work with such groups after college. It was also pointed out by those who favored such programs that, given immigration and birthrate patterns, the proportion of Americans of European background in this country will shrink dramatically in the next twenty years. Universities and colleges have to prepare for that future.

The same argument was used on many campuses—most notoriously Stanford—to justify redesigning courses associated with reading the great books of European culture so as to promote a concern with the literature of non-European peoples. Western culture, it was argued, was the culture of white male racists and homophobes. Students had to be made aware of this even as they were made aware of the contributions of other societies. Such awareness would help the dominant whites, even as it built up the self-esteem of minority students and hence improved their ability to learn.

Since Asian Americans are doing quite well with the traditional curriculum, it is difficult to determine how the changes are expected to benefit them. In any event it is by no means clear that those who urge such programs are genuinely interested in studying other cultures for their own sake. While there are exceptions, the emphasis seems less on including the *Analects* of Confucius or the *Bhagavad Gita* than on adding the writings of militant feminists, lesbians, Americans of Hispanic background, or other groups defined as oppressed, including African revolutionaries.[54] It is asserted that all of these represent a cultural orientation which differs from white-male-dominated Western culture. The changes seem designed less to broaden the scope of Euro-American students' knowledge than to activate their guilt. This is especially true of white males, who, whatever their background, are all characterized ethnically as "Anglos."

A number of colleges and universities, especially elite institutions, have also created special programs designed to encourage student and even faculty appreciation of cultural differences. While such programs are not usually compulsory, tremendous pressure is placed upon students to participate. The programs are often couched so as to convict American society of male-centered, Eurocentric racism and homophobia.

The programs are supplemented by new courses on racism, or by remaking some few traditional required courses (for example, freshman English at the University of Massachusetts) so as to stress all of the themes noted above. In some cases the changes have been blocked, modified, or delayed by angry faculty (for example, at the University of Texas).[55] In other cases the courses have been established without opposition.

Colleges and universities have also developed new rules and regulations designed to prevent members of the student body and/or faculty from making "insensitive remarks" which might psychologically injure minority persons regarding any of these categories. In some cases rules were adopted which merely prohibited the use of insulting epithets. In other cases (for example, at Smith College) they went much further, prohibiting the use of "stereotypes," that is, general group characterizations. Issues of sexual harassment have taken on special importance in this regard because of the increased power of campus feminists, various state and federal laws (including the Civil Rights Act of 1991), and court decisions on sexual harassment in the workplace and in schools.[56]

As a consequence, many colleges and universities have created regulations for punishing faculty or students who engage in sexual harassment. Such regulations are often quite vague, and university procedures often violate due process. In one case a professor was punished by his institution for "staring" at a female swimmer in the college pool. At the University of Minnesota, professors were charged with sexual harassment because of "insensitivity." In some cases the charges were eventually dropped, but not before considerable time and effort and, sometimes, funds had been expended.[57] Not to be outdone, the Modern Language Association started a "New Project on Anti-Feminist Harassment." Harassment included "easy dismissal of feminist writers, journals and presses."[58]

However, attempts to institutionalize censorship were seriously hampered by a series of court decisions. In 1989, a U.S. district court struck down the University of Michigan's speech code (*Doe v. University of Michigan*). It found that terms such as "victimize" and "stigmatize" lacked "precise meaning" and were unconstitutionally vague. "Students of common understanding were forced to guess whether a comment about a controversial issue would later be found to be sanctionable under the policy." Similar decisions were handed down in Wisconsin (*UWM Post Inc. et al. v. Board of Regents of the University of Wisconsin*, 1991) and in Virginia (*Iota Xi Chapter of Sigma Chi Fraternity v. George Mason University*, 1991).

Given these rulings, faculty opposition, and the ridicule of the press, administrations at public institutions quickly retreated.[59] At some private institutions which seemed likely to follow suit, faculties protested vociferously, and administrations either seriously limited the grounds of possible action against students or faculty or completely withdrew the new rules. Even though the decisions only applied to public schools, administrators at private institutions clearly believed that they could not exempt themselves from the rulings.

These were only district court rulings, but their unanimity was clearly sufficient to give many administrators pause. The pattern of decisions was capped by a 1992 Supreme Court decision overturning a municipal "hate speech" law in Saint Paul, Minnesota (*R.A.V. Petitioner v. City of Saint Paul*). While that decision and others did not necessarily prohibit all speech codes, it was clear that such codes would have to be written very carefully.[60]

This is by no means to say that colleges and universities are free of the kind of informal censorship that is a function of the aggressiveness of powerful minorities and/or administrative policy. The atmosphere at many colleges is such that students are afraid to speak in "socially and politically incorrect" ways, and faculty, despite the protection of tenure, tend to avoid controversial issues. Perhaps the most well known case in this regard is that of Professor Stephan Thernstrom at Harvard, a former civil-rights activist who was publicly accused by a few students of racial insensitivity on the flimsiest of grounds. The accusation was published by the *Harvard Crimson*. Thernstrom was defended by most (though not all) of his colleagues. Nevertheless, he decided that the publicity given the charges and the general harassment which followed upon them were not worth the effort. He no longer participates in the offending course.[61]

There are a large number of other cases. At the State University of New York at Binghamton, a meeting of the National Association of Scholars was disrupted by a violent mob of black students who had been told that it was a Klan meeting. At the University of Western Ontario, a Canadian professor who argued for the reality of racial differences in intelligence, as part of a general pattern of black-white differences, was threatened with dismissal and was given very low ratings for his teaching and scholarship, though his ratings had, in the past, been among the highest in the university. At the University of Delaware, a professor was (temporarily) denied a grant because she was suspected of racist scholarship. In another case a senior professor at Duke University, Stanley Fish, wrote a letter to the administration urging that James David Barber and other members of a newly formed chapter of the National Association of Scholars be denied important committee posts. The fact that most of these incidents (though not all) ended well is no cause for celebration.[62]

The establishment of new rules and programs followed an established trajectory. Black or other "minority" students would charge that some students had engaged in racist, homophobic, or other oppressive actions. The institution as a whole was then charged with creating an atmosphere in which such actions could occur, and minority students demanded the course changes, hiring and admission policies, and rule changes which have been described. The administration and much of the faculty have often supported such students and sometimes have even led them.

Racial incidents seem to have increased at some colleges and universities, though the extent of this increase is hard to document. Most of the incidents are anonymous—for example, writing epithets on walls or sending unsigned notes. At worst these are the work of one or a few students who clearly do what they do in secret, at least in part because they are a small minority and are afraid to express their hatred openly.

It is at least possible that some of these incidents have been staged by minority students who wish to draw attention to what they consider the general racism of the campus. Such behavior is not unknown: a case of this kind occurred at Amherst College.[63]

Why do racial and other incidents seem to be multiplying? Thomas Sowell and Shelby Steele both suggest that some of the increase in white racist acts stems from resentment of quota-like programs for blacks, and from the fact that white students are constantly being subjected to attacks upon themselves and upon the culture of which they are part.[64]

On the other hand, it can be argued that the behavior of black students, including their "rejection" of Western culture, may, as Sowell suggests, have something to do with patterns of recruitment, both of black students and of faculty. In both cases, many are being recruited for schools for which they would not necessarily qualify on the basis of purely merit-based standards.[65] Given their failure to perform as well as they had expected in comparison to other students, it is natural that they should turn against the "system," especially when attacks on the system are so ardently invited by some administrators and faculty.

Many white faculty and students deeply resent what they regard as reverse discrimination, and so do some black faculty. Other academics continue to claim that, in fact, the dice are loaded against both black students and black faculty. However, here we do have hard evidence. It is clear that black students are a protected category at many schools.[66] In addition, a series of studies has demonstrated that as long ago as the mid-1970s, college and university sociology departments were more likely to express interest in a black candidate than a white one with the same credentials. Unsolicited applications requesting positions were sent to various sociology departments. They differed only in that in some cases it was indicated that the candidate was black. Sociology departments expressed far more interest in the applications from "blacks," than in those from "whites." It should be noted that the job applications were spurious. In any event, today "real" white male candidates often receive rejection letters as follows:

> We try to give every applicant thorough consideration. We recognize, however, that our assessments of the degree to which a given candidate meets our criteria are subjective . . . and that the process of reaching department-wide decisions can be subject to influences that have little to do with quality considerations.[67]

For some "radical" faculty members, multiculturalism has clearly become a substitute for Marxism and even neo-Marxism, both of which are now in a period of at least temporary decline, given events in Eastern

Europe and elsewhere. These are faculty who are alienated from their own society and are clearly seeking any issue which enables them to attack it. Given the sharp opposition between traditional Marxism (and neo-Marxism) and cultural and/or racial explanations of events, the alienation hypothesis would seem the only reasonable explanation of the ease with which they have shifted from one theoretical stance to the other. It is extremely difficult, after all, to square explanations of events primarily in terms of economic organization and class division (Marxism) with explanations which stress ethnicity, race, or culture. It is also difficult to suggest at one and the same time that the experiences of Asians or Africans cannot be understood by white Europeans, *and* that the experience of being a woman or a homosexual transcends such fundamental cultural (and/or racial) differences.

That, however, is by no means the full story. Fueled by feminist rhetoric, the race issue, environmental concerns, and European theoretical developments (most notably the writings of Jacques Derrida and Michel Foucault, among others), a full-scale attack has been leveled against Western culture. Western philosophy is but one system of thought, a "phallocentric system" which emphasizes exploitation and dominance. Even its science is suspect. The goals of various critics differ, but all agree that Western "rationality" and other forms of behavior must be changed. To some, at least, there are no unambiguous "rational" systems of thought. All are merely creations of linguistic conventions. Perhaps because of this relativism, their commitment to freedom of inquiry is limited. Whether it be Stanley Fish suggesting that absolutist notions of free speech have never prevailed and should not, or the vehemence of Richard Perry and Patricia Williams's attack on unnamed academics who "put a revisionist happy face upon . . . the Nazi genocides," the message is the same.[68]

IV. The Present and the Future

The American system of higher education is facing difficult times. Academic hiring and student admissions are becoming political matters, as is the question of how knowledge is defined. In these areas the radical critics of American institutions are achieving many more victories than they did in the 1960s.

The shift in faculty orientations in the 1950s contributed to the weakening of even elite colleges' sense of community and concern about teaching. The growth in size of academic institutions also made them far more impersonal places. None of these trends has been reversed. There is little evidence that the new generation of academics feels even as much loyalty to either their institutions or their students as did an earlier generation. Indeed, they are contributing to the destruction of the last remnants of community on the campus. Their critique of Western culture has only contributed to fragmentation among both faculty and students, as groups of students (though by no means all students) more fully identify with their own group than with the college or university as a whole.

There are countervailing forces. Conservative foundations, for example, are supporting at least some student groups, including student newspapers, which take views counter to those dominating campuses. The success of these groups has been mixed. At Dartmouth College, the conservative student newspaper has probably angered more people than it has persuaded. Elsewhere conservatives have had a more positive impact. At some institutions, alumni have been roused to criticize policies which they do not support. However, such arousal is neither widespread nor likely to be lasting. For the most part, alumni prefer to ignore current controversies and to contribute to institutions because of their fond memories of things past. Whether this will be the case in the next generation remains to be seen.

Academics resisting the new conventional wisdom have formed a rapidly growing organization, the National Association of Scholars (NAS), which has thus far had some limited success in fighting the new trends. It remains to be seen how effective NAS will be.[69]

The national media, while viewing the changes in academia with mixed feelings, have publicized the fact that "politically correct" views are being promulgated on campuses. They have reacted negatively both to the authoritarian aspects of the new dispensation and to the humorless self-righteousness of many of its proponents. They have succeeded in embarrassing some faculty and administrations, but only enough to slow the pace of change.

What then of the future? It seems unlikely that the idea that the university constitutes a community of teachers and students will soon again become dominant at American institutions of higher learning. These institutions are now, for the most part, too large, and the social and geographic mobility of academics is too great. A few institutions will maintain an older tradition, but they will, indeed, be few in number. It is also unlikely that colleges and universities will lose interest in public policy and retreat to some pure realm which involves *only* transmitting knowledge. American universities have been involved in public affairs since the 1860s, and, again, with some exceptions, they will not be able to separate themselves from those concerns.

The preservation of the university as a transmitter of knowledge relatively free from political polarization will very much depend on what happens in the larger society. The problems of the university are, after all, a manifestation, however magnified, of the changes which are taking place in the society, including the emergence of new elites, and of the continued problems of racial and ethnic accommodation. The key issues revolve heavily around the condition of African Americans and Americans of Puerto Rican background. While some members of these groups have achieved middle-class status, life conditions in the ghetto have continued to deteriorate. In part, the emphasis on "multiculturalism" for them must be seen as a defense against a tremendous sense of failure.[70]

What is disturbing is that so many blacks and whites have taken some of the more extreme rhetoric about multiculturalism seriously. The problem is not that Professor Leonard Jeffries may be anti-Semitic. He is clearly incompetent, without any claim to scholarly credentials. His argument, for which there is no scientific evidence, is that Europeans are ice people who brought death and destruction to the world, whereas Africans (who grew up with the intellectual and physical superiority provided by melanin) are warm and creative. That he could have been given tenure, much less appointed head of the Afro-American studies department at the City College of the City University of New York, speaks volumes about the state of the academic community. The fact that he was appointed to a blue-ribbon committee to develop a program for multicultural education in New York public schools speaks additional volumes. Even more incredible are the assertions in new baseline guides for the Oregon public schools that black African Egyptians developed a theory of evolution thousands of years before Darwin, in addition to being able to foresee the future. Unfortunately, as Henry Louis Gates and others have pointed out, these are far from isolated examples.[71]

On the one hand, it is difficult to believe that quotas and extreme forms of multiculturalism can be long sustained. Asian Americans have more to gain from a meritocracy than they do from affirmative action. And, while the status of victim offers some advantages, Asians in general and Asian Americans in particular are more wedded to acquiring Western skills (and surpassing Europeans in their application of them) than they are to overturning Western knowledge in favor of their traditional cultures. Given the fact that Asian Americans mix relatively easily with Euro-Americans (a term I prefer to "Anglos" or "whites") and are intermarrying at a very high rate, it is difficult to believe that they will long join with (some) blacks and (some) Hispanics in criticizing the Western orientation of the university, whether as students or as academics.[72]

Further, while some African Americans may find allies among some Hispanics, the politicization of admissions and hirings will eventually lead to conflict among these groups as to which is entitled to how much of the pie. Additionally, Hispanic culture is largely European in origin, a fact which many Hispanics recognize. Indeed, many middle-class African Americans also realize that they are Americans not Africans, and that, in any event, success in the society requires developing the skills hitherto taught so well by Western universities. It is no accident that the traditional Western university is so highly regarded in Third World countries. Insofar as Western culture is becoming a world culture, demands for seriously reducing its place in American universities are likely eventually to be seen by many students as archaic and even silly.

Societal ferment almost inevitably accompanies increasing diversity and awareness of diversity. The United States has, in the past, overcome the centrifugal tendencies characteristic of such diversity. It may do so again.

There is, however, another side to the coin. There is good reason to believe that the patterns of ego control, so laboriously constructed in Europe and the United States, are breaking down, even as are conventional superego restraints. The result is an erosion of the capacity to sublimate both aggressive and erotic drives in the service of the work of civilization, and the replacement of bourgeois commitments to achievement and constancy by increased defensive projection, "acting out," and drives for power and control. There is at least some evidence that the number of persons fitting this pattern in the United States is on the increase.[73] It is not unreasonable to suggest that the current attacks on "Western phallocentric society" reflect this breakdown as much as they are contributing to it.

Liberal democracy and capitalism in Europe emerged out of a particular cultural and personality matrix. The pattern was unique. Their limited success has depended both on particular public policies and upon the character and underlying cultural commitments of their citizens. The mere belief that a society should be democratic and rely upon markets is not enough. If both are to work in the relatively successful manner in which they have in the West in the past, a particular personality structure is required. The liberal democrat can be an individualist precisely because his individualism is supported by an internal psychic structure which defines limits and moderates desire by a sense of social responsibility. When this internal psychic structure collapses, no system of institutions will sustain a liberal political order based upon a capitalist economic system.

It can be argued that the virtues and vices of American society are both now telling against it. After all, while European universities, once far more political than American ones, may be following the American example in some ways, they are following slowly, and they have not traveled nearly the distance of their American counterparts.[74] In a way this reflects the lack of conservative ballast in American society. The self-destructive penchant of liberal ideology can play itself out more easily here than in countries where older values still command loyalty. Joseph Schumpeter may have been partly right when he argued that capitalism needed an aristocratic class committed to intellectual activities to save it from its own self-destructive proclivities.[75]

In addition, the people of many European nations (by no means all), like the Japanese, share a common ethnic identity forged over many centuries, which binds them to their culture, even as it makes them more ethnocentric. Whatever ideological changes take place in their society, they are still French (or Japanese), as they have been for "time out of mind." America, on the other hand, has always relied on a set of ideas to bind it together. It has also accepted a massive influx of immigrants from other, non-European nations and cultures, and has not yet successfully resolved the conflicts engendered by slavery. As the integrating ideas that have bound it together in the past erode, what does it have to fall back on?[76]

In any event, the incidence of criminal violence continues to escalate in America and Europe, after declining steadily for a hundred years.[77] And, in America, the manner in which this culture is changing is exemplified by the popularity of Madonna and the growing popularity of explicitly violent "rap" music. It is not accidental that a Florida jury decided with ease that the following lyrics of the rap group 2 Live Crew, from their album "As Nasty as They Wanna Be," are not obscene:[78]

> Grabbed her by the hair, threw her on the floor / opened her thighs and guess what I saw. . . . He'll tear the cunt open 'cause it's satisfaction.
> From "Dick Almighty"

> Bust your cunt then break your backbone. . . . I wanna see you bleed!
> From "The Fuck Shop"

These lyrics do not represent the sentiment of Americans now, but they are a metaphor for the profound changes that are taking place.

We face still other dangers. Given what has occurred in the former Soviet Union and Eastern Europe, the possibility of an escalating breakdown into mutually hostile ethnic enclaves in the United States cannot be ignored. The decline of the idea of a unified America could produce disastrous results.

If this scenario is correct, we cannot, as noted earlier, expect more from American universities than we can expect from the larger society. At one time, European universities retained considerable autonomy within the dominant culture. Nevertheless, their very creation and functioning derived from that culture. In the United States, the autonomy of the university has never been as great as it was in Europe; and, today, in most of the world, and perhaps especially in the United States, the autonomy of the university is highly circumscribed. It is influenced far more by social currents than it ever was. Thus, without cultural and social renewal in the larger society, the drop in general intellectual levels of scholarship of students and faculty will probably continue, as will the growth of irrationality and even violence.[79] The prospect is not a pleasant one. I hope I shall prove to be a poor prophet.[80]

NOTES

1. Allan Bloom, *The Closing of the American Mind* (New York: Simon and Schuster, 1987); Roger Kimball, *Tenured Radicals: How Politics Has Corrupted Our Higher Education* (New York: Harper and Row, 1990); Page Smith, *Killing the Spirit: Higher Education in America* (New York: Viking, 1990); Irving Kristol's views were expressed in a personal communication.
2. Henry Rosovsky, *The University: An Owner's Manual* (New York: W. W. Norton, 1990).
3. The historical sections of the next several pages rely heavily upon such books as Joseph Ben-David, *Trends in American Higher Education* (Chicago: University of Chicago Press, 1972); Richard Hofstadter and Walter P. Metzger, *The Development of Academic Freedom in the United States* (New York: Columbia University Press, 1955); Christopher Jencks and David Riesman, *The Academic Revolution* (New York: Doubleday, 1968); and Murray G. Ross, *The University: The Anatomy of Academe* (New York: McGraw Hill, 1967), among others.
4. However, from the beginning some very good scholarship was completed at universities, and the notion of the university as a place where thought was untrammeled established itself early, though it was often honored in the breach. The issues are, of course, quite complex. Rather different traditions developed in Paris and Bologna, and in the wake of the Reformation and Counter-Reformation, and state domination of the universities, their centrality declined. It also declined because of the rigid adherence of many universities to traditional Aristotelian modes of thought as the new science was emerging. Between 1500 and 1800, for example, some of the best research was completed in various royal academies and private academies. It was not until the late eighteenth century that the university regained its

predominance as a source of scholarship. These issues are dealt with in more detail in the books cited in note 3 above.

5. I realize that the term "intelligentsia" has been applied primarily to Russian intellectuals. I am using it more broadly in this essay to describe a self-conscious intellectual stratum.

6. The best summaries of Weber's analysis, though they differ slightly in detail, are Reinhard Bendix, *Max Weber: An Intellectual Portrait* (New York: Doubleday, 1962); and Randall Collins, *Weberian Sociological Theory* (Cambridge: Cambridge University Press, 1986).

7. These themes are treated in far more (comparative) detail in Stanley Rothman, S. Robert Lichter, and Linda Lichter, *Elites in Conflict: Social Change in America Today* (Greenwich, CT: Greenwood/Praeger, forthcoming 1993), and in my forthcoming book, *The End of the Experiment.*

8. See Bendix, *Max Weber: An Intellectual Portrait.* See also the essays by Benjamin Nelson and S. N. Eisenstadt in Charles Y. Glock and Phillip E. Hammond, eds., *Beyond the Classics: Essays in the Scientific Study of Religion* (New York: Harper and Row, 1973); Randall Collins, "Weber's Last Theory of Capitalism: A Systematization," *American Sociological Review,* vol. 45 (December 1980), pp. 925–42; Collins, *Weberian Sociological Theory;* and Randall Collins, *Max Weber* (Beverly Hills, CA: Sage Publications, 1985). One must be clear on this, however. Protestantism is a Christian heresy. As Weber notes, the "rationalization" of social institutions and thought in the West begins with the Catholic Church.

9. See Robin May Schott, *Cognition and Eros: A Critique of the Kantian Paradigm* (Boston: Beacon Press, 1989); and Harold J. Berman, *Law and Revolution: The Formation of the Western Legal Tradition* (Cambridge: Harvard University Press, 1983). Schott's book is, unfortunately, marred by a radical feminist ideology. Because the university emerged from an ascetic tradition, she argues, it (and modern science in general) has always been patriarchal and anti-woman. Since all historical societies, ascetic or not, have been more patriarchal than the West, it is difficult to maintain that Western rationality is the source of patriarchy.

The origins of the university in the West are somewhat more complex than suggested in the text. One can find antecedents in Greece and Rome, and, at one point, Islam seemed on the verge of developing universities. Further, while certain unique characteristics of Western Christendom may have fostered the development of the university, it was only when secular universities emerged that the institution realized its full scholarly potential.

10. Max Weber, *The Sociology of Religion* (Boston: Beacon Press, 1963), p. 125.

11. According to Edward Shils, intellectuals possess an alienative disposition, derived from the nature of being intellectuals. The culture of the intellectual is characteristically a culture once-removed from the immediacies of everyday life. Intellectuals are more concerned with the wider universe and the larger questions of life. They are less concerned with the practical and possible.

Given their role in the elaboration and legitimation of action, intellectuals are in the position to dream of alternatives. But to dream of alternatives opens each intellectual to the possibility of rejecting the current world, with its inevitable flaws and imperfections. See Edward Shils, "The Intellectuals and the Powers," in his *The Intellectuals and the Powers and Other Essays* (Chicago: University of Chicago Press, 1972), pp. 3–22. See also Lewis A. Coser, *Men of Ideas: A Sociologist's View* (New York: Free Press, 1965). Both authors are generalizing from the modern experience of the West. In most historic literate cultures, intellectuals (priests, Confucian literati, etc.) were supportive of the traditional order, even if they criticized particular rulers or practices.

12. The specific differences between the French and Russian modes of class conflict are far too complex to discuss in detail here. I intend to address them in a later study. See also my *European Society and Politics* (Indianapolis: Bobbs-Merrill Co., 1970), pp. 53–67 and 145–93.

13. Joseph Ben-David, "Professions in the Class Systems of Present Day Societies," *Current Sociology*, vol. 12, no. 3 (1963–64), pp. 247–98; S. M. Lipset and Richard B. Dobson, "The Intellectual as Critic and Rebel with Special Reference to the United States and the Soviet Union," *Daedalus*, vol. 101, no. 3 (Summer 1972), pp. 137–98.

14. This is fully developed in the political writings of John Locke. Modern natural rights must, as Leo Strauss has pointed out, be distinguished from classical and Catholic natural law. See Leo Strauss, *Natural Right and History* (Chicago: University of Chicago Press, 1953).

15. For discussions of the role of intellectuals in America, see Louis Hartz, *The Liberal Tradition in America* (New York: Harcourt Brace and Co., 1955); Lewis Perry, *Intellectual Life in America: A History* (New York: Franklin Watts, 1984); James Ceaser, "Alexis de Tocqueville on Political Science, Political Culture, and the Role of the Intellectual," *The American Political Science Review*, vol. 79, no. 3 (September 1985), pp. 656–72; Richard Hofstadter, *Anti-Intellectualism in American Life* (New York: Alfred A. Knopf, 1963); and Robert Kroes, ed., *The Intellectual in America* (Amsterdam: Amerika Instituut, 1979).

16. Alexis de Tocqueville, *Democracy in America*, trans. Phillips Bradley et al. (New York: Alfred A. Knopf, 1948), vol. 2, p. 315. De Tocqueville credits this lack of interest in general ideas as a factor which contributes to the success of American democracy.

17. The spread of liberal-capitalist ideas to Asia was, in part, determined by the same concerns, though the issues are too complex to be discussed here. However, see Benjamin I. Schwartz, *In Search of Wealth and Power: Yen Fu and the West* (Cambridge: Harvard University Press, 1964). I do not mean to suggest that other concerns, e.g., new conceptions of justice, were unimportant. However, this too is an issue which will have to be postponed until a later volume.

18. Contemporary liberal reformers in the United States are still disconcerted by the Church's "progressive" economic views as compared to its "retrograde" social views, and are constantly finding radical shifts in the Church's position when it criticizes capitalism. They fail to realize that the Church never supported liberal capitalism, for it remained faithful to a perspective which (deriving from Aristotle and European feudalism) always subordinated economic activity to moral purposes. See Ernest Troeltsch, *The Social Teachings of the Christian Churches*, 2 vols. (New York: Harper and Brothers, 1960); and Alec R. Vidler, *The Church in an Age of Revolution* (Baltimore: Penguin Books Ltd., 1961). It is true, however, that the Ameri-

can Catholic Church is well to the "left" of the current Pope on a number of social issues, though it remains much more conservative than mainline Protestant churches have become. See Robert Lerner, Stanley Rothman, and S. Robert Lichter, "Christian Religious Elites," *Public Opinion,* vol. 11, no. 6 (March/April 1989), pp. 54–58. For a good general discussion of the American Catholic Church today, see Avery Dulles, *The Reshaping of Catholicism: Current Challenges to the Theology of the Church* (New York: Harper and Row, 1988).

19. The "heresy" centered around the thinking of Archbishop Corrigan of New York and others who wanted the Church to adjust to American ways on parochial school issues and questions of personal conscience. After a commission study of the issues, Pope Leo XIII addressed a personal letter to Cardinal Gibbons, "Testem benevolentiae," in which he gently and indirectly chided some American Church officials and emphasized the importance of traditional doctrine. See Stanley Rothman, "The Politics of Catholic Parochial Schools," *The Journal of Politics,* vol. 25 (1963), pp. 49–71, and the references cited therein.

20. See, for example, Robert L. Beisner, *Twelve Against Empire* (New York: McGraw Hill Book Company, 1968); and John G. Sproat, *The Best Men* (New York: Oxford University Press, 1968). The quote is from Richard Hofstadter, *The Age of Reform* (New York: Alfred A. Knopf, 1985), p. 195.

21. William Nisbet Chambers and Walter D. Burnham, *The American Party System* (New York: Oxford University Press, 1967).

22. Stanley Rothman and S. Robert Lichter, *Roots of Radicalism* (New York: Oxford University Press, 1982).

23. See, for example, David J. Rothman, *The Discovery of the Asylum: Social Order and Disorder in the New Republic* (Boston: Little Brown, 1971), and his *Conscience and Convenience: The Asylum and Its Alternatives in Progressive America* (Boston: Little Brown, 1980).

24. Daniel Bell, *The Coming of Post-Industrial Society* (New York: Basic Books, 1973); Christopher Lasch, *Haven in a Heartless World* (New York: McGraw-Hill, 1977); and Morris Janowitz, *The Last Half Century: Societal Change and Politics in America* (Chicago: University of Chicago Press, 1978). For my use of the term "cosmopolitan," see note 40 below.

25. I refer here primarily to the work of Erich Fromm and Abraham Maslow, although there were hundreds of imitators. See, for example, Erich Fromm, *Escape from Freedom* (New York: Avon Books, 1971), *The Art of Loving* (New York: Harper, 1956), and *The Sane Society* (New York: Holt Rinehart and Winston, 1960). See also Abraham Maslow, *Motivation and Personality* (New York: Harper and Row, 1954), and *The Further Reaches of Human Nature* (New York: Viking, 1971). Of course, T. W. Adorno et al., *The Authoritarian Personality* (New York: Harper and Row, 1950) quickly became popularized.

26. Daniel Aaron, *Writers on the Left* (New York: Avon, 1961); Daniel Bell, *Marxian Socialism in the United States* (Princeton: Princeton University Press, 1967); Irving Howe, *Politics and the Novel* (Cleveland: World, 1962); David Caute, *The Fellow Travellers* (New York: Macmillan, 1973); and Harvey Klehr, *The Heyday of American Communism* (New York: Basic Books, 1984).

27. H. Stuart Hughes, *The Sea Change* (New York: Harper and Row, 1975);

Lewis A. Coser, *Refugee Scholars in America* (New Haven: Yale University Press, 1984).

28. Everett Carll Ladd, Jr., and S. M. Lipset, *The Divided Academy* (New York: W. W. Norton, 1976), p. 22.

29. Lionel S. Lewis, *Cold War on Campus: A Study of the Politics of Organized Control* (New Brunswick, NJ: Transaction Books, 1988).

30. See Stanley Rothman, "Professors in the Ascendant," *Academic Questions,* vol. 2, no. 4 (1989), pp. 45–51; and "Academics on the Left," *Society,* vol. 23, no. 3 (March/April 1986), pp. 5–8.

31. Steven Goldstein, "Reforming Socialist Systems: Some Lessons of the Chinese Experience," *Studies in Comparative Communism,* vol. 21, no. 2 (Summer 1988), pp. 221–37; S. Frederick Starr, "Reform in the Soviet Union," *The Wilson Quarterly,* vol. 13, no. 2 (1989), pp. 569–96; and Stephen White et al., *Developments in the Soviet Union* (Durham: Duke University Press, 1990).

32. In the late nineteenth century a number of American universities, led by Johns Hopkins, took German universities as their models, stressing the importance of research.

33. They are still private institutions. However, since they now receive extensive government funding, without which they could not retain many of their current programs, they are subject to government regulation.

34. The data in this and the next few paragraphs is derived from Daniel Bell, *The Coming of Post-Industrial Society;* The National Center for Educational Statistics, *Digest of Educational Statistics* (Washington: U.S. Government Printing Office, 1982); *The Statistical Abstract of the United States* for 1942, 1975, and 1985; and U.S. Department of Commerce, Bureau of the Census, *Historical Statistics of the U.S.: Colonial Times to the Present* (Washington: U.S. Government Printing Office, 1975).

35. Aside from some small denominational Protestant colleges and Catholic colleges and universities, this power structure is somewhat more likely to characterize private rather than public institutions.

36. Ladd and Lipset, *The Divided Academy,* p. 29.

37. C. Wright Mills, *White Collar* (New York: Oxford University Press, 1951).

38. Ladd and Lipset, *The Divided Academy,* pp. 55–124 and 149–68.

39. Waldemar A. Nielsen, *The Golden Donors* (New York: E. P. Dutton, 1985).

40. The term "cosmopolitan" is defined as a counterfoil to locally and, hence, parochially oriented, as in Elihu Katz and Paul F. Lazarsfeld, *Personal Influence* (Glencoe, IL: Free Press, 1955). As I use the term, cosmopolitan individuals share broadly "sophisticated" views and transcend narrow local and parochial attitudes and attachments.

41. Robert Bellah et al., *Habits of the Heart* (Berkeley: University of California Press, 1985).

42. Edward Shils, "Learning and Liberalism," in his *The Calling of Sociology and Other Essays on the Pursuit of Learning* (Chicago: University of Chicago Press, 1980), pp. 289–355. The term was actually first used by John Dewey in his *Liberalism and Social Action* (New York: G. P. Putnam and Sons, 1935), p. 20.

43. Aaron Wildavsky, *The Rise of Radical Egalitarianism* (Washington: The American University Press, 1992).

44. Some early studies of college students seemed to indicate that while they became more liberal during their college years, they reverted "to type" once they left college. However, later analyses agreed that the liberal transformation of students which occurs in many colleges is never fully reversed. For a summary of the major studies through the 1950s and 1960s, see Kenneth A. Feldman and Theodore M. Newcomb, *The Impact of College on Students*, 2 vols. (San Francisco: Josey Bass, 1969).

45. This tradition, however, dates only as far back as eighteenth-century England. It was not part of the understanding of medieval universities, or, in general, of universities on the continent.

46. This is certainly the view of both Jencks and Riesman, as well as that of Ross (see note 3 above). Francis Oakley disputes their analysis, noting that studies by the Carnegie Foundation seem to indicate that most college professors place higher priority on teaching than on research. See Oakley, "Against Nostalgia: Reflections on Our Present Discontents in American Higher Education," in Darryl J. Gless and Barbara Herrnstein Smith, eds., *The Politics of Liberal Education* (Durham: Duke University Press, 1992), pp. 267–89.

47. In the United States most members of the working class think of themselves as lower middle class. As used here, the term "working class" is based on socioeconomic status and includes primarily blue-collar workers and low-status service employees.

48. Clark Kerr, *The Uses of the University* (Cambridge: Harvard University Press, 1963).

49. In the 1980s it would be argued that capitalism had been foisted on the world by authoritarian white (European) males. As John Taylor describes it:

> In the view of such activists, the universities . . . had hopelessly compromised their integrity by accepting contracts from the Pentagon, but those alliances . . . were seen as merely one symptom of a larger conspiracy by white males. Less obviously they had appointed themselves guardians of the culture and compiled the list of so-called great books as a propaganda exercise to reinforce the notion of white-male superiority.

John Taylor "Are You Politically Correct?" *New York*, January 21, 1991, p. 36.

50. They also opposed recruitment on campus by business firms having defense contracts.

51. Any educational institution receiving funds from the United States government is not permitted to discriminate against members of protected minority groups. Goals and time tables are supposed to be set for hiring minority faculty and admitting minority students. Each institution is also required to hire an affirmative-action officer. If charges of discrimination are brought against the institution, the proportion of minority students and/or staff may be examined to determine whether or not a prima facie case of discrimination can be established. Many states have similar laws. To protect themselves, more than a few institutions attempt to hire and admit by the numbers, despite recent court rulings asserting that statistical disparity is not enough by itself to establish discrimination. The failure to exhibit "diversity" in staff and students has also been used to threaten institutions with removal of accreditation.

52. Office of Scientific and Research Personnel, *Summary Report 1986: Doctorate Recipients from United States Universities* (Washington, 1987), p. 44, appendix A, table 1A.
53. For general discussions, see Dinesh D'Souza, *Illiberal Education: The Politics of Race and Sex on Campus* (New York: Free Press, 1991). For the official Smith College document on affirmative action, see *The Smith Design for Institutional Diversity*, Smith College, Northampton, MA, 1989. For discussions of Berkeley, see Vincent Sarich, "The Institutionalization of Racism at the University of California at Berkeley," *Academic Questions*, vol. 4, no. 1 (Winter 1990–91), pp. 72–81; John H. Bunzel, "Affirmative-Action Admissions: How It Works at UC Berkeley," *The Public Interest*, no. 93 (Fall 1988), pp. 111–29; and John H. Bunzel, "Minority Faculty Hiring: Problems and Prospects," *American Scholar*, no. 59 (Winter 1990), pp. 39–52. A discussion of the law school at the University of Arizona will be found in Maurice Auerbach, "Affirmative Discrimination in the University: The Case of the College of Law, University of Arizona," *Measure*, no. 90 (November/December 1990), pp. 6–12.
54. For a description and discussion of the new Stanford freshman course, providing an alternative to the traditional Western culture course, see Sidney Hook, "The Politics of Curriculum Building," *Measure*, no. 77 (January 1989), pp. 1ff.; and D'Souza, *Illiberal Education*.
55. See Joseph S. Salemi, "Lone Star Academic Politics: Persecution at the University of Texas," *Measure*, no. 87 (August 1990), pp. 4–10.
56. For example, *Christine Franklin v. Gwinnett County Public Schools and William Prescott*, 112 S.Ct. 1028 (1992).
57. For example, see Allan Mandelstamm, "McCarthy's Ghost: Reminiscences of a Politically Incorrect Professor," *Crisis*, vol. 9, no. 8 (September 1991), pp. 14–18; and John Leo, "PC Follies: The Year in Review," *U.S. News and World Report*, January 27, 1992, pp. 22ff. For the Minnesota case, see Barry R. Gross, "Salem in Minnesota," *Academic Questions*, vol. 5 (Spring 1982), pp. 67–75.
58. *MLA Newsletter*, Summer 1991, p. 21. Feminist scholars have made other statements at least as irrational. What are we to make, for example, of a book review in the *New York Times*, July 5, 1992, by the head of the department of foreign languages and literatures at MIT?

> Lest we reassuringly relegate female genital mutilation in Africa . . . bride burning in India and the elimination of female babies in China to . . . third world countries . . . in this country women are faring terribly as well. . . . Why, for example, such vigorous prosecution and jailing of women who improperly care for a fetus by using drugs or alcohol . . . ?

Or the following in a book written by a noted feminist scholar and published by Harvard University Press:

> [T]he major distinction between intercourse (normal) and rape (abnormal) is that the normal happens so often that one can not get anyone to see anything wrong with it.

Catherine A. MacKinnon, *Toward a Feminist Theory of the State* (Cambridge: Harvard University Press, 1989), p. 146.
Or, finally:

I begin the course with the basic feminist principle that in a racist, classist and sexist society we have all swallowed oppressive ways of being, whether intentionally or not. Specifically, this means it is not open to debate whether a white student is racist or a male student is sexist. He/she simply is.

The above is quoted from the syllabus of a Brandeis University sociology course. It is reprinted in Patricia Hill Collins and Margaret L. Andersen, *An Inclusive Curriculum: Race, Class, and Gender in Sociological Instruction* (Washington: American Sociological Association, 1987).

59. For a detailed review of the cases, see Stephen F. Rohde, "Campus Speech Codes: Politically Correct, Constitutionally Wrong," *Los Angeles Lawyer,* December 1991, pp. 23–51. I should note that I am not a First Amendment absolutist. I see no particular reason to dignify racial epithets by placing them under the protection of the First Amendment. On the other hand, the First Amendment is designed to protect individuals who, for example, argue civilly and rationally that racial differences are significant.
60. "Universities Reconsidering Bans on Hate Speech," *New York Times,* June 24, 1992, p. A13.
61. Chester Finn, Jr., "The Campus: 'An Island of Repression in a Sea of Freedom,' " *Commentary,* September 1989, pp. 17–23; Taylor, "Are You Politically Correct?"
62. Thomas Short, "Big Brother in Delaware," *National Review,* March 18, 1991, p. 32; *Wall Street Journal,* November 13, 1990, and April 10, 1991; Barry Gross, "The Case of Philippe Rushton," *Academic Questions,* vol. 3 (Fall 1990), pp. 35–46. The National Association of Scholars was created by a group of scholars to fight some of the trends discussed above.
63. *Daily Hampshire Gazette,* April 18, 1979, May 22, 1979, and May 25, 1979.
64. Thomas Sowell, *Preferential Policies: An International Perspective* (New York: William Morrow, 1990); Shelby Steele, *The Content of Our Character* (New York: St. Martin's Press, 1990). The same explanation may hold for homophobic or supposed homophobic incidents.
65. See the cited essays by Sowell (note 64), Bunzel (note 53), and Sarich (note 53), among others.
66. See D'Souza, *Illiberal Education.* See also Timothy Maguire, "My Bout with Affirmative Action," *Commentary,* April 1992, pp. 50–52.
67. For differing perspectives on this issue, see Philip Altbach et al., *The Racial Crisis in American Higher Education* (Albany: State University of New York Press, 1991) on the one hand, and Frederick Lynch, *Invisible Victims* (New York: Greenwood Press, 1988) on the other. For empirical studies from the 1970s, see Stuart H. Gould and Pierre L. Van Den Berghe, "Particularism in Sociology Departments' Hiring Practices," *Race,* no. 16 (July 1973), pp. 6–11; and Barbara R. Lorch, "Reverse Discrimination in Hiring in Sociology Departments: A Preliminary Report," *The American Sociologist,* vol. 8 (August 1973), pp. 117–20. The rejection letter quoted in the text was received by a young colleague of mine and shown to me.
68. The literature on this issue is vast, and I will cite only a few authors. For commentaries on Foucault, see Mark Cousins and Athar Hussein, *Michel Foucault* (London: St. Martin's Press, 1984). For a feminist use of Foucault, see Irene Diamond and Lee Quinby, eds., *Feminism and Foucault: Reflec-*

tions on Resistance (Boston: Northeastern University Press, 1988). The radical ecological perspective is summarized by Christopher Mannes, *Green Rage: Radical Environmentalism and the Unmaking of Civilization* (Boston: Little Brown, 1992). A general discussion of the gurus of the deconstructionist and related movements will be found in Richard J. Bernstein, *The New Constellation: The Ethical-Political Horizons of Modernity/Post Modernity* (Cambridge: Cambridge University Press, 1992). One should also read Dieter Freundlieb, "Rationalism v. Irrationalism: Habermas's Response to Foucault," *Inquiry,* vol. 31, no. 2 (June 1988), pp. 171–92. The Fish and Perry/Williams essays are to be found in Paul Berman, ed., *Debating P.C.: The Controversy Over Political Correctness on College Campuses* (New York: Dell Publishing, 1992). The quote from Perry/Williams is from p. 227. See also Gless and Smith, eds., *The Politics of Liberal Education.*

69. Radical academics have formed two organizations to counter the NAS. These are Teachers for a Democratic Culture, and the Union of Democratic Intellectuals.

70. Hispanics (Latinos?) are not a homogeneous group. Cuban Americans are clearly making it. The future status of Mexican Americans and Americans from other Latin American countries is unclear.

71. For a discussion of Afrocentrism, etc., see, among others, Henry Louis Gates, Jr., "Black Demagogues and Pseudo-Scholars," *New York Times,* July 20, 1992, p. A15; Albert Shanker, "Current Multicultural Curricula and the Danger of Multiple Perspectives," *Measure,* no. 102 (January 1992), pp. 1ff.; Diane Ravitch, "Multiculturalism: E Pluribus Plures," *American Scholar,* vol. 59, no. 3 (Summer 1990), pp. 337–54; and the very angry book by Arthur Schlesinger, Jr., *The Disuniting of America: Reflections on a Multicultural Society* (New York: W. W. Norton, 1992).

72. Nevertheless, at least some are attracted to the status of victim. See the essay by Sucheng Chan and Ling-Chi Wangin in Altbach et al., *The Racial Crisis in American Higher Education.* Need I say that Asian cultures differ widely from each other; it is only for lack of space that I lump them together.

73. See Rothman, Lichter, and Lichter, *Elites in Conflict* (see note 7 above). Some years ago Christopher Lasch argued, in *The Minimal Self* (New York: W. W. Norton, 1984), that current political conflicts were really those between the parties of the superego, the liberal ego, and the id. I would agree, though I do not share his position on certain matters. I would only add that attempts to preserve the culture by giving in on certain issues are likely to be fruitless in the present climate. Cultural restraints are subject to the most violent attacks when those who are supposed to enforce them are seen to have lost their will to do so.

74. I refer here to the breakdown of academic standards, the attack on Western culture, and the impact of feminism. Issues of racism and affirmative action are not relevant to these countries.

75. Joseph Schumpeter, *Capitalism, Socialism, and Democracy* (New York: Harper and Brothers, 1947). For a fuller development of all these themes, see Rothman, Lichter, and Lichter, *Elites in Conflict.*

76. America differs from other ethnically divided nations in the following sense. In most ethnically divided nations, each group has a very strong sense of ethnic identity. Euro-Americans certainly do not. Most of them have given up their heritage for the idea of America, as have most other groups in the

society. Even those minority groups that assert the importance of the culture out of which they have sprung, do so in a very American way.

77. Robert Ted Gurr, ed., *Violence in America,* 3d ed. (Newbury Park, CA: Sage Publications), vol. 1, pp. 21–54.

78. Quoted in Michael Medved, "The New Sound of Music," *The Public Interest,* no. 109 (Fall 1992), p. 45.

79. For a popular discussion of the declining achievement level of American college students as mirrored in SAT scores, see Daniel J. Singal, "The Other Crisis in American Education," *Atlantic Monthly,* November 1991, pp. 59–74. For a more technical discussion, see Charles Murray and R. J. Herrnstein, "What's Really Behind the SAT-Score Decline?" *The Public Interest,* vol. 10 (Winter 1992), pp. 32–56.

80. I know that some of my colleagues will regard my remarks as hyperbolic. I challenge them to find a better explanation of the growing irrationality of discourse in the academy, only a few examples of which have been presented in this essay. Incidentally, while the sciences have thus far been relatively less affected, it is not necessarily true that they will continue to be, given the attitudes of radicals in the environmental movement and of feminist academics. For the latter, see, among many other essays, Paul R. Gross, "On the Gendering of Science," *Academic Questions,* vol. 5 (Spring 1992), pp. 10–23.

The Sources of Political Correctness
on American Campuses

Seymour Martin Lipset

The contemporary discussion over "political correctness," PC, on college campuses has reached far beyond the university into the mass media and the political world. The term refers to the efforts by campus advocates of left-liberal politics to control the content of speech, courses, and appointments, and to impose their views with respect to multiculturalism, minority rights, and feminism. This essay is an effort to account for this new wave of repressive moralism, to explain some of the issues involved, to locate the sources of support and opposition, and to voice a judgment about the current situation in American academe.

I. Moralism

The concern for political correctness is the latest expression of moralism in the United States, and moralism, as United States history demonstrates, is as American as apple pie. Starting with the Alien and Sedition Acts of the 1790s, through various waves of xenophobia and of heightened nationalism (of which McCarthyism was the most recent), and including abolitionism, prohibition, anti-war movements from 1812 through Vietnam, and most recently pro- and anti-choice advocacy, Americans of both the right and left have exhibited a Protestant-sectarian-bred propensity for crusades. The United States is the only country in which the majority of the citizens have adhered to the sects, those which the British refer to as the "dissenting" or "nonconformist" denominations, rather than to groups that are or once were state churches. The American sectarian religious ethos has assumed, in practice if not in theology, the perfectibility of humanity and the obligation to avoid sin, while the churches whose followers predominate in Europe, Canada, and Australia have accepted the inherent weakness of people and the need for the church and the polity to be forgiving and protecting. The values of the sectarians, (e.g., the Baptists, Methodists, and hundreds of others) have deeply informed our political behavior. American wars and ideological conflicts are conducted as battles between good and evil, and such conflicts engender demands for "correctness."

The sectarian emphasis on moralism is reinforced by elements derivative from the fact that the United States defines its *raison d'être* ideologically. As Richard Hofstadter notes: "It has been our fate as a nation not to have ideologies but to be one."[1] In so saying, he was reiterating Ralph Waldo Emerson's and Abraham Lincoln's emphases on the country's "political religion," alluding in effect to the former's statement that becoming American was a religious—that is, ideological—act. Except for the now deceased Soviet Union, other countries' senses of themselves have been derived from a common history, not an ideology. In Europe and Canada, nationality is related to community, to ancestry. Being an American, however, is an ideological commitment. The emphasis on Americanism as a political ideology has led to a utopian and absolutist orientation among American liberals and conservatives. Both seek to extend their version of the good society. Those who reject American values are incorrect, are un-American and may be denied rights.

The current efforts to impose political correctness on the campus go back to the controversies of the 1960s when the anti-war and radical university-based movements opposed the Vietnam War as immoral. In the strict American moralistic tradition, they sought to prevent any supporter of the war from speaking on campuses, to end all forms of collaboration by universities with the war-making government, and to politicize academic organizations like the Modern Language Association or the American Sociological Association.

Political correctness is not a new phenomenon in American academe. As all histories attest, American private higher education largely began in church-affiliated schools. Most of these insisted that their faculty be denominationally correct, be members of the church which paid for the institution. Faculty who deviated from religious doctrine could be fired. When institutions changed, grew less orthodox, the churches' right-wings set up new schools. Yale came into existence in 1701 to counterbalance Harvard, which had moved toward Unitarianism. Few, if any, schools would hire Jews and Catholics, not to speak of overt atheists, until well into the nineteenth century. Abolitionists lost jobs in southern schools, and sometimes in northern ones as well.

Intellectual arenas have been centers of opposition, of an "adversary culture."[2] Daniel Patrick Moynihan has noted that since "about 1840, the cultural elite have pretty generally rejected the values and activities of the larger society."[3] Writing in 1873, Whitelaw Reid, then editor of the *New York Tribune,* emphasized that "exceptional influences eliminated, the scholar is pretty sure to be opposed to the established. . . . Free thought is necessarily aggressive and critical. The scholar . . . is an inherent, an organic, an inevitable radical."[4] Twenty-eight years later, after observing such political tendencies at work in the campus opposition to the Spanish American War and the occupation of the Philippines, an older and more conservative Reid commented: "It is a misfortune for the colleges, and no less for the country, when the trusted instructors are out of sympathy with its history, with its development, and with the men who made the one and are guiding the other."[5] Richard Hofstadter, writing in 1963, concluded that academe had been on the left for the previous three quarters of a century.[6]

As the social sciences emerged in the latter part of the nineteenth century, trustees, alumni, and politicians found the teaching and writing of some scholars offensive. Sociology became identified with radicalism at Stanford, when E. A. Ross was fired at Mrs. Stanford's insistence in 1900 because he had attacked Leland Stanford and other railroad barons. Other California universities followed Stanford's lead in rejecting sociology. Concern that morals would be corrupted led to repression of teaching and research about sex-related issues. A celebrated University of Chicago sociologist, W. I. Thomas, was dismissed in the early 1920s because of publicized relations with prostitutes, which he claimed were part of his research. Pacifists, socialists, and other opponents of the U.S. foreign policy of intervention in World War I were discharged by major universities, including Columbia, which let Charles Beard go. The American Association of University Professors (AAUP) was founded in 1915 to defend academic freedom and to protect the rights of leftists and agnostics to secure and retain faculty positions.

Meritocracy, equal opportunity for the most-qualified to enter the university, an issue raised by the Jacksonians in the 1830s, continued to be a cause of the populist and intellectual left. It took the form of favoring the founding and expansion of public institutions of higher education, which were more universalistic in their admission and hiring practices with respect to ethnic and religious and, to some extent, gender and racial (outside of the South) criteria than the elite private colleges.

Jews, who were particularly insistent on participation in higher education at all levels and produced large numbers of qualified people, supplied considerable evidence that it was necessary to be ethnically or religiously "correct" to study or teach at many of the leading universities. Harvard, which was the most open of the private schools, was faced with large numbers of qualified Jewish applicants at the turn of the century and admitted many. When Charles Eliot, its president of four decades, from 1869 to 1910, was told that this would eventually make Harvard the most Jewish school in the nation, he responded that he would regret that very much, but he saw no alternative to a meritocratic admission process.[7] Other university presidents, including Eliot's successor at Harvard, A. L. Lowell, saw the situation differently, and tried to hold down Jewish admissions.[8] First and second generation Americans of recent non-Anglo-Saxon immigration background, such as Italians and other Catholics, also faced restrictions. There were overt debates about restrictive quotas, in which administrators like Lowell at Harvard and Butler at Columbia argued that the educationally ambitious minorities should not be concentrated in the major northern schools, that as groups they would be better off, that there would be less prejudice against them, if they were dispersed around the country. Harvard and other northeastern schools adopted a national emphasis in their admission policies consciously designed to cut back on those from New York City and other northeast urban areas.[9]

The Great Depression of the 1930s seemingly reinforced the belief that the children of the newer non-Nordic immigrants did not fit, were not "correct." Campuses at which they congregated, City College in New York, Boston University, the University of Wisconsin, and the University of California at Berkeley, became notorious as centers of radicalism. The American Student Union, largely dominated by Communists, Socialists, left liberals, and pacifists, faced repressive measures on many campuses and was often not allowed to meet or hold demonstrations on school property.[10] The teacher's union, the American Federation of Teachers, had to operate surreptitiously in some areas. With the coming of World War II, radical faculty, Communists and Socialists, both then against American military preparations and actions, faced hostile investigations and exposés. These ended for a time when the Nazi attack on the Soviet Union in June 1941 turned the Communists into ardent interventionists and patriots. In general, various experiences (e.g., the Depression, the rise of the New Deal, the World War II alliance with the Soviet Union, reactions to Nazism, and the enormous postwar increase in the size of higher education with the opening to strata and ethno-cultural groups previously held back) seemingly led to a further shift to the left among faculty and students.

II. Social Science Evidence and Analysis

The earliest surveys of faculty values (questionnaire polls of attitudes toward religion) were conducted in 1913–14 and again in 1933 by James Leuba. They attest to the validity of Hofstadter's report. Leuba found that more than half the professors queried in both periods did not believe in God. Only 42 percent in 1914 and 33 percent in 1933 reported faith.[11] Studies of American religious behavior indicate that these professors and scientists were far more irreligious than the general population, a pattern which would reappear in every subsequent survey of faculty political opinion. While Leuba did not inquire directly about politics, antireligious views have been associated with left politics. It is noteworthy that both in 1914 and in 1933 the more distinguished professors were much more irreligious than their less eminent colleagues. Later local and national questionnaire surveys taken in the late 1930s and 1940s, which dealt with partisan orientations directly, found that social and natural scientists and people in the arts were much more left and Democratic than people in the nonacademic occupational strata.[12] A late 1930s effort to account for the leftist views of the more intellectually oriented undergraduates by two psychologists suggested that to be "bookish" meant to be exposed to radical thought:

> To be bookish in this era has meant to steep oneself in the disillusioned gropings of postwar thinkers, most of whom, from philosophers to lyricists, are clearly "radical." . . . The literary groups to which these men belong, the day-by-day conversations in which they train one another to think and to feel, are full of the modern doubt and disquietude, and even more frequently, of the modern challenge and rebellion. To be bookish today is to be radical.[13]

In 1949, just before the advent of McCarthyism, Friedrich Hayek, then visiting at the University of Chicago, commented that as he traveled around the universities of America the dominant tone in faculty club conversation was "socialist," by which he probably meant supportive of the Keynesian planning welfare state.[14] And Hayek went on to say that the brightest academics he encountered were the most likely to be socialist. A national survey of 2,500 social scientists conducted in 1955 by Paul Lazarsfeld and Wagner Thielens found that 8 percent had backed left third-party candidates in 1948, compared to 2 percent in the electorate generally. Most, 63 percent, voted for Harry Truman; only 28 percent supported Thomas Dewey.[15] And once again, those at leading universities were considerably to the left of their colleagues at other institutions.

Hypotheses to explain these findings have been suggested by Joseph Schumpeter, Paul Lazarsfeld, and C. P. Snow. They contend, in different ways, that academe and the intellectual world reward originality, innovation, a rejection of the past, of what one has been taught—ways of thinking linked to political radicalism.[16] Consequently, the best and the brightest are disproportionately found among the more radical or anti-establishmentarian, usually located on the left in the West, but sometimes on the right as well, particularly where the left has held longtime power. Inherent in the obligation to create is the tendency to reject the status quo, to oppose the traditional as philistine.[17] Hayek, who had made the same empirical observation (though limited in the American case to the left), explains the phenomenon as stemming from selectivity. Among college-educated youth cohorts, the brightest leftists choose intellectual pursuits while the brightest conservatives concentrate on practical areas, such as business, engineering, and the free professions.

The Lazarsfeld-Thielens study was in fact conducted to evaluate the impact of McCarthyism on social scientists. As might be expected, the overwhelming majority were strongly anti-McCarthy. What was much more surprising—given the assumption that McCarthy and other government investigations of Communism were intimidating even politically moderate faculty, pressing professors to expound conformist views—was the conclusion that any intimidation or sense of "apprehension among the social science teachers . . . is hardly of a paralyzing nature; the heads of these men and women are 'bloody but unbowed.' "[18] The further left the faculty were in their opinions, the more concern they expressed about external intimidation, but being to the left also correlated with subscribing to left-of-center magazines and reporting membership in political groups "which advocated a program or cause which has been unpopular or controversial."[19] Only 6 percent of the 743 who had so belonged indicated that such membership adversely affected their academic careers.[20]

Given that liberalism is associated with scholarly productivity and prestige and the quality of academic institutions, it is logical that Lazarsfeld and Thielens found even during the age of McCarthyism that young faculty consciously recognized "that professional success is more often attained" by liberal than by conservative colleagues.[21] There was, of course, apprehension among academics, since some professors lost jobs. But these tended to be scholars who could be formally charged with or asked about present or past Communist Party affiliations. Those who refused to answer were frequently let go. Other well-known radicals, including socialists, Trotskyists, and anarchists, were rarely sanctioned. Val Lorwin of the University of Oregon, whose red Socialist Party card was reported to investigators as a Communist one by his landlady, is a notable exception.

III. Politicization and Quiescence: The 1960s, 1970s, and 1980s

The militant civil-rights movement of the early 1960s, which engaged in civil-disobedience tactics, was heavily campus-based. Black and white students joined in demonstrations and sit-ins. They were backed by most of their professors, who saw in the activity of the movement revenge for the passivity and outward conformism of the early 1950s. And through a process which led from civil-rights sit-ins in business establishments to student takeovers of administration buildings, actions which led almost everywhere to the calling in of the police and which produced the recurrent condemnation of campus officialdom by faculty meetings, the American campus was radicalized by the end of the decade.

The major catalytic events that gave rise to the movements of the 1960s were the civil-rights and anti–Vietnam War struggles. The student mass base was dedicated to the substantive issues, but radicals of diverse varieties took over the leadership in many local and national demonstrations. They became carried away with the illusion that they were creating a revolutionary mass movement. And as support for authority began to weaken, a broad coterie of anti-establishment causes was added to the movement, such as gay and women's rights, environmentalism, and greater freedom in personal behavior, particularly in the realms of sexual activity and use of drugs.

The movement issues affected faculty as well. They led to the politicization of many academic organizations, particularly in the social sciences and the humanities. Selection of officers, which had previously been perceived as honors to be given for contributions to scholarship, much like prizes, became vigorously contested elections with the left winning out in a number of associations. Major scholars were defeated because of their alleged conservatism. Similar issues divided campuses. Formal faculty political parties were established to contest elections for faculty senates and to affect the outcomes of faculty meetings. The ideological splits within the academic organizations continue to affect the choice of officers in elections in some, such as the Modern Language and American Historical Associations; parties have disappeared on the campuses, but the lines of political cleavage which undermined collegial relations in departments and universities remain, to be activated when new issues dealing with matters such as multiculturalism and free-speech rights arise. They also continue to affect votes on appointments and promotions, particularly in the humanities and social sciences.

A number of opinion surveys taken in the late 1960s and the 1970s, some by Everett Ladd and myself, found again that militancy and radicalism were strongest at the most prestigious campuses among the brightest students and the intellectually most distinguished faculty. In discipline terms, they had their greatest strength among the more purely academic, least practical, subjects, i.e., the humanities and nonquantitative social sciences.[22] As Thorstein Veblen emphasized at the end of World War I, intellectual creativity and social and political marginality appeared to be functionally interrelated.[23]

The "movements" exulted in their apparent ability to stop the war and to reduce segregation and racially discriminatory hiring practices. But victory brought frustration. The great majority of the student protesters dropped away once the war and the great civil-rights causes ended. A political quiescence descended on the American campuses from the mid-1970s on, with the end of the Vietnam conflict. And the triumph of Reagan-Bush Republicanism seemed to indicate that the country at large had turned conservative. During the 1980s, young voters, eighteen to twenty-four, were the most Republican of all age groups. A 1989 national faculty survey reports that 83 percent agreed that undergraduates have become more conservative politically.[24] Two national surveys of all undergraduates taken in the mid-1980s appeared to confirm this view. They found that self-identified "moderate conservatives" outnumbered "liberals" by three to two (31–32 percent to 23–21 percent), while "strong conservatives" had more support, 5 or 6 percent, than those who described themselves as left, 2 percent.[25]

IV. Recent Shifts to the Left

Yet opinion data gathered over a quarter of a century by Alexander Astin and his colleagues in the Cooperative Institutional Research Program (CIRP) contradict this impression, or, perhaps more accurately, indicate that the situation may be changing. Their findings suggest that a new liberal-left protest wave may be in the making on American campuses in the early 1990s. CIRP has been analyzing the responses of college freshmen in over five hundred institutions. Their twenty-fifth annual survey (Fall 1990) reports that the "number of students who plan to participate in campus protests in college . . . reached an all-time high. . . ."

> The survey also yielded an all-time high in the number of freshmen who say that it is an "essential" or "very important" goal in life to "influence social values" (43 percent) or to "influence the political structure" (21 percent). . . . These trends suggest that there is a rapidly expanding number of American college students who are dissatisfied with the status quo and who want to become personally involved in bringing about change in American society.[26]

Astin et al. report a syndrome of attitudes which attest to increasing student liberalism with respect to environmental issues and racial discrimination. The proportion who say it is "essential" or "very important" for them personally to "become involved" in efforts to clean up the environment increased from 16 percent in 1986, to 26 percent in 1989, to 33.5 percent in 1990, while those saying the same about the need to personally "help promote racial understanding" climbed steadily from 27 percent in 1986 to 38 percent in 1990. Support for busing in the schools to achieve racial balance jumped from 37 percent in 1976 to 57 percent in 1990. Conversely, interest in establishment careers, business-related and engineering, dropped steadily during the late 1980s. Aspirations for "master's and doctoral degrees reached all-time highs (37 percent and 12 percent, respectively)" in 1990.[27]

The pattern among the professoriate resembles that of the students. Faculty became less liberal or more conservative between 1969 and 1984 according to a series of national surveys conducted for the Carnegie Corporation, although they remained far to the left of the general population. The proportion describing themselves as left or liberal fell off from 46 percent in 1969, to 41 percent in 1975, to 39 percent in 1984. Conversely, those identifying themselves as conservative increased from 28 percent in 1969, to 31 percent in 1975, to 33 percent in 1984.

The move to the right among faculties seemingly was reversed in the latter half of the 1980s. In the most recent Carnegie poll (taken in 1989), the percentage agreeing with the statement "I am apprehensive about the future of this country" moved up from 50 in 1984 to 63 in 1989. The proportion describing themselves as liberal jumped to 56 percent, while that of identified conservatives fell to 28 percent.[28] Again, the data show that scholars at the most prestigious universities are to the left of those at other institutions. At the research universities, 67 percent are liberals while only 17 percent are conservatives. Conservatives are strongest at the predominantly teaching institutions, 27 percent at four-year colleges and 35 percent at two-year community colleges, although liberals predominate at them as well, 59 and 48 percent respectively.[29] Conversely, most polls indicate the general population to be more conservative, about 35 to 40 percent, than liberal, 10 to 20 percent.

As the 1980s progressed, sections of the professoriate had been quietly moving toward the left. The "new" faculty liberalism does not reflect revived mass protest. To some degree, the change may have been a reaction to Reaganism, to the triumphs of the Republican Right in the larger polity. For even when moving away from radical left and activist views, the bulk of academe, particularly in the upper echelons, remained much more liberal and Democratic than the general electorate and more critical of business-related institutions and values. Hence, many faculty perceived the 1980s as a decade of increased materialism, and as less egalitarian with respect to income distribution and minority rights.

Preliminary findings from the exit polls taken on election day 1992 indicate a sizable move to the Democrats on the part of first-time voters, students in the eighteen-to-twenty-four-year-old category, and those who have some post-graduate education. Such behavior is in line with the evidence indicating greater strength for the left in the 1990s.

The growth of faculty activism, a related but partially independent development, appears to be a product of the increased presence of the "veterans" of the 1960s, of former student radicals as well as of feminists, racial minorities, and gays, in the tenured ranks. In their rejection of the "bourgeois" world, many student activists had turned to the academy. Historian John Diggins notes: "Consisting to a large extent of graduate students, the New Left entered the academic profession en masse. . . ."[30] As leading cultural activist Henry Louis Gates, now at Harvard, notes: "Ours was the generation that took over buildings in the late 1960s and demanded the creation of black and women's studies programs and now, like the return of the repressed, has come back to challenge the traditional curriculum."[31]

Left faculty are to be found in greater numbers in the humanities and "soft" social sciences, as well as in some of the professional schools (such as law and social work), while their relative strength in the increasingly quantitative social sciences has fallen off. Existential and class analyses linked to Marxist thought have made considerable gains in humanities departments in the emergence of deconstructionism, and in the law schools in the form of critical legal studies, which also seek to "expose" the system-supporting aspects of the law rather than explaining how it operates or exploring the normative principles which underlie it. In their teachings and writings today, many historians, legal scholars,

English professors, and qualitative sociologists try to expose the dominant "hegemonic" culture that—in their view—legitimizes the traditional establishments of wealthy white males. American society and culture remain the enemy.

Berkeley philosopher John Searle, once an ardent supporter of student activism but more recently a champion of the more traditional canons, has sought to answer the question why "the 'cultural left' is not heavily influential outside the departments of French, English, and comparative literature and a few history departments and law schools . . . [since] the study of poetry, plays, and novels is hardly the ideal basis for understanding modern structures of power or the mechanisms of revolutionary change." His tentative answers make good sense in explaining "the migration of radical politics from the social sciences to the humanities":

> First, as empirical theories of society or blueprints for social change, Marxism and other such theories have been discredited by recent events. The collapse of the Soviet empire only marks officially something that most intellectuals have known quietly for a long time. The standard versions of radical leftist ideology in the form of theories of society and social change, such as Marxism, Leninism, Stalinism, Maoism, and Castroism, are all in disrepute. The most congenial home left for Marxism, now that it has been largely discredited as a theory of economics and politics, is in departments of literary criticism.
>
> Secondly, for reasons I do not fully understand, many professors of literature no longer care about literature in the ways that seemed satisfactory to earlier generations. It seems pointless to many of them to teach literature as it was understood by such very different critics as Edmund Wilson, John Crowe Ransom, or I. A. Richards; so they teach it as a means of achieving left-wing political goals or as an occasion for exercises in deconstruction, etc. The absence of an accepted educational mission in many literary studies has created a vacuum waiting to be filled. Perhaps the original mistake was in supposing that there is a well-defined academic discipline of "literary criticism"—as opposed to literary scholarship— capable of accommodating Ph.D. programs, research projects, and careers for the ambitious. When such a discipline fails to be "scientific" or rigorous, or even well defined, the field is left wide open for various fashions, such as deconstruction, or for the current political enthusiasms.[32]

Observers, both on the left and the right, native and foreign, have repeatedly noted in the 1980s and early 1990s that Marxism is alive and relatively well in the American intellectual world, even beyond the activism of the humanities. Marxist scholars Bertell Ollmann and Edward Vernoff introduce a comprehensive work on Marxists in academe saying: "A Marxist cultural revolution is taking place today in American universities."[33] Journalist Garry Abrams notes: "American universities may be one of the last bastions of intellectual Marxism, at least in the developed world."[34] Oxford political theorist John Gray, writing in the *Times Literary Supplement,* also concludes that "the academic institutions of capitalist America will be the last redoubt of Marxist theorizing. . . ."[35] Radical feminist historian Elizabeth Fox-Genovese observes that "a good case could be made that, as a group, they [conservatives] are more vulnerable to exclusion from or marginalization within the academy than even the most radical of their left-wing opponents."[36] Radical sociologist Richard Flacks, a former leader of Students for a Democratic Society (SDS), states that by "the eighties, the tradition of the left was rather well-entrenched in American academe, having come to have a taken-for-granted influence on the curriculum, on dominant outlooks of the social sciences and humanities, and the micro-politics of academic life. . . . [I]n the major universities (if nowhere else in this country), it is intellectually respectable to express an affinity with 'Marxism' and to be some kind of socialist."[37] Gerald Marzorati, senior editor of *Harper's Magazine,* emphasizes that the American academic radicals have dropped "liberalism, with its notions of tolerance" in favor of "a mix of neo-Marxism and semiotics, . . . a Continental language, precisely that being abandoned" by the younger European intellectuals who have resuscitated liberalism, the emphasis on individual rights, and pragmatism. Ironically, he notes, these overseas "writers and thinkers seem to harbor none of the easy anti-Americanism of their intellectual forefathers and of America's academic radicals."[38]

The "news" that Marxism is still alive and well in America has spread to purged Communists in Eastern Europe. A *New Yorker* article reports that "a philosopher from Humboldt University [in East Berlin] who had been informing on his department chairman . . . was now looking forward to a semester teaching in America, where he had heard there were still Marxist philosophers like him to talk to."[39] Writing in the *New York Review of Books* on the attitudes and writings of American elite scientists, Cambridge University Nobel laureate M. F. Perutz also concludes: "Marxism may be discredited in Eastern Europe, but it still seems to flourish at Harvard."[40] Commenting in a similar way in *The New Republic* on the differences between American and Russian literary analysts, Robert Alter, a leading student of comparative literature, points out that "[l]iterature in our own academic circles is regularly dismissed, castigated as an instrument of ideologies of oppression. . . ." But after a trip to Moscow, he "came away with the sense that there are still people in the world for whom literature matters urgently."[41] Flacks wrote in *Critical Sociology* in 1988: "If there was an Establishment sociology twenty years ago, we helped do it in, and so, for good or ill, the field is to a great extent ours."[42] And leftist historian Jonathan Wiener noted in *The Journal of American History* in 1989 that "radical history in the age of Reagan occupied the strongest position it has ever held in American universities."[43] He documented his thesis elsewhere by noting that in "the past several years an impressive number of prizes have gone to radical and feminist historians. . . . [E]specially in the crucial field of American history, radical and feminist historians have made their work the center of discussion and debate. . . . The Organization of American Historians has elected several leftists to its presidency in recent years. . . ."[44] A survey of emphases in the humanities conducted under the auspices of the Modern Language Association found Marxist approaches used in more than one-quarter of all humanities departments and in over two-fifths of those in major universities.[45] And self-identified radicals have been elected to office in communities with concentrations of academics and the creative intelligentsia—e.g., Ann Arbor, Amherst, Austin, Berkeley, Boulder, Burlington (Vermont), Cambridge, Hyde Park (Chicago), Ithaca, Madison, Manhattan (New York City), Santa Cruz, and Santa Monica.[46]

If Marxism remains strong among American academics, particularly in the leading research universities, the bulk of the intellectuals in Europe and Japan appear to have dropped their former allegiance to the ideology. Polls indicate that British intellectuals and academics have backed center-left parties, while Swedish professors have also supported nonsocialist groups.[47] French intellectuals turned very anti-Marxist and were anti-Soviet hard-liners during the 1970s and 1980s.[48] Japanese academics have also moved to the right.[49] The behavior of intellectuals in different countries may stem in part from their past links to strong socialist, labor, and, in Italy and France, Communist parties.[50] Socialism as a utopia clearly has failed, both in its authoritarian and democratic forms. Many intellectuals previously involved with left politics have turned away. An analyst of Swedish society, Ron Eyerman, in explaining why European intellectuals, unlike American, have not been "an alienated stratum with an independent tradition vis-à-vis the state," points out that the continental intellectual world, even when on the left, "found itself at the center, rather than the margins, of society." Intellectuals there could take part in the large labor and social-democratic movements. The "alienated intelligentsia that did exist was limited to the arena of high culture," not academe.[51]

The American situation has been quite different. As Richard Flacks emphasizes: "The left has had more meaning in the United States as a cultural than as a political force."[52] Leftist party politics, particularly since World War II, has been too small a matter to count, and trade unions disdain intellectuals. There has been little application of radical theory to policy. As a consequence, Gray indicates, the American "academic class . . . uses the rhetoric and theorizing of the radical intelligentsia of Europe a decade or a generation ago to legitimate its estrangement from its own culture. . . . American academic Marxism . . . [is] politically irrelevant and marginal . . . [and] compensates for its manifest political nullity by seeking hegemony within academic institutions."[53] Leftist ideologies, therefore, have been academic in both senses of the word. As noted, they remain important in the university world and the creative culture generally, and a large and perhaps growing segment of the American intelligentsia, including the media and entertainment elite, appear more inclined to support leftist ideologies than their compeers in most European countries.[54]

Radical sentiments do not appear to affect the bulk of the students nor the majority of the faculty on most teaching-oriented campuses. But they have reached out to many in the leading universities and have received the support of many discipline leaders. As Hayek noted half a century ago, the conservative bourgeoisie control the economy while the campus anti-establishmentarians dominate intellectual life in the humanities and much of the social sciences, particularly in the research universities.

V. The Emergence of Political Correctness

The emergence of cultural critiques in the main centers of academe seemingly also stimulated what was left of the "movements," particularly of ethnic civil-rights protesters, the blacks and the Hispanics, the feminists and the environmentalists. The traditional radicals, undermined by events in Eastern Europe and the Soviet Union, also have turned to the movements and have added a strong intolerant strain to their activity. Frustrated by the Reaganite domination of the polity, the movement radicals concentrated on the campus, raising issues about South African investment, preferential hiring and admission practices, and multicultural programs which challenge the dominance of the traditional American canon and its standards of intellectual judgment.

Conservative (and even moderate liberal) speakers, faculty, and books have become "politically incorrect." Major political spokespersons with impeccable academic credentials, like former professors Jeane Kirkpatrick, Henry Kissinger, and Daniel Patrick Moynihan, have been forced to cancel lectures because of actual or threatened protest demonstrations.[55] A survey taken of a national sample of senior college and university administrators during the 1990–91 academic year indicates that "controversies over the political or cultural context of remarks made by invited speakers are reported by one in 10 institutions, and by 20 percent of the nation's doctoral universities." Complaints from faculty "about pressures to alter their course content [occurred] at five percent of institutions. Among doctoral universities, 12 percent reported such complaints." Similarly, 4 percent of all institutions and 10 percent of doctorate-granting ones report having "experienced significant controversy over the political or cultural content of information presented in the classroom."[56] A year earlier in 1989, a comparable survey of college and university presidents, which questioned whether "disruptive protest demonstrations" were a problem on their campuses, found that 91 percent of all institutional chief officers replied they were not a problem, but many fewer, 60 percent of the heads of research and doctorate-granting institutions, gave this response.[57] Such variations between the research universities and others may be credited to the greater liberalism of the students at the former and/or to encouragement given to activists by a more leftist faculty.

How strong are the movements behind such efforts? Not very, if we examine the distribution of opinions among students. More powerful, if we recognize the ability of activist minorities to mobilize militant student demonstrations against "incorrect" opinion and teaching, which though including only 5 or 10 percent of the undergraduate population, means a few thousand demonstrators on large campuses. An indication of the incendiary role played by some faculty may be found in an article by a prominent professor of English and Law, Stanley Fish, a founding leader of the left academic association, Teachers for a Democratic Culture. In an essay titled "There's No Such Thing as Free Speech and It's a Good Thing Too," Professor Fish writes:

> [A]bstract concepts like free speech do not have any "natural" content but are filled with whatever content and direction one can manage to give them. Free speech, in short, is not an independent value but a political prize, and if that prize has been captured by a politics opposed to yours, it can no longer be involved in ways that further your purposes for it is now an obstacle to those purposes. . . .
>
> [P]eople cling to the First Amendment pieties because they do not wish to face what they correctly take to be the alternative. That alternative is *politics,* the realization . . . that decisions about what is or is not protected in the realm of expression will rest not on principle or firm doctrine, but on the ability of some persons to interpret—recharacterize or rewrite—principle and doctrine in ways that lead to the protection of speech they want heard and the regulation of speech they want silenced. . . . When the First Amendment is successfully invoked the result is not a victory for free

speech in the face of a challenge from politics, but a *political victory* won by the party that has managed to wrap its agenda in the mantle of free speech.[58]

Such views are not an aberration among the cultural left. During the 1960s and early 1970s, opposition to free speech had wide circulation in Herbert Marcuse's ideas about "repressive tolerance," a critique of the free circulation of ideas as suffocating revolutionary approaches, which had considerable support among New Left students.[59] In 1969, Louis Kampf, professor of literature at MIT and president of the Modern Language Association in the late 1960s, told the activist students to disrupt all establishment cultural institutions, not just the universities. Speaking of Lincoln Center, which he said "was built upon the ruins of a low-cost residential area," he proposed: "Not a performance should go without disruption. The fountains should be dried with calcium chloride, the statuary pissed on, the walls smeared with shit."[60] Writing of the situation, two decades later, Berkeley sociologist and former SDS leader Todd Gitlin has noted: "A bitter intolerance emanates from much of the academic left."[61] And socialist intellectual Paul Berman in 1992 observes that "if the intolerance is bitter among some of the professors, how much worse it is in the world of their own students—among the hard-pressed student leftists especially."[62]

Historian Eugene Genovese, a former Marxist who remains on the left, and who stands out as a defender of the rights of those with whom he disagrees, has summed up the current situation in strong terms in reacting to "the repression of professors and students who take unpopular stands against quotas, affirmative action, busing, abortion, homosexuality and the like." He sees the situation as worse for the right than it was for the left in the 1950s, noting: "As one who saw his professors fired during the McCarthy era, and who had to fight, as a pro-Communist Marxist, for his right to teach, I fear that our conservative colleagues are today facing a new McCarthyism in some ways more effective and vicious than the old."[63]

The major problem, however, does not lie in the beliefs and behavior of left-wing teachers or students, but in the weakness of college administrators, who fear the notoriety resultant from resistance to activist student protest, particularly when associated with ethnic, racial, and gender issues.[64] Many are reluctant to get into conflicts even to prevent limitations on campus freedom of speech. To understand the reasons for such behavior would require a separate and longer discourse on the sociology of university governance, on the ways administrators are chosen and the types of faculty drawn to such roles.

Here it is relevant to note that the 1989 survey of the professoriate found that one-third of those queried did not agree that "the administration here supports academic freedom"; 17 percent rejected the statement entirely, while 16 percent were uncertain. Those least likely to say that their administration backs academic freedom are in the most conservative fields—engineering, business, and the physical sciences.[65]

The nature of the concerns for academic freedom and free speech on campus has changed particularly with reference to the leading universities and colleges. Complaints once came from the more liberal or left faculty and students, who worried about extramural efforts (undertaken by conservative trustees, alumni, and state legislators, as well as administrations) to dominate the university and to repress various forms of deviance and political radicalism. Today, the more conservative and apolitical faculty are the most likely to report harassment by students and coileagues, as well as feelings of malaise about the behavior of administrators.

Increasingly, nonscholarly particularistic criteria, e.g., political views, ethnic, religious, and gender characteristics, are affecting faculty selection.[66] Of course, they always have done so to some extent. The norms, however, remain as they must, universalistic and meritocratic. But they are now being challenged by demands for increased representation of women and minorities, and, less openly, for political correctness.

Progress has been made with respect to gender for some time. Changes in the position of women attest to this. Jessie Bernard, a leading feminist sociologist, documented the considerable increase of women in academe which occurred after World War I as an outgrowth of the suffragette movement. The proportions, however, declined greatly after World War II, a phenomenon described by Bernard as "the great withdrawal." What she documented was the way in which the values espoused by female leaders, including the heads of women's colleges, were modified to emphasize the creative roles of mother and wife, which were put on par with a career. These leaders argued that denigrating child-rearing, community activity, and homemaking in favor of jobs was an anti-female view. And Bernard contended that the college women of the 1940s and 1950s responded willingly, *rejecting* the greater emphasis on careers of earlier cohorts. She noted a change in values which pressed women in the years following World War II into "a headlong flight into maternity. Whether they wanted babies or not, they felt they should have them."[67] She pointed out that the drop-off in the proportion of women in the professoriate in the 1940s and 1950s appeared to be "the result of a declining supply of women offering their services" much more than of a "declining demand. . . . The picture seems to be one not of women seeking positions and being denied but rather one of women finding alternative investments of time and emotion more rewarding."[68] The situation, of course, changed dramatically once again from the mid-1960s on, as a new wave of feminists rejected the home in favor of careers and demanded not just meritocratic equal opportunity, but preferential treatment to make up for past discrimination. The record shows that white women—who, unlike African Americans, are distributed in the same class and formal educational attainment groups as the traditionally dominant group, white males—have been able to take advantage of increased opportunities.[69]

The condition of blacks has, of course, been different from that of white women. They entered the affirmative-action era considerably behind whites in educational attainments. Proportionately, relatively few were qualified (had Ph.D.s from highly ranked universities or departments) for academic positions in major universities. And as more have won entrance to the better institutions, they have sought to qualify for the more economically rewarding positions, not for academe or intellectual pursuits. Doing so is typical first-college-generation behavior among all groups. Going to college is seen by those without a history of intellectuality as an avenue of upward mobility. And the positions they know about and aspire to are in business and the professions. This has been true for all immigrant groups except the Jews, who brought respect for learning with them. Henry Louis Gates explains the shortage of black Ph.D.s by the fact that "we don't have a long tradition of academic families."[70] The best and the brightest among African Americans seek to succeed in business management, medicine, law, and the like. This pattern has continued the situation in which African Americans remain heavily under-represented in the pool of those qualified for the professoriate. And their low presence among the faculty contributes to campus tension and activism among minority students and left-inclined faculty. It seems to confirm the belief that discrimination is still widespread in hiring in higher education.

Ever since the adoption of special preferences and quotas for minorities and women introduced by the Nixon Administration in 1969 and strongly pressed on academe by the Department of Health, Education, and Welfare, higher education, like the rest of society, has been severely divided between those favoring meritocratic norms and others who press for social diversity and affirmative-action quotas.[71] While opinion surveys of faculty indicate that significant majorities back meritocracy, administrators, members of the affected minorities, feminists, the more left-inclined academics, and activist students press for proportional-representation targets. The latter goals have become "politically correct." Political correctness also involves support for multiculturalism, the emphasis on including in the curriculum the contributions of Third World cultures, while reducing or rejecting any emphasis on Western ones. As John Diggins concludes: "To be PC was to denounce Western Culture. . . . [M]ulticulturists attacked racism, sexism, and DWEM-ism—partiality to dead, white, European males who wrote most of the books on a course's reading list."[72] Opponents face stigmatization as racists or chauvinists and frequently fear to speak up at faculty or student meetings.

VI. Conclusion

As far as I can judge, an emphasis on political correctness is much more prevalent in American universities than elsewhere in the economically affluent democracies.[73] Such behavior is not unique to academe or to leftists, feminists, or environmentalists. Social conservatives in this country are much more aggressive outside the academy in efforts to impose their morality on the body politic with respect to issues like the right to life than their ideological compeers elsewhere, even in predominantly Catholic countries like Italy, France, or the former West Germany. Such repressive aspects of American culture may be related to two exceptional national characteristics noted earlier: (1) the utopian ideological context of the American Creed, which defines the country in ways that nations characterized by a common history, not an ideology, lack; and (2) the predominance in the United States of Protestant sectarianism, a minority elsewhere in Christendom. The political emphasis on loyalty to Americanism, the defining of deviants as "un-American," the insistence on ideological conformity, and the sectarian stress on personal morality represent forms of behavior which are less prevalent in historically defined countries whose religious ethos and orientation toward personal morality reflect the values of hierarchically organized state-related churches which assume humans and their institutions are inherently imperfect.[74] American values encourage concern for "correctness," both on and off campus, by the right as well as the left. Both are more moralistic, insistent on absolute standards, than their ideological compeers elsewhere in the developed world.

The war between the redefined lefts and rights will continue. As in earlier times, the left draws disproportionately, often heavily, from the campus, from intellectuals, from the "nonprofit sectors" and those training to join them. The right draws its sustenance from the monied sectors, from students seeking to enter them, as well as from the less educated who are more socially conservative. Ironically, the right, strong in the economy and polity, complains that the institutions of the intellectual world put forth an anti-patriotic, un-American critique of the historically dominant values and censor conservative views. The left intelligentsia, who once argued that economic power frustrated their access to the media and undermined academic freedom, currently seek to deny these to those who challenge their beliefs with respect to ethnic, racial, and gender issues, and sexual behavior and preferences. It is now the moderates and conservatives on campus who feel the need to organize to defend their freedoms in organizations like the National Association of Scholars. English and history departments, once justifiably criticized as bastions of WASP, anti-Semitic male chauvinism, upholding the traditional canons and denying the academic legitimacy of modern literature and history, are now the major doors open to militant minorities, women, homosexuals, and intellectual anti-nationalist radicals. Conversely, economics, once perceived as radical, as supportive of trade unions and the welfare state, accepts market economics as its fundamental dogma.

Will these developments continue? If we take history as a guide, such trends rarely do. As we have seen, many members of the European and Japanese intellectual worlds have moved rightward, though they are far from being rightists. These changes occurred before Marxist power collapsed in the Communist world.

The one thing we can be certain of is that the intellectual world, like the polity and market, behaves somewhat cyclically. Student generations frequently do not follow their teachers. The leftist undergraduates of the 1960s and early 1970s became the radical professors of the 1980s and early 1990s. The less politicized students of the 1980s may be the apolitical professors of the early years of the next century. They will live in an intellectually and ethnically more heterogeneous university in which the definitions of political and intellectual correctness will also be much different from the present.

Two decades ago, I dealt with the efforts of the activist left to politicize the American university in some detail. I will not repeat the arguments here.[75] The debate then was almost identical to that waged today. Principles apart, I noted that "the myth of the apolitical university, though a myth, serves to protect unpopular minorities," much more often than not, radicals. And I cited various prominent leftists, including Noam Chomsky, to this effect. He wrote: "One legacy of classical liberalism that we must fight to uphold with unending vigilance, in the universities and without, is the commitment to a free market place of ideas. . . . Once the principle is established that coercion is legitimate,

. . . it is rather clear against whom it will be used. And the principle of legitimacy of coercion would destroy the university as a serious institution. . . ."[76]

Universities must be free places; they must be open to talent, to critical ideas, to the possibility of revisionism from many sources. Censorship, even self-censorship, has no place on the campus. Repression from the left, even though drawing its legitimacy from populist values, must suffer the same fate as repression from the right once did. If it does not, it will revivify the latter. The only policy possible in a university worthy of the name was enunciated in 1975 by the Committee on Freedom of Expression at Yale, chaired by C. Vann Woodward:

> No member of the community with a decent respect for others should use, or encourage others to use, slurs and epithets intended to discredit another's race, ethnic group, religion, or sex. It may sometimes be necessary in a university for civility and mutual respect to be superseded by the need to guarantee free expression. The values superseded are nevertheless important and every member of the university community should consider them in exercising the fundamental right to free expression. . . . The conclusions we draw, then, are these: even when some members of the university community fail to meet their social and ethical responsibilities, the paramount obligation of the university is to protect their right to free expression. . . . If the university's overriding commitment to free expression is to be sustained, secondary social and ethical responsibilities must be left to the informal processes of suasion, example, and argument.[77]

NOTES

1. Quoted in Michael L. Kazin, "The Right's Unsung Prophet," *The Nation*, February 20, 1989, p. 242.
2. Lionel Trilling, *Beyond Culture* (New York: Viking Press, 1965), pp. xii–xiii.
3. "Text of a Pre-Inauguration Memo from Moynihan on Problems Nixon Would Face," *New York Times*, March 11, 1970.
4. Whitelaw Reid, "The Scholar in Politics," *Scribner's Monthly*, vol. 6 (1873), pp. 613–14.
5. Whitelaw Reid, *American and English Studies* (New York: Scribner's, 1913), vol. 1, pp. 241–42.
6. Richard Hofstadter, *Anti-Intellectualism in American Life* (New York: Knopf, 1963), p. 39. See also Richard Flacks, *Making History: The American Left and the American Mind* (New York: Columbia University Press, 1988), pp. 116–17.
7. Seymour Martin Lipset, "Political Controversies at Harvard, 1636 to 1974," in Lipset and David Riesman, *Education and Politics at Harvard* (New York: McGraw-Hill, 1975), p. 106.
8. *Ibid.*, pp. 144–50.

9. Heywood Broun and George Britt, *Christians Only* (New York: Vanguard Press, 1931), pp. 89–90.

10. Seymour Martin Lipset, *Rebellion in the University* (Chicago: University of Chicago Press, 1971; New Brunswick, NJ: Transaction Publishers, 1992), pp. 179–82.

11. James Leuba, *The Belief in God and Immortality* (Chicago: Open Court Publishing Co., 1921), pp. 219–87; and *The Reformation of the Church* (Boston: Beacon Press, 1950), pp. 44–48.

12. Everett Carll Ladd, Jr., and Seymour Martin Lipset, *The Divided Academy: Professors and Politics* (New York: W. W. Norton, 1976), pp. 27–28.

13. Gardner Murphy and Rensis Lickert, *Public Opinion and the Individual* (New York: Harper and Brothers, 1938), pp. 107–8.

14. Friedrich Hayek, "The Intellectuals and Socialism," *University of Chicago Law Review,* vol. 16 (Spring 1949), pp. 426–27.

15. Paul Lazarsfeld and Wagner Thielens, Jr., *The Academic Mind* (Glencoe: The Free Press, 1958), pp. 14–17, 95, 104, and 402.

16. Joseph Schumpeter, *Capitalism, Socialism, and Democracy* (New York: Harper and Row, 1962), p. 148; C. P. Snow, *The New Men* (London: Macmillan, 1954), p. 176; Lazarsfeld and Thielens, *The Academic Mind,* p. 149.

17. For an elaboration of the argument and a presentation of research findings, see Seymour Martin Lipset, "The Academic Mind at the Top: The Political Behavior and Values of Faculty Elites," *Public Opinion Quarterly,* vol. 46 (Summer 1982), pp. 143–68.

18. Lazarsfeld and Thielens, *The Academic Mind,* p. 95.

19. *Ibid.*, pp. 150–52.

20. *Ibid.*, p. 95.

21. *Ibid.*, p. 384.

22. Ladd and Lipset, *The Divided Academy,* pp. 125–48.

23. Thorstein Veblen, *Essays in Our Changing Order* (New York: Viking Press, 1934), pp. 226–27.

24. *The Condition of the Professoriate: Attitudes and Trends 1989* (Princeton: Carnegie Foundation for the Advancement of Teaching, 1989), p. 35.

25. Ernest L. Boyer, *College: The Undergraduate Experience in America* (New York: Harper and Row, 1987), p. 189; and "Students' Views on Social and Educational Issues," *Chronicle of Higher Education,* February 5, 1986, p. 6.

26. Alexander W. Astin, William S. Korn, and Ellyne R. Berz, *The American Freshman: National Norms for Fall 1990* (Los Angeles: Higher Education Research Institute, University of California, 1990), p. 4.

27. *Ibid.*, pp. 5–6.

28. From files of the Roper Data Center at the University of Connecticut.

29. *The Condition of the Professoriate,* pp. 143–44.

30. John Patrick Diggins, *The Rise and Fall of the American Left* (New York: W. W. Norton, 1992), p. 289. See pp. 288–306 and *passim* for the role and influence of the academic left. See also Paul Hollander, *Anti-Americanism Critiques at Home and Abroad, 1965–1990* (New York: Oxford University Press, 1992), pp. 151–55.

31. Henry Louis Gates, Jr., "Whose Canon Is It, Anyway?" in Paul Berman, ed., *Debating P.C.: The Controversy Over Political Correctness on College Campuses* (New York: Dell Publishing, 1992), p. 193. See also Flacks,

Making History, pp. 185–86; and Roger Kimball, *Tenured Radicals* (New York: Harper and Row, 1990), pp. xiv–xv.

32. John Searle, "The Storm Over the University," in Berman, ed., *Debating P.C.*, pp. 105–6.
33. Bertell Ollmann and Edward Vernoff, eds., *The Left Academy—Marxist Scholarship on American Campuses* (New York: McGraw-Hill, 1982), vol. 1, p. 1. See this volume and volume 2, which has a different publisher (New York: Praeger, 1984), for documentation on different disciplines.
34. Garry Abrams, "After the Wall: As New Era Emerges U.S. Political Thinkers Ponder Fate of Marxism," *Los Angeles Times*, December 6, 1989, pp. E1, E6; Tony Judt, "The Rediscovery of Central Europe," *Daedalus*, vol. 119 (Winter 1990), p. 34; Diggins, *Rise and Fall of the American Left*, pp. 296–97. For conservative views, see Peter Shaw, *The War Against the Intellect: Episodes in the Decline of Discourse* (Iowa City: University of Iowa Press, 1989); Paul Hollander, *The Survival of the Adversary Culture* (New Brunswick, NJ: Transaction Books, 1988); and Kimball, *Tenured Radicals*. For radical views, see Ollmann and Vernoff, eds., *The Left Academy*; Jonathan M. Wiener, "Radical Historians and the Crisis in American History, 1959–1980," *Journal of American History*, vol. 76 (September 1989), pp. 399–434; Michael Burawoy, "Introduction: The Resurgence of Marxism in American Sociology," *American Journal of Sociology*, vol. 88 (Supplement 1982), pp. S1–S30; Michael Denning, " 'The Special American Conditions': Marxism and American Studies," *American Quarterly*, vol. 38, no. 3 (1986), pp. 356–80; and Flacks, *Making History*, pp. 185–86 and 190–91.
35. John Gray, "Fashion, Fantasy, or Fiasco?" *Times Literary Supplement*, February 24–March 2, 1989, p. 183.
36. Elizabeth Fox-Genovese, *Feminism without Illusions: A Critique of Individualism* (Chapel Hill: University of North Carolina Press, 1991), p. 150.
37. Flacks, *Making History*, p. 185.
38. Gerald Marzorati, "Europe is Reclaiming the Language of Liberalism," *International Herald Tribune*, July 11, 1990, p. 4.
39. Jane Kramer, "Letter from Europe," *New Yorker*, May 25, 1992, p. 46.
40. M. F. Perutz, "High on Science," *New York Review of Books*, August 16, 1990, p. 15.
41. Robert Alter, "Tyrants and Butterflies," *The New Republic*, October 15, 1990, p. 43.
42. Richard Flacks, "The Sociology Liberation Movement: Some Legacies and Lessons," *Critical Sociology*, vol. 15 (Summer 1988), p. 17.
43. Wiener, "Radical Historians," p. 434.
44. Jon Wiener, *Professors, Politics, and Pop* (New York: Verso, 1991), pp. 117–18.
45. Carolyn J. Mooney, "Study Finds Professors Are Still Teaching the Classics, Sometimes in New Ways," *The Chronicle of Higher Education*, November 6, 1991, p. A20.
46. Hollander, *Survival of the Adversary Culture*, pp. 16–18.
47. In 1992, the large majority of British faculty voted for the Labour Party, but Labour has become a centrist, nonsocialist party. For reports on the voting behavior of British academics from 1983 to 1992, see Tony Tysome, "Academic Land-Slide to Labour," *Times Higher Education Supplement*, March 27, 1992, pp. 1–3.

48. For a description of the way the latter change occurred, see Tony Judt, *Marxism and the French Left* (New York: Oxford University Press, 1986). See also Mark Kesselman, "Lyrical Illusions or a Socialism of Governance: Whither French Socialism?" in Ralph Milibrand, John Saville, Marcel Liebman, and Leo Panitch, eds., *Socialist Register 1985/86* (London: Merlin Press, 1986), pp. 240–42.

49. Masakazu Yamazaki, "The Intellectual Community of the Showa Era," *Daedalus,* vol. 117 (Summer 1990), pp. 260–62.

50. Diggins, *Rise and Fall of the American Left,* p. 294. Diggins classifies English academe with American as arenas where Marxism is still strong. This is true in some fields, but on the whole, radicalism is weaker in British universities than in American ones.

51. Ron Eyerman, "Intellectuals and the State: A Framework for Analysis, with Special Reference to the United States and Sweden," unpublished paper, University of Lund, p. 18.

52. Flacks, *Making History,* p. 189.

53. Gray, "Fashion, Fantasy, or Fiasco?" pp. 183–84.

54. A striking example is John Kenneth Galbraith, who, at a conference in July 1990 on economic reforms in Eastern Europe, railed against the "primitive ideology" of the rapid movement toward market economics. He made "a veiled attack on the privatisation programmes planned by some east European governments." See "East Europe Warned Over Fast Economic Change," *Financial Times,* July 6, 1990, p. 2. See also Galbraith's critique of developments in Eastern Europe in "The Rush to Capitalism," *New York Review of Books,* October 25, 1990, pp. 51–52.

55. See Hollander, *Anti-Americanism,* pp. 159–66.

56. Elaine El-Khawo, *Campus Trends, 1991* (Washington, DC: American Council on Education, 1991), pp. 17–40.

57. *Campus Life in Search of Community* (Princeton: Carnegie Foundation for the Advancement of Teaching, 1990), Table A-2.

58. Stanley Fish, "There's No Such Thing as Free Speech and It's a Good Thing Too," *Boston Review,* vol. 17 (February 1992), pp. 3, 25 (emphasis in original).

59. Herbert Marcuse, "Repressive Tolerance," in Robert Paul Wolff, Barrington Moore, Jr., and Herbert Marcuse, *A Critique of Pure Tolerance* (Boston: Beacon Press, 1965), pp. 81–117. See also Marcuse, *One Dimensional Man* (Boston: Beacon Press, 1964), pp. 7, 9, and *passim.*

60. Louis Kampf, "Notes Toward a Radical Culture," in Priscilla Long, ed., *The New Left* (Boston: Porter Sargent, 1969), p. 426.

61. Cited in Paul Berman, "Introduction: The Debate and Its Origins," in Berman, ed., *Debating P.C.,* p. 22.

62. *Ibid.*

63. Eugene D. Genovese, "Heresy, Yes—Sensitivity, No," *The New Republic,* April 15, 1991, p. 30.

64. Dinesh D'Souza, *Illiberal Education* (New York: The Free Press, 1991), pp. 15–17; Genovese, "Heresy, Yes," pp. 32–33.

65. *The Condition of the Professoriate,* p. 97.

66. Abigail Thernstrom, "Permaffirm Action," *The New Republic,* July 31, 1989, pp. 18–19.

67. Jessie Bernard, *Academic Women* (University Park: Pennsylvania State

University Press, 1964), p. 62. See also Mabel Newcomer, *A Century of Higher Education for American Women* (New York: Harper's, 1959), p. 204.

68. Bernard, *Academic Women*, p. 67.
69. Seymour Martin Lipset and Everett C. Ladd, Jr., "The Changing Social Origins of American Academics," in Robert K. Merton, James S. Coleman, and Peter H. Rossi, eds., *Qualitative and Quantitative Research: Papers in Honor of Paul F. Lazarsfeld* (New York: The Free Press, 1979), pp. 329–36.
70. Quoted in D'Souza, *Illiberal Education*, p. 171.
71. Seymour Martin Lipset, "Affirmative Action and the American Creed," *The Wilson Quarterly*, vol. 16 (Winter 1992), pp. 52–62.
72. Diggins, *Rise and Fall of the American Left*, p. 297.
73. For a comprehensive description and analysis of the way political correctness has taken over in Hollywood and intimidates conservatives, see Allessandra Stanley, "Hidden Hollywood," *New York Times*, May 19, 1992, section 9, pp. 1, 9.
74. See Seymour Martin Lipset, *Consensus and Conflict: Essays in Political Sociology* (New Brunswick, NJ: Transaction Books, 1985), pp. 299–304.
75. Lipset, *Rebellion in the University*, pp. 201–18.
76. Noam Chomsky, "The Function of the University in a Time of Crisis," in Robert M. Hutchins and Mortimer J. Adler, eds., *The Great Ideas Today: 1969* (Chicago: Encyclopedia Britannica, 1969), p. 59.
77. As quoted in *Campus Life* (see note 57 above), p. 21.

The Limits of Diversity:
The New Counter-Enlightenment and
Isaiah Berlin's Liberal Pluralism

Eric Mack

I. Introduction

My purpose in this essay is to examine critically the limits and dangers of the ideology of diversity which has played so prominent a role in recent debates about the character and future of education in American universities. However, my method is to proceed indirectly. In particular, I shall proceed by investigating the structure and development of the thought of the great historian of political ideas, Isaiah Berlin.[1] My contention is that to a large measure the structure and development of Berlin's thought can be understood as an attempt by Berlin to articulate a conception of moral and cultural diversity and to address conscientiously the pitfalls of diversity—pitfalls which he himself discovers in the course of his articulation. More specifically, Berlin begins with a conception of moral and cultural diversity which is very much akin to the conception at the core of today's friends of diversity and multiculturalism. This is a conception which, according to both Berlin and today's friends of diversity, radically challenges central tenets of Western thought. At least in its unalloyed form, this doctrine of diversity rejects belief in universal epistemological and moral norms; it rejects belief in objectivity about facts and about values; it rejects the possibility of genuinely rational dialogue among representatives of diverse forms of life; it insists upon the fundamental incommensurability of different cultures, different ways of thought, feeling, and evaluation.[2]

However, Berlin is very much aware of the profound limits and dangers of diversity. His awareness grows out of his understanding of the historical impulses which gave rise to earlier efforts to advocate diversity and of the historical consequences of those efforts; and it is informed by his understanding of the logical implications of unalloyed forms of the doctrine of diversity. It is vitally important that we recognize these shortcomings and perils. In this essay, the route to that recognition largely consists in an examination of central themes within Berlin's historical and philosophical studies. Through this examination, I shall summon a great champion of diversity to bear witness against the current ideology of diversity and multiculturalism.

Berlin's testimony goes beyond a rejection of unalloyed diversity. We shall see how Berlin's awareness of the limits and dangers of the ideology of diversity leads him to reintroduce and reemphasize crucial elements from within the Western intellectual and moral tradition. Among these elements are: objectivism about both factual and moral matters; the search for an underlying human nature as the foundation for universal (or near-universal) practical norms; and the attempt to identify a sphere of freedom for each individual into which neither other individuals nor the state may intrude. What concerns me in this essay is not the ultimate success of Berlin's positive case for objective values and human liberty, but rather Berlin's reasons for distancing himself from unalloyed diversity and the *extent* to which, to achieve this distance, he must return to the mainstream of the "dominant Western tradition." Berlin continues to believe, with good reason, that an appreciation of cultural and moral diversity is essential for a liberal and tolerant social order. Nevertheless, the primary lesson to be gleaned from Berlin's studies is that the sort of celebration of separatist and disintegrating diversity and multicultural-ism which is common among today's friends of diversity, radically undercuts *liberalism* and *tolerance*. These supreme social values must be defended—if they are to be defended at all—as elements or implications of the core Western intellectual tradition.

The structure of my indirect investigation of the limits of diversity is complex. For this reason, it may be helpful at the outset to indicate the themes of the various sections of this essay and certain of the intercon-nections among those themes. In Section II, "Diversity and Berlin's Rejection of Monism," I present Berlin as an advocate of diversity by describing his celebration of the rejection of the "monism" which he takes to be at the core of the dominant Western tradition. According to Berlin, this monism reached its apogee during the eighteenth-century French Enlightenment. For this reason, Berlin labels the historic reac-tion against monism, which occurred during the eighteenth and early nineteenth centuries, the "Counter-Enlightenment." In Section III, "The New Counter-Enlightenment and the University," I highlight the parallels between the historical Counter-Enlightenment and what I shall call the "New Counter-Enlightenment" embodied in current multiculturalist doctrine. In addition, I sketch the multiculturalist program for restructuring the university.

In Section IV, "The Political Dangers of Diversity," I recount Berlin's recognition of the authoritarian and aggressively nationalistic (or tribalist) implications of the unalloyed revolt against monism's core commitments to universality, rationality, and objectivity. Given the parallels between the Old and the New Counter-Enlightenments, similar implications also issue from the current ideology of diversity. In the absence of common methodological norms and of a perception of objective constraints on the permissible treatment of individuals and societies, nothing remains but for the world to be ruled by faith and force. Just as the ideology of the Old Counter-Enlightenment was incapable of providing general norms in support of tolerance and peace among diverse nations and nationalities, so the New Counter-Enlightenment is bound to prove incapable of promoting tolerance and peaceful coexistence among the various racial, ethnic, and gender groups that make up the modern university.

In Section V, "Wounded Pride and the Retreat from Common Norms," I reinforce the parallels between the Old and New Counter-Enlightenments by showing how Berlin's account of the psychological impulses which drove the Old Counter-Enlightenment (and which drive contemporary irrationalist nationalism and tribalism) applies with equal plausibility to the New Counter-Enlightenment. In Section VI, "The Need for Common Norms," I provide a sketch of the sort of common norms without which the liberal society and the liberal university cannot survive. This vindicates Berlin's perception that a *liberal* pluralism, a *liberal* rejection of monism, must find a way to align itself with elements of the "dominant" Western tradition.

In Section VII, "Beyond Diversity: Objective Value Pluralism," I describe Berlin's arguments against normative relativism—the primary moral danger of unalloyed diversity—and on behalf of the objectivity of the incommensurable values which individuals and cultures discover. In Section VIII, "Beyond Diversity: Human Nature and Liberty," I provide a speculative sketch of Berlin's argument from objective pluralism, through a conception of our nature as beings who must choose among incommensurable objective values, to an endorsement of liberty and tolerance. In these two "Beyond Diversity" sections, my purpose is not to provide a definitive analysis of Berlin's positive argument. Rather, it is to document the extent to which Berlin's recognition of the pitfalls of diversity and the need for common norms brings this opponent of monism back to the perennial project of Western political thought, the grounding of common norms on a conception of human nature. Finally, in Section IX, I summarize and conclude.

II. Diversity and Berlin's Rejection of Monism

Of all the terms which have been employed by those who demand the transformation of the university and of society at large from their currently oppressive forms to "liberated," "postmodern," "inclusive," "multicultural" forms, none has been employed more frequently or more thoughtlessly than the term "diversity." In light of this constant appeal to diversity, it is remarkable that advocates of radical multiculturalism have totally ignored or are simply ignorant of one of the greatest intellectual champions of diversity of our century, Isaiah Berlin. It is Berlin who declares that at the core of "the central tradition of western thought" is "the notion that One is good, Many—diversity—is bad. . . ."[3] Berlin's insistence that the central error of Western thought has been to embrace the One and disdain the Many (i.e., disdain "diversity") is a theme which has been present from his earliest studies of political thought.[4] And Berlin has devoted many of his essays to powerfully sympathetic accounts of thinkers, from Niccolo Machiavelli, to Giambattista Vico, Johann Georg Hamann, and Johann Gottfried Herder, to Alexander Herzen and Georges Sorel, who challenged and rejected this dominant tradition. According to Berlin, the dominant, Western, monist tradition has adhered to

> the notion of timeless objective truths, eternal models, by following which alone men attain to happiness or virtue or justice or any proper fulfillment of their natures. . . . [This] dominant *philosophia perennis* [consists in] the belief in the generality, uniformity, universality, timeless validity of objective and eternal laws and rules that apply everywhere, at all times, to all men and things. . . .[5]

Against the Enlightenment vision of "a single, scientifically organized world system governed by reason,"[6] Berlin offers with approval the vision of the Counter-Enlightenment, namely,

> a new view of men and society, which stressed . . . the charm and value of diversity, uniqueness, individuality, a view which conceived of the world as a garden where each tree, each flower, grows in its own peculiar fashion

and incorporates those aspirations which circumstances and its own individual nature have generated, and is not, therefore, to be judged by the patterns and goals of other organisms.[7]

This new view of men and society—first developed in reaction to the French Enlightenment and to French political and cultural hegemony over central and eastern Europe in the eighteenth and early nineteenth centuries—celebrates the diversity of incommensurable cultures,

> each making its own peculiar contribution to human civilisation, each pursuing its own values in its own way, not to be submerged in some general cosmopolitan ocean which robs all native cultures of their particular substance and colour. . . .[8]

Presenting and drawing out the implications of the views of Herder, Berlin writes:

> If each culture expresses its own vision and is entitled to do so, and if the goals and values of different societies and ways of life are not commensurable, then it follows that there is no single set of principles, no universal truth for all men and times and places. . . . [I]f authenticity and variety are not to be sacrificed to authority, organisation, centralisation, . . . then the establishment of one world, organised on universally accepted rational principles—the ideal society—is not acceptable.[9]

The subversion of monistic rationalism, as it was epitomized by the French Enlightenment and its cosmopolitan delusions and imperialist ambitions, validates

> the will to live one's own regional, local life, to develop one's own *eigentümlich* [characteristic] values, to sing one's own songs, to be governed by one's own laws in one's own home, not to be assimilated to a form of life that belongs to all and therefore to no one.[10]

Moreover, according to Berlin, we owe our current ideals of tolerance and of liberty precisely to this relatively recent denial of monism. Among the "elements in [the] great mutation in western thought and feeling that took place in the eighteenth century" are "[t]he notion of toleration . . . as an intrinsic value" and "the concepts of liberty and human rights as they are discussed today."[11] J. S. Mill was shocked when Auguste Comte infamously suggested that freedom of opinion was no more sacrosanct in morals and politics than in mathematics—and that, since it was not sacrosanct in the latter, it was not sacrosanct in the former either. According to Berlin, within this vignette, the authoritarian Comte represents "the central tradition of western thought," while the libertarian Mill is part of a "deep and radical revolt" against this tradition.[12]

Let us pause for a moment to note how extraordinary this last claim is and how it reflects the recurring and fundamental flaw within Berlin's own, immensely learned, historical vision. Berlin's conception of the dominant Western tradition is of a rigid chain of monistic, confining rationalism which is anchored at one end by Plato and his philosopher-kings and guardians, and at the other end by Henri de Saint-Simon (of whom Comte was a disciple) and his Council of Newton and *industriels*.[13] Berlin always assumes and perceives an ineluctable association between: (1) the belief that humanity is capable of rationally comprehending the universe, especially the social universe; and (2) the belief that, through this comprehension, humanity is capable of systematically constructing and reconstructing the social universe and is called upon by Reason, or Justice, or History to engage in this construction and reconstruction. In short, for Berlin, rationalism inevitably amounts to what F. A. Hayek calls "constructivist rationalism," that is, the conviction that reason reveals to society or to society's experts an authoritative goal toward which all members of society should be consciously directed, and for the sake of which all social relations and institutions should be constructed or reconstructed.

In parallel fashion, for Berlin, the Enlightenment is always the French Enlightenment, never the predominantly nonconstructivist English or Scottish Enlightenments—branches of the Enlightenment which showed little or no propensity to conceive of individuals as malleable building-blocks to be rearranged by social engineers to best promote society's purportedly cohesive purposes. Thus, Locke's *Letter on Toleration,* a masterful defense of tolerance, liberty, and individual rights—which preceded Mill's comparable, but more vacillating *On Liberty* by about 160 years and which could hardly have drawn upon the "deep and radical revolt" which Berlin ascribes to Vico, Hamann, and Herder—is, to my knowledge, never mentioned by Berlin. Hume, the centerpiece of the Scottish Enlightenment *and* an enemy of constructivist rationalism if ever there was one, primarily appears in Berlin's writings as a philosophical skeptic whose work was appropriated and interpreted to suit the eighteenth-century anti-rationalistic, Germanic pietism of Hamann.[14] Nor does Adam Smith's systematic attack on the constructivist model play any role in Berlin's representation of the Enlightenment.[15] It is Berlin's special reading of both rationalism and the Enlightenment[16] which allows him to operate, as he often does, with the simple and ultimately misleading dichotomy of universalist-imperialist-anti-pluralist-anti-individualist-intolerant rationalism versus particularist-egalitarian-pluralist-individualist-tolerant voluntarism.[17]

Berlin, then, has presented the central Western tradition as an extravagant and exaggerated rationalism which imposes, either directly or through the oppressive institutions it promotes, universal, eternal, and authoritative standards for thought and action—standards which take no account of (except to condemn and seek the destruction of) particular circumstances, purposes, and individualities. And this, of course, corresponds to the current representation of the central Western tradition—as a male, Eurocentric vision—by today's friends of diversity. No formulation could better capture the current disparaging characterizations of "masculinist" and "logocentric" thinking than Berlin's description of the *philosophia perennis* as "the belief in the generality, uniformity, universality, timeless validity of objective and eternal laws and rules."[18] Moreover, the product of the "deep and radical revolt" against this inflexible and despotic world-view—the celebration of "the will to live one's own regional, local life, to develop one's own *eigentümlich* [characteristic] values, to sing one's own songs, to be governed by one's own laws in one's own home"[19]—corresponds to the positive vision offered today in the name of multiculturalism.

III. The New Counter-Enlightenment and the University

All one need do to arrive at the core contentions of contemporary multiculturalism is substitute for the collective regional or national experiences depicted by Vico and Herder[20] the communal forms of life and thought associated with racial, ethnic, or gender-defined subcultures or forms of life—subcultures which share, or (more and more frequently) struggle over, a common territory. Add to this anti-universalist and communalist multiculturalism, the conviction (also advanced by Berlin in his commendation of the anti-monist revolt) that universalist objectivism opposes, while particularist relativism befriends, tolerance and liberty, and one arrives at the self-understanding of today's advocate of diversity. For this reason, no one at all familiar with current controversies about the nature and mission of the liberal order and the liberal university can fail to see powerful intellectual support for the cause of diversity in Berlin's championing of these anti-monist themes of the Counter-Enlightenment.

Let us pause here for a more extensive account of the current ideology of diversity as it is advocated on university campuses today, and for an account of its implications for the values and structure of the university. The current ideology of diversity substitutes more parochially defined groups for Vico's cultures and Herder's nations. Each racially, ethnically, and sexually defined group has, if not through genetic determination, at least through powerful and pervasive cultural reproduction, its own form of life, its own ways of perceiving, thinking, and feeling, its own ways of choosing and valuing. There are feminist and masculinist ways of thinking and valuing. There are black, white, Hispanic, Native American, Indian, and East Asian ways of thinking and valuing. There are heterosexual and homosexual ways of thinking and valuing. Indeed, a thorough sensitivity to diversity would reveal more fine-tuned permutations—for example, white-male-homosexual forms of cognition and feeling versus East-Asian-feminist-heterosexual forms of cognition and feeling. The cluster of perceptions, conceptions, and norms of each biologically defined tribe—with one notable exception—are internally self-validating, incommensurable with other world-views, and impervious to external criticism and refutation. The one exception is the Eurocentric world-view, that is, the *Weltanschauung* of the white male heterosexual. This mode of thought and evaluation invalidates itself in virtue of its pretension to universal validity—its insistence that its epistemic and pragmatic norms provide the ultimate, unchanging standards by which all world-views are to be judged, and by which all fundamental alternatives to it are found wanting.

A university which properly recognized diversity would make room for and welcome each diverse world-view or, at least, each world-view significantly present within the multicultural society which it serves. Since each world-view is fundamentally tied to a group which is identified in terms of gender, race, sexual orientation, or national origin, intellectual or cultural diversity within the university depends upon full representation within the student body and, especially, within the faculty, of each significant gender, race, sexual-orientation, or national-origin caucus. Each non-Eurocentric world-view and each of their respective witnesses is under constant, imperialist assault by the Eurocentric world-view and by the universalist standards by which it has maintained its hegemony. Thus, the first task of the bearers of each non-Eurocentric vision is to reveal the oppressive nature of uniformistic Eurocentrism, to deconstruct its anthems and rob them of their power to disparage deviation from masculinist and logocentric thought. This requires that the increased representation of non-Eurocentric world-views take the form of special courses or, better yet, new and independent programs devoted to the consciousness-raising study of how the Eurocentric vision and the despotic institutions it has spawned have oppressed and exploited women, blacks, Hispanics, East Asians, gays, and so on. Among the crucial tasks of these programs in oppression studies is the critique or, at least, the denunciation of the traditional Eurocentric academic standards in terms of which the qualifications of the consciousness-raisers, and/or the quality of their scholarship, might be challenged. Since each world-view is a world unto itself, with its own indigenous meanings and standards, neither it nor its representatives should be subject to external judgment on the illusory basis of measures that transcend particular tribal visions.

Thus, the university which duly recognizes diversity will move in the direction of cultural and biological apartheid—albeit not under that all too straightforward description. Each biologically identified community will have its own reservation, its own fief within which it will sing its own songs of resentment and anxious self-glorification. There will, of course, be no room for biological/cultural traitors—for blacks who do not think like blacks, for women who do not think like women, and so on. There will, presumably, be room for a white male reserve, albeit a chastised and self-criticizing one—that is, for white males who somehow do not think like white males. Across these separate-but-equal domains there will be no common questions, no common controversies, no common projects. There will be no common discourse because it will be recognized that there are no common standards of evidence, of relevancy, of demonstration, or even of civility. The historically ensconced norms of rational discourse will be recognized simply as instruments of racial and sexual hegemony.

IV. The Political Dangers of Diversity

With both Berlin's endorsement of the revolt against monism and the contemporary vision of diversity before us, we must ask why Berlin has not been inducted into the pantheon of divinities of diversity. Why has he not been enshrined along with such giants as Jacques Derrida, Michel Foucault, and Paul de Man? Very probably the correct answer is that Berlin simply is not known to the friends of diversity or is known to them only as a defender of liberal individualism and even of the coldly capitalistic idea of "negative liberty."[21] However, there are far more profound reasons why Berlin could never qualify as an official hero of diversity. These reasons have to do with the genuinely critical character of Berlin's investigation of the revolt against monism and with Berlin's own commitment to measure ideological movements in terms of their capacity to sustain rational dialogue and tolerant coexistence among diverse individuals and cultures.

In accordance with this critical approach, Berlin has been concerned to investigate the profound dangers which arise from the rejection of the dominant Western tradition as exemplified in the Enlightenment. In this section, I want to describe briefly Berlin's recognition of the Counter-Enlightenment's capacity to give rise to authoritarianism and aggressive nationalism.

To begin with, Berlin is well aware of features of the Counter-Enlightenment that have "strongly conservative and, indeed, reaction-ary implications."[22] In its systematic rejection of faith and revelation and in its moral secularism, "[w]hat the entire Enlightenment has in common is denial of the central Christian doctrine of original sin. . . ." For this reason, "the sharpest single weapon in the root-and-branch attack on the entire Enlightenment by the French counter-revolutionary writers" was the reassertion of original sin. This weapon was most boldly em-ployed in the decades following the French Revolution by the diplomat Joseph de Maistre. De Maistre rejected the liberal bourgeois conception of man "as naturally disposed to benevolence, cooperation and peace, or, at any rate, capable of being shaped in this direction by appropriate education or legislation. . . ."[23] Rather, with postmodern clairvoyance, de Maistre perceived that

> men are by nature evil, self-destructive animals, full of conflicting drives, who do not know what they want, want what they do not want, do not want what they want, and it is only when they are kept under constant control and rigorous discipline by some authoritarian elite . . . that they can hope to survive and be saved. Reasoning, analysis, criticism shake the foundations and destroy the fabric of society.[24]

Suppose, as de Maistre did, that we have only two alternatives. One is conscientious analysis and criticism which deconstructs the social order and its myths, which lays bare the insubstantiality and inconsistency of our being and sets us forever wandering through meaningless terrain. The other is bad-faith, yet life-preserving, acceptance of established norms and of established authority which is brutal and frightening enough to suppress corrosive criticism. If those are our choices, must not anyone not at war with life itself turn to the latter? Thus, de Maistre's reactionary authoritarianism is a logical consequence of a process which begins with the Counter-Enlightenment attack on reason and criticism in accord with universal norms.

As virulent and more dangerously seductive than reactionary authori-tarianism is the modern populist nationalism which, according to Berlin, issues directly from the rejection of the Enlightenment—a nationalism which emerges as an attempt to protect meaning and coherence against their purported subversion by universalism and cosmopolitanism.[25] It is the Counter-Enlightenment's contention that each culture, each people, each nation has its own collective form of life, its own values, myths, and aspirations. Moreover, it is only in terms of and within his own native communal values, myths, and aspirations that each individual finds his voice, his meaning, and his purpose. Thus,

> if I am separated from it [i.e., from my nation's form of life] by circumstance or my own wilfulness, I shall become aimless, I shall wither away, being left, at best, with nostalgic memories of what it once was to have been truly alive and active, and performing that function in the pattern of national life, understanding of which alone gave meaning and value to all I was and did.[26]

Furthermore, the Counter-Enlightenment's revolt against monism also contends that the values and aspirations of diverse cultures and nations do not form a harmonious whole, that the realization of some fundamental values can only emerge through the suppression of other fundamental values. In such a universe of diverse and incommensurable values, each bearer of a form of life must, it seems, promote its own meaningful ends and aspirations, whatever the dimly understood effects may be on other nations' values:

> If the satisfaction of the needs of the organism to which I belong turns out to be incompatible with the fulfilment of the goals of other groups, I, or the society to which I indissolubly belong, have no choice but to force them to yield, if need be by force.[27]

The rejection of value monism yields the understanding that some ultimate values will always, tragically, have to be sacrificed on the altar of other ultimate values. Must not each bearer of a set of values, of a way of life, reason that it is better (by *our* standards) that *our* ultimate understandings and values prevail over theirs, that the tragedy be theirs, not ours? As Berlin puts it, the denial of monism has led not only to "the conservatism of [Edmund] Burke and [Justus] Möser [and Hamann and de Maistre]" but also "to Fascism and brutal irrationalism and the oppression of minorities."[28]

Are there no principles of constraint that issue from value diversity— principles that apply across variegated value communities and require that each bearer of values and meanings live at peace or in justice with the others? Such principles seem impossible if difference and particularity are truly and thoroughly more fundamental than uniformity and universality. For if one genuinely rejects the dominant Western tradition, as today's friends of diversity demand, it seems that one must agree with the relativistic nationalist that

> [t]here is no over-arching criterion or standard, in terms of which the various values of the lives, attributes, aspirations, of different national groups can be ordered, for such a standard would be super-national [that is, trans-cultural], not itself immanent in, part and parcel of, a given social organism, but deriving its validity from some source outside the life of a particular society—a universal standard, as natural law or natural justice are conceived by those who believe in them.[29]

As we shall see shortly, for Berlin the first step back toward such a standard is his qualification of his anti-monism so as to distinguish it sharply from all forms of relativism. His second step is an attempt to ground a universal principle of liberty and tolerance upon a conception of human nature which is tied to this qualified pluralism.

V. Wounded Pride and the Retreat from Common Norms

Before turning to Berlin's attempt to escape from relativism, it is interesting to examine Berlin's account of the psychology that propels the nationalist rejection of universalism and cosmopolitanism. What, according to Berlin, drives this denial of

> the reality of universal truths, the eternal forms which knowledge and creation, learning and art and life, must learn to embody if they are to justify their claims to represent the noblest flights of human reason and imagination?[30]

The primary condition for the development of nationalism, as exemplified by the late eighteenth and early nineteenth century German Counter-Enlightenment, is "wounded pride and a sense of humiliation in its [the nation's] most socially conscious members, which in due course produce anger and self-assertion."[31] This "wound to group consciousness" is the communal equivalent of the blow to self-esteem experienced by an individual newly exposed to enshrined and authoritative standards in terms of which his self-evaluation is poor or precarious. In particular, the wounded pride essential to the Counter-Enlightenment was the product of the encounter of German thought, culture, and institutions with "the eternal forms [of] knowledge and creation" advanced by the French establishment, coupled with a felt inability or unwillingness among those newly exposed to these externally imposed standards to measure up to them. According to Berlin, there are two further conditions for the nationalist reaction to "the infliction of a wound on the collective feeling of a society, or at least of its spiritual leaders." One of these is the existence, within that society, of "a group or class of persons who are in search of a focus for loyalty or self-identification, or perhaps a base for power."[32] The other further condition for a society's chauvinist recalcitrance is the presence,

> in the minds of at least some of its most sensitive members, [of] an image of itself as a nation, at least in embryo, in virtue of some general unifying factor or factors—language, ethnic origin, a common history (real or imaginary). . . .[33]

In the case of the Germanic resistance to the French Enlightenment, this reaction centered on the contrast between

> the depth and poetry of the German tradition, with its capacity for fitful but authentic insights into the inexhaustible, inexpressible variety of the life of the spirit, [and] the shallow materialism, the utilitarianism, and the thin, dehumanised shadow play of the worlds of the French thinkers.[34]

Thus, the Germans' denial of central themes within Western tradition aimed, consciously or unconsciously,

> to create a new synthesis, a new ideology, both to explain and justify resistance to the forces working against their [pre-Enlightenment] convictions and ways of life, and to point in a new direction and offer them a new centre for self-identification.[35]

What is extraordinary is how closely Berlin's entire motivational analysis applies to particularist, group-defined modes of thought and feeling which today's friends of diversity want to license and empower.[36] Almost all young people are anxious when they enter the university, either as students or as faculty. This anxiety, this felt encounter with standards and expectations, which one is uncertain one will be able to satisfy, will be all the greater for individuals with limited academic backgrounds. Such individuals will tend to be less familiar with these standards and with the entire form of life that universities at least pretend to represent; and they will, therefore, be less prepared to meet these criteria and to be successfully integrated into university life.

For anyone in such circumstances, there is a powerful attraction toward ideologies that will explain anticipated shortfalls, not in terms of one's own deficiencies (however blameless one may be for those deficiencies), but rather in terms of the faults, indeed the damnability, of those standards and expectations and of the institutions and individuals whose judgments press upon one. The most seductively attractive of such ideologies will vindicate one's withdrawal from the project of proving oneself in and integrating oneself into the alien world—and will characterize that withdrawal as being, in truth, the liberating rediscovery of the special, deeper modes of perceiving, thinking, and feeling that define the collective world-view of one's racial, ethnic, or gender group. The more the demanding external environment is depicted as foreign, hostile, oppressive, and exploitative, the greater will be one's felt vindication in rejecting it or in demanding its radical transformation into structures that affirm and celebrate the distinctive, albeit ineffable, meanings, insights, and songs of one's native *Weltanschauung*. And, of course, the more effectively one defies the imperialistic demands of the male, Eurocentric university establishment—the more one alienates oneself from it in order to be at home and in tune with, for example, one's black soul or one's feminine voice—the greater will be one's need continually to recompose reality into a tale of nefarious colonialist assault and heroic tribal resistance.[37]

This is not the occasion to recount the unhappy consequences of this social and intellectual self-ghettoization. Instead, I have another purpose in displaying the structural and motivational parallels between the emergence of modern nationalism and the balkanization of our universities in the name of diversity. This reinforces the insight that the current ideology of diversity is no more capable of validating a regime of peaceful coexistence and tolerance among the racial, ethnic, and gender-based cultures which it proposes to enshrine within the multicultural society and university than the Old Counter-Enlightenment was capable of yielding norms valid across competing nations (or alliances of nations), each of which embodied its own incommensurable ambitions and forms of well-being. This profound defect within the ideology of diversity is manifest for both the case of society at large and the case of the liberal university.

VI. The Need for Common Norms

Of course, one of the great virtues of liberal society is that it minimizes the need for a social consensus on substantive ends. In this way, it is the natural social structure for accommodating the incommensurability among value systems of diverse persons and subcultures. But liberal society accomplishes this by recognizing for each individual (and each freely formed association) a sovereign domain within the boundaries of which that person (or association) may determine for himself (or itself) how to act, and by recognizing rules for the mutually agreeable redrawing of those boundaries. Through the recognition of such domains, the liberal regime avoids the need to arrive at a legally enforceable consensus about how particular persons (or associations) should live their lives or employ their resources. But the rights constituted by these boundaries (e.g., rights over one's own body parts, talents, and justly acquired property) and by the restraints on how boundaries may be redrawn must themselves have validity across the individuals (and associations) comprising liberal society.

This morally authoritative framework is liberal society's alternative to the "monistic" enthronement of some single substantive value, for example, the glory of the race or the triumph of the revolutionary class, for the sake of which the lives, resources, and aspirations of different individuals and their subcultures are to be sacrificed. While the liberal rejects any such value monism, he insists upon an intersubjectively valid framework of rights which define and secure domains of choice for value-pursuing individuals (and associations). Furthermore, there must be sufficient convergence of motivational schemes, aspirations, and social understandings among the participants within liberal society for there to be general compliance with the rules of the liberal framework. However, no such universally binding constraints or supportive (partial) convergence of values and understandings will be possible if, paraphrasing Berlin's expression of Herder's views,[38] each subculture of our society (as defined by race, ethnicity, and gender) expresses its own vision and is entitled to do so, and has goals, values, and ways of life that are fundamentally incommensurable, so that there is no single set of principles, no universal truth for all of these subcultures. If this is our multicultural condition, the optimist will hope for Hobbes's absolute sovereign, the pessimist for the executioner upon whose services, according to de Maistre, all social order rests.

To a considerable degree, the liberal university is an analogue of the liberal social order. It is a highly heterogeneous structure within which colleges, departments, special programs of study, and individual faculty are presumed to have their own distinctive missions and character, and are vested with considerable independent authority to advance their respective projects in the manner they judge best. There are ascriptions of jurisdictional spheres and elaborate rules governing the establishment of new spheres and the redrawing of boundaries between existing ones. However, while the liberal society accommodates itself to value pluralism, the liberal university goes beyond this. It commits itself to encouraging intellectual pluralism. The independence granted to particular colleges, departments, and especially to individual faculty members is intended, not merely to allow, but to foster, ongoing critical inquiry and debate and an understanding of the historical experiences and controversies that have conditioned, and that illuminate, current inquiry and debate. Such independence is intended to foster the difficult and uncertain processes of sustaining, conveying, and even advancing human knowledge and understanding. The commitment to intellectual pluralism, and to the institutional rules and forms that tend to foster it, requires of members of the university a form of the virtue of tolerance—it requires intellectual tolerance, the willingness to allow others to go their own scholarly way within their own sphere. It requires a willingness to accept, as equal members of the university community, individuals whose disciplinary assumptions, methodologies, interests, arguments, and/or conclusions one in no way shares. But, once again, this norm of tolerance has to be understood as not itself the creature of particular world-views that are incommensurable with other world-views represented within the university, but rather as having validity and, thus, binding force on all parties, whatever their indigenous world-views.

Unlike the liberal social order, the liberal university does have a goal, albeit the highly abstract and multifarious goal of sustaining, conveying, and advancing human knowledge. Having this goal, the university may make a demand upon its members beyond the liberal demand for tolerance of others' choices. It may demand that its members contribute to (or show due promise of contributing to) the process of inquiry and debate by which its goal is advanced. It may—it *must*, to be true to its mission—establish mechanisms for the evaluation of how fully its members satisfy the diverse aspects of this complex demand. This means that participants within the liberal university must be subject to intellectual standards, to measures of scholarly and scientific integrity, responsibility, comprehension, clarity, ingenuity, explanatory illumination, and even truthfulness, and that these measures cannot themselves be thought of as world-view-specific. Of course, the conscientious application of these measures requires sensitivity to the particular character of the intellectual project being evaluated, to its specific methodology, and to the demands of its distinctive subject matter. Nevertheless, what duly conscientious evaluation is in search of—namely, intellectual worth—is a value which has validity across all racial, ethnic, or gender lines.

Suppose, to the contrary, there were many forms of intellectual worth—for example, black intellectual worth, Native-American intellectual worth, feminist intellectual worth—forms that were incommensurable all the way down. Clearly this would require the dissolution of anything like the evaluation process I have described. For no representative of one medley of songs could possibly be entrusted with the evaluation of the singer of another medley. Even if, through a heroic imaginative effort, the lesbian feminist could capture some of the ineffable feeling of the black, male heterosexual, the world revealed would be utterly alien to, and utterly discordant with, her own inescapable evaluative categories, her own deeply embedded feminist conceptions of comprehension, explanation, and even truth. Here it is well to recall Berlin's remark about the analogous problem of trans-cultural understanding:

> Unless we are able to escape from the ideological prisons of class or nation or doctrine, we shall not be able to avoid seeing alien institutions or customs as either too strange to make any sense to us, or as tissues of error, lying inventions of unscrupulous priests. . . .[39]

As we shall see, Berlin believes that we *can* escape these "ideological prisons," but only because the relativistic pluralism which currently marches under the banner of "diversity" is false. But if we cannot escape those prisons, the only possible resolution is the one already proposed by the friends of diversity (although not described in these terms) to avoid the evils inherent in evaluation by male, Eurocentric standards: namely, the establishment of separate racial, ethnic, and gender reserves, and/or separate evaluative standards and processes.[40]

VII. Beyond Diversity: Objective Value Pluralism

In Section IV, we took note of Berlin's reasons for thinking that what I have been calling "unalloyed diversity," namely, the systematic rejection of universal norms and objectivity, is *politically* ominous. But beyond this, and especially in his later essays, Berlin insists that the epistemological and normative relativism inherent in unalloyed diversity is also deeply intellectually flawed. Berlin's disavowal of these forms of relativism and his own affirmation of epistemological and normative objectivism often take the form of representing his chief stalking-horses, Vico and Herder, as *anti-relativist* pluralists.[41]

To begin with, Berlin distinguishes between relativism with regard to "judgements of facts" and with regard to "judgements of value," and he immediately disavows the former, both on behalf of Vico and Herder and on behalf of himself. He insists that neither Vico nor Herder were relativists, or even pluralists, with regard to "judgements of facts." This speaks well of them because, according to Berlin, the relativist denial of the possibility of objective knowledge of facts is not merely false; it is "ultimately self-refuting."[42] The only live issue, then, is whether the great critics of monism should be understood as relativists with regard to "judgements of value." Berlin contends that they should not, for he contends that the value pluralism which they and he endorse is a species of value objectivism and not of value relativism. Pluralism's incommensurable values can be "equally genuine, equally ultimate, [and] equally objective."[43]

Berlin clears the way for objective pluralism by reasserting the central discovery of normative anti-monism, namely, that ultimate objective values need not all be reducible to a *summum bonum* or be otherwise commensurable. Hence, to affirm the incommensurability of values is not to be committed to their relativity.[44] It is not to be committed to the relativist contention that the affirmation of any one of these values by

> a man or a group, since it is the expression or statement of a taste, or emotional attitude or outlook, is simply what it is, with no objective correlate which determines its truth or falsehood.[45]

Nevertheless, even if incommensurability does not *entail* relativism, why not accept relativism as providing a plausible explanation of value incommensurability? At first blush, Berlin's answer seems to be that, if relativism were true, we would not even be able to comprehend the values of other cultures. Since, with sufficient learning and effort, we can comprehend these values, relativism must be false. He argues that

> [m]embers of one culture can, by the force of imaginative insight, understand . . . the values, the ideals, the forms of life of another culture or society, even those remote in time or space. They may find these values unacceptable, but if they open their minds sufficiently they can grasp how one might be a full human being, with whom one could communicate, and at the same time live in the light of values widely different from one's own, but which nevertheless one can see to be values, ends of life, by the realisation of which men could be fulfilled.[46]

Yet the possibility of imaginative insight into another's alien values does not in itself testify to their objectivity or to the objectivity of one's own values. Something further is needed, and at least part of this is supplied within Berlin's account of what makes such trans-cultural (and trans-subcultural) comprehension possible:

> Intercommunication between cultures in time and space is only possible because what makes men human is common to them, and acts as a bridge between them.[47]

What makes others and their values intelligible is our capacity to understand them as modes of human self-realization, as "ends of life, by the realization of which men could be fulfilled." The reason that objective values are many, but not infinitely many, is that to be understood as ultimate values, they must be understood as among those ends that promise human fulfillment; and not all ends hold out this promise:

> Incompatible these ends may be; but their variety cannot be unlimited, for the nature of men, however various and subject to change, must possess some generic character if it is to be called human at all.[48]

Indeed, despite his continued attempts to be pluralist all the way down, at times Berlin's language suggests that there is an ultimate human good, albeit one that is concretized in different ways and forms, for different individuals and societies. It is by seeing how the specific ways and forms which have been adopted by particular individuals or communities are modes of this single ultimate good that we comprehend them:

> There are many kinds of happiness (or beauty or goodness or visions of life) and they are, at times, incommensurable: but all respond to the real needs and aspirations of normal human beings; each fits its circumstances, its country, its people; the relation of fitting is the same in all these cases. . . .[49]

Perhaps most suggestive of a monistic bedrock beneath value's local formations is this description of Herder's anti-relativism:

> When Herder says 'each nation' (and elsewhere 'each age') 'has its centre of happiness within itself, just as every sphere has its centre of gravity', he recognises a single principle of 'gravitation': the anthropology which Herder wishes to develop is one which would enable one to tell what creates the happiness of what social whole, or of what kinds of individuals. . . .[50]

However monistic Berlin's ultimate re-commitments may be, the basic shape of his theory of value is reasonably clear. The fulfillment of the real needs and aspirations of normal human beings is the schema of value. These needs and aspirations have reality only as they are articulated within particular people by their judgments, their choices, and their context of social meanings. It is only in the fulfillment of those concrete needs and aspirations that value obtains, not in participation in the abstraction "the fulfillment of real needs and aspirations." Since people's judgments, choices, and contexts of social meanings vary enormously across both time and space (and, within modern pluralist societies, from block to block), value has many incommensurable realities.

There are also, within Berlin's argument, the seeds of an important critique of radical multiculturalism. Most advocates of unalloyed diversity continue to insist that among their most treasured goals is the goal of increased understanding, if not agreement, across individuals and cultures with disparate modes of thought, feeling, and evaluation. However, Berlin argues that even comprehension across individuals and cultures is possible only in terms of a general framework which allows us to apprehend the values and aspirations of others as issuing from "the real needs and aspirations of normal human beings." Genuine intercommunication among individuals and cultures is possible only because "what makes men human is common to them, and acts as a bridge between them." This means that if genuine communication and understanding are possible, it is only because there are sound intellectual bridges by which people can escape the confines of ways of thought, feeling, and evaluation which reflect only their given race, gender, and nationality.

VIII. Beyond Diversity: Human Nature and Liberty

What sort of social-political doctrine emerges from this value pluralism? Even after we remind ourselves that Berlin never presents himself as a political theorist, it is striking how little he offers in the way of a self-critical response to this question. Nevertheless, we can identify two alternative lines of argument in Berlin. The first line of argument simply includes liberty, understood as freedom from coercion, among the many incommensurable objective values. The second, more structurally complex and interesting line of argument assigns a special status to this "negative" liberty.

The first approach naturally calls forth the questions: How do we choose between competing values, one of which may be liberty? Which values are to be sacrificed to which other values? When two values collide, to what extent should the lesser value be sacrificed to the greater? Berlin's response to these and like questions, which he describes as "no clear reply," is that

> the collisions, even if they cannot be avoided, can be softened. Claims can be balanced, compromises can be reached. . . . Priorities, never final and absolute, must be established.[51]

Unfortunately, this seems to be no reply at all. For why should we believe that balance is, in general or in any particular case, better than wholehearted pursuit of certain values at the acknowledged cost of the total neglect or destruction of other values? Furthermore, how could the ranking of any particular balance among competing values above an alternative balance ever be shown to be more reasonable than the reverse ranking? Berlin's endorsement of balance, presupposing as it does the ranking of balanced over unbalanced resolutions and the existence of criteria for grading alternative balances, seems fundamentally at odds with belief in the deep incommensurability of values. Berlin does offer one rationale for balance and compromise. This is that they serve "the first requirement of a decent society," which is the prevention of "desperate situations, of intolerable choices."[52] Unfortunately, the prevention of one person's desperate situation or intolerable choice will almost certainly diminish the fulfillment of the needs and aspirations of other people—even other "normal" people. How can it be reasonable—given the ultimate incommensurability of the values in conflict—to judge that this or that prevention is worth the cost? Nothing about the objectivism which Berlin attaches to his pluralism facilitates his answering these vital questions.[53]

Furthermore, even if some rationale for balance and compromise were available, we would be far from arriving at any principled doctrine of liberal tolerance. Negative liberty (and the tolerance mandated by it) would be only one of many conflicting values which would have to be balanced on the social scales. Of course, a value pluralism which includes an affirmation of negative liberty can provide some protection for that value by discrediting any monistic doctrine which denies this good in the name of some One True Good. Much of the force of Berlin's critique of doctrines of positive liberty in "Two Concepts of Liberty" derives from his display of the monistic impulse within such doctrines. This impulse leads to the falsehood that anything which must be sacrificed to advance True Rational Freedom—including negative liberty—can have no genuine worth. Still, this discrediting of monism is simply pluralism at work. It does not signify any special regard or place for the values of liberty and tolerance.

Berlin's second and more promising approach is carried out primarily within his "Two Concepts of Liberty." Even here Berlin reaffirms that

> [t]he extent of a man's, or a people's, liberty to choose to live as they desire must be weighed against the claims of many other values, of which equality, or justice, or happiness, or security, or public order are perhaps the most obvious examples.[54]

However, he also wants to insist that "there must be some frontiers of freedom which nobody should be permitted to cross," that belief in "the inviolability of a minimum extent of individual liberty entails [an] absolute stand," and that this belief constitutes "the recognition of the moral validity—irrespective of the laws—of some absolute barriers to the imposition of one man's will on another."[55]

This defense of "absolute barriers"—boundaries which would define "a certain minimum area of personal freedom which must on no account be violated"[56]—puts into play the liberal strategy for dealing with the incommensurability of values. As previously described, this strategy disavows the search for authoritative substantive *values* whose service requires the sacrifice by individuals and groups of their own distinctive aspirations and projects. Instead, it seeks to identify general *rules* which define personal domains within which each is free to do as he chooses, that is, free to pursue his own chosen ends. The connections between this liberal strategy (on the one hand) and freedom *and* diversity (on the other) have recently been emphasized by F. A. Hayek:

> Whereas enforced obedience to common concrete ends is tantamount to slavery, obedience to common abstract rules [which define spheres of free choice] provides scope for the most extraordinary freedom and diversity. Although it is sometimes supposed that such diversity brings chaos threatening the relative order that we also associate with civilization, it turns out that greater diversity brings greater order.[57]

Berlin's argument for some "absolute barriers" also assigns a special status to liberty. It is not merely a value among many other values. For, according to Berlin, the absolutist affirmation of some measure of negative liberty is not a component of pluralism, but rather is *entailed by* pluralism.[58] It is the necessity of choice between incomparable ultimate values which, in turn, gives liberty its intrinsic importance. Liberty is not among the many first-order values, but rather has a higher-order value or importance in virtue of our need to choose among these incommensurable first-order values.

> The necessity of choosing between absolute [i.e., ultimate] claims is then an inescapable characteristic of the human condition. This gives its value to freedom as Acton had conceived of it—as an end in itself. . . .[59]

Unfortunately, in itself, this argument hardly seems compelling. For one thing, even if choice is inescapable for each individual, we cannot infer that choice is valuable for, much less the birthright of, each and every individual. For another thing, what is inescapable may merely be that *some* individuals have to make choices—choices that may be imposed upon others. I conjecture, however, that Berlin's argument can be given a more generous reading—a reading which connects pluralism, a conception of human nature, and the fundamental norm that persons be treated in accordance with their nature.

Early in "Two Concepts of Liberty," Berlin approaches the question of the ground for a measure of negative liberty in terms of human nature and human essence:

> We must preserve a minimum area of personal freedom if we are not to 'degrade or deny our nature'. . . . What then must the minimum be? That which a man cannot give up without offending against the essence of his human nature.[60]

Value pluralism turns out to be a key to, or a mirror of, this human essence or nature:

> To assume that all values can be graded on one scale . . . seems to me to falsify our knowledge that men are free agents, to represent moral decision as an operation which a slide-rule could, in principle, perform.[61]

Thus, the "inescapable characteristic of the human condition" is not our actually being engaged in moral choice, but our possessing the status of beings capable of moral choice. Our recognition of this status is reciprocal with our recognition of the plurality of incommensurable values. *"These collisions of values are of the essence of what they are and what we are."*[62] Thus, throughout "Two Concepts of Liberty," the fundamental consideration offered against coercion is that to coerce a person is to fail to acknowledge his or her status as a freely choosing being:

> To threaten a man with persecution unless he submits to a life in which he exercises no choices of his goals . . . is to sin against the truth that he is a man, a being with a life of his own to live.[63]

In the course of what must be read as a highly sympathetic exposition of Kantian themes, Berlin is even more explicit in his linkage of human nature, choice, and the wrongfulness of coercion:[64]

> [I]f the essence of men is that they are autonomous beings—authors of values, of ends in themselves, the ultimate authority of which consists precisely in the fact that they are willed freely—then nothing is worse than to treat them as if they were not autonomous, but natural objects . . . whose choices can be manipulated by their rulers whether by threats of force or offers of rewards. To treat men in this way is to treat them as if they are not self-determined. . . .
>
> [T]o manipulate men, to propel them towards goals which you—the social reformer—see, but they may not, is to deny their human essence, to treat

them as objects without wills of their own, and therefore to degrade them. . . .

In the name of what can I ever be justified in forcing men to do what they have not willed or consented to? Only in the name of some value higher than themselves. But if, as Kant held, all values are made so by the free acts of men, and called values only so far as they are this, there is no value higher than the individual. . . . [U]sing other men as means . . . is a contradiction of what I know men to be, namely ends in themselves.

In these passages Berlin speaks of men as "authors of values"; he speaks of the authority of values consisting in their being "willed freely," and of values being "made so by the free acts of men." The pluralism invoked in these passages is voluntarist and, hence, relativist. As written, these lines embody the view (present at least through Berlin's "The Apotheosis of the Romantic Will") that "morality is moulded by the will and that ends are created, not discovered."[65] Nevertheless, one can easily substitute into these passages Berlin's more recent objectivist pluralism. Men are choosers among many objective values. The authority of the values chosen (for the choosing agent) consists in their being freely chosen from among incommensurable objective values. Particular values are made the valuable ends of agents' actions by being freely chosen objective values. Berlin must favor the substitution of this objectivist pluralism, given his disavowal of and concern about the implications of relativist pluralism. With this substitution, we find Berlin providing a pluralist defense of individual freedom which rests upon two bulwarks of the Western intellectual tradition—a theory of objective value and a theory of human nature.

IX. Conclusion

The critical assessment of Berlin's attempt to ground the claims of liberty upon the doctrines of objective pluralism and free agency is a larger project than can be encompassed here. And this attempt, of course, is only one of many in the not-so-monistic Western tradition. My project has been the much more modest one of asking what the course and structure of Berlin's thought tells us about the limits of the ideology of diversity. The most central and persistent element throughout Berlin's thought is his belief that a profound error lies at the base of the Western intellectual tradition—the delusion of monism. Against this error, Berlin celebrates the pluralist thought of the Counter-Enlightenment, as exemplified by Vico and Herder, with its emphasis on the irreducible particularity of communal forms of life. Berlin shares with Vico, Herder, and Romanticism in general, a picture of the rationalist Enlightenment as inherently authoritarian, constructivist, and oppressive precisely in virtue of its commitment to universal, trans-cultural standards for thought and action. Furthermore, Berlin maintains that tolerance and regard for personal liberty are the offspring, not of the dominant Western tradition, but of the anti-monistic revolt against it. In all these ways, and throughout the pattern and coloration of the fabric of his sympathies, Berlin seems at one with, albeit infinitely deeper, more learned, and more eloquent than, today's friends of diversity.

Yet Berlin is not counted among, and will never be counted among, the divinities of diversity. This is because Berlin's writings are also responsive to the limits of diversity. They are responsive to the dangers attached to relativist diversity, to its epistemic and moral nihilism, to its cultural (or subcultural) solipsism, and to its propensity to give rise either to authoritarian reaction or to revolutionary populist nationalism. Moreover, his writings are responsive to intellectual pressures felt by any conscientious thinker (of any culture, race, or gender) who has pursued a coherent grasp of human values and of principles protective of those values in all their diversity. Thus, in pursuit of an account of trans-cultural understanding and of the objectivity of the incommensurable values affirmed by different people of different cultures, Berlin rejects relativistic conceptions of knowledge and of value and seems to advance a schema of the human good: namely, that which fulfills human needs and aspirations. And in pursuit of an absolute stance in favor of freedom from coercion for all value-pursuers, Berlin offers a conception of the human essence as the capacity for free choice among ultimate values.

In all of these ways, in response to both the significance and the limits of diversity, Berlin returns to or remains within the great enterprise of social and metaphysical theorizing that is central to the Western tradition. If today's friends of diversity were equally responsive to the significance and limits of diversity, then two hallmarks of that tradition, the liberal social order and the liberal university, would have more auspicious futures. For, at its base, the current ideology of diversity, the New Counter-Enlightenment, denigrates the possibility of common epistemological norms and of rational dialogue among representatives of differing racial, gender, or national groups. It denigrates the project of elucidating and employing a common framework for comprehending human values and aspirations, and the ambition of ordering relationships within the university or within society at large in ways that are just for all. This is not a formula for increased harmonious existence among individuals or groups, either within the university or within the wider society. Rather, it is a formula for factional strife, irresoluble tribal conflict, and rule by interest-group manipulation and coercion.

NOTES

1. Sir Isaiah Berlin is a Fellow of All Souls College, Oxford University. He was a Fellow of New College from 1938 to 1950, Chichele Professor of Social and Political Theory at Oxford from 1957 to 1967, and first President of Wolfson College from 1966 to 1975. He was President of the British Academy from 1974 to 1978.

    I am indebted to Mary Sirridge, Ronna Berger, and Ellen Paul for their helpful comments on early or intermediate drafts of this essay.
2. Of course, today's friends of diversity are a diverse lot. They would not all be willing to affirm each of the views I identify with this syndrome. Neither at this point nor in Section III of this essay will I attempt to catalog all the variants on the diversity theme. I feel confident that anyone at all familiar with current campus controversies will recognize the elements that I cite as central to the *underlying* world-views of those who embrace diversity and multiculturalism as slogans in the battle against what they perceive to be the inherently racist, sexist, exploitative, hegemonic, brutal, and dehumanizing character of the existing order. Jerry L. Martin's "The University as Agent of Social Transformation: The Postmodern Argument Considered" (in this volume) provides a further exposition of some aspects of the multiculturalist ideology.
3. Isaiah Berlin, "The Apotheosis of the Romantic Will: The Revolt against the Myth of an Ideal World," in *The Crooked Timber of Humanity,* ed. H. Hardy (New York: Knopf, 1991), p. 208. This essay, originally published in 1975, may embody the apotheosis of Berlin's endorsement of unalloyed "diversity."

    Throughout this essay I refer to the views of various historical figures, such as Vico and Herder, *as those views are presented by Berlin.* My central concern is what we can infer about Berlin's views. I have no authority whatsoever for joining a scholarly discourse on the validity of Berlin's interpretation of figures such as Vico and Herder. Aside from the essays by Berlin cited throughout this essay, see his *Vico and Herder* (New York: Viking Press, 1976). For a concise treatment of some of the German Counter-Enlightenment figures, especially of Hamann and Herder, see the chapter on "The Counter-Enlightenment" in Lewis White Beck, *Early German Philosophy* (Cambridge: Harvard University Press, 1969), pp. 361–92.
4. It is present in, e.g., Berlin's 1955 essay, "Herzen and Bakunin on Individual Liberty," reprinted in *Russian Thinkers* (New York: Penguin, 1980), and his 1958 essay, "Two Concepts of Liberty," reprinted in *Four Essays on Liberty* (Oxford: Oxford University Press, 1969).
5. Isaiah Berlin, "Nationalism: Past Neglect and Present Power," in *Against the Current,* ed. H. Hardy (New York: Penguin Books, 1982), p. 348.
6. *Ibid.,* p. 353.

7. *Ibid.,* p. 348
8. Berlin, "The Apotheosis of the Romantic Will," p. 223.
9. *Ibid.,* p. 224.
10. *Ibid.,* p. 225.
11. Berlin, "Nationalism: Past Neglect and Present Power," p. 333.
12. Berlin, "The Apotheosis of the Romantic Will," p. 208.
13. In his 1802 work, *Letters from an Inhabitant of Geneva to his Contemporaries,* the apostle of rational social engineering Henri de Saint-Simon (1760–1825) proposed the scientific reorganization of society under the guidance of a Council of Newton. In later works, for example, *Catechisme Politique des Industriels,* Saint-Simon placed more emphasis on the guiding role of the elite members of the productive class, the *industriels.*
14. See Berlin's "Hume and the Sources of German Anti-Rationalism," in *Against the Current,* pp. 162–87. Of course, it was with Jeremy Bentham (of whom Mill was an only somewhat wayward disciple) that constructivist rationalism became dominant in British thought.
15. Cf. Smith's attack on the "man of system [who] is apt to be very wise in his own conceit" and who, therefore, imagines that "he can arrange the different members of a great society with as much ease as the hand arranges the different pieces upon the chess-board"; see Adam Smith, *The Theory of Moral Sentiments* (Indianapolis: Liberty Classics, 1976), VI.ii.2.17, pp. 233–34.
16. For a contrary view—namely, that in the course of the French Enlightenment rationalism was infected with, and thereby subverted by, the scientistic misperception that human beings and society are subject to the same sort of understanding and the same sort of beneficial conscious control as inanimate nature—see F. A. Hayek, *The Counter-Revolution of Science* (New York: The Free Press, 1955).
17. Berlin is far from consistently clear about what the central error of the dominant tradition is. The problem arises from the fact that this tradition consists of several interconnected elements and Berlin is neither clear nor consistent about which element or elements he is challenging. Note, for example, the distinct components within the dominant conviction

> that there exist true, immutable, universal, timeless, objective values, valid for all men, everywhere, at all times; that these values are at least in principle realisable whether or not human beings are, or have been, or ever will be, capable of realising them on earth; that these values form a coherent system, a harmony which, conceived in social terms, constitutes the perfect state of society. ("Vico and the Ideal of the Enlightenment," in *Against the Current,* p. 121)

18. Berlin, "Nationalism: Past Neglect and Present Power," p. 348.
19. Berlin, "The Apotheosis of the Romantic Will," p. 225.
20. For Vico, the bearers of diversity are cultures: "Each culture expresses its own collective experience." Isaiah Berlin, "The Counter-Enlightenment," in *Against the Current,* p. 5. Similarly, for Herder:

> Art, morality, custom, religion, natural life . . . are created by entire societies living an integrated communal life. . . . Who are the authors of the songs, the epics, the myths, the temples, the *mores* of a people . . .?

The people itself, the entire soul of which is poured out in all they are and do. (*Ibid.*, p. 11)

21. For Berlin's most renowned essay, "Two Concepts of Liberty," is fundamentally a defense of negative liberty, i.e., the liberty of noninterference, against the substitution of positive liberty, the liberty of being guided by one's "true" self. For Berlin's own acute discomfort with the perception that this essay is, even in part, an apology for capitalism, see his introduction to *Four Essays on Liberty*, especially pp. xlv–xlvi.
22. Berlin, "The Counter-Enlightenment," p. 14.
23. *Ibid.*, p. 21.
24. *Ibid.* See also Berlin, "Joseph de Maistre and the Origins of Fascism," in *The Crooked Timber of Humanity* (see n. 3 above), pp. 91–174.
25. De Maistre's position is akin to the nationalist's in that each seeks to protect ineffable personality against the purported disintegrating effects of reason and analysis.
26. Berlin, "Nationalism: Past Neglect and Present Power," p. 343.
27. *Ibid.*
28. Berlin, "The Apotheosis of the Romantic Will," p. 225.
29. Berlin, "Nationalism: Past Neglect and Present Power," pp. 343–44. Recall the view, ascribed by Berlin to Herder, that

    [i]f each culture expresses its own vision and is entitled to do so, and if the goals and values of different societies and ways of life are not commensurable, then it follows that there is no single set of principles, no universal truth for all men and times and places. ("The Apotheosis of the Romantic Will," p. 224)

30. Berlin, "The Apotheosis of the Romantic Will," p. 214.
31. Berlin, "Nationalism: Past Neglect and Present Power," p. 346.
32. *Ibid.*
33. *Ibid.*, p. 347.
34. *Ibid.*, p. 349.
35. *Ibid.*
36. Similarly, with the appropriate substitutions, the analysis illuminates today's most powerful anti-Western and intolerant nationalism, viz., Islamic fundamentalism.
37. The term "recomposition" is Shelby Steele's. Anyone familiar with his *Content of Our Character: A New Vision of Race in America* (New York: St. Martin's Press, 1990) will recognize the extent to which the last couple of paragraphs generalize portions of the analysis offered by Steele. Steele emphasizes that the vulnerability felt by, for example, black students entering largely white universities is real—and is the heritage of past racial injustice. His objection is not to the feeling of the vulnerability but rather to the attempt to deal with it through self-deluding recomposition rather than painful acknowledgment.
38. Cf. the passage previously cited (in n. 29) from Berlin "The Apotheosis of the Romantic Will," p. 224.
39. Berlin, "Alleged Relativism in Eighteenth-Century European Thought," in *The Crooked Timber of Humanity* (see n. 3 above), p. 86.
40. In reality, the friends of diversity are not as threatened with internecine

warfare as their ideology would predict—precisely because the ideology is mistaken. The devotee of lesbian feminist thought and the partisan of male Afrocentrism in fact operate with a common anti-liberal ideology which is universal and unchanging across anti-liberals of all cultures and ages.

41. See especially Berlin's 1980 essay, "Alleged Relativism in Eighteenth-Century European Thought," and his 1988 essay, "The Pursuit of the Ideal," both reprinted in *The Crooked Timber of Humanity*. The rejection of all forms of relativism and the advocacy of objective value pluralism continues in *Conversations with Isaiah Berlin,* conducted by Ramin Jahanbegloo (New York: Scribner's, 1992). In this work, issued in English after the composition of the present essay, Berlin insists upon his membership within the "liberal rationalist" camp and aligns himself with the "great liberators" of the French Enlightenment (p. 70).

42. Berlin, "Alleged Relativism in Eighteenth-Century European Thought," p. 74.

43. *Ibid.,* p. 79.

44. Berlin never provides us with an explicit analysis of incommensurability. In addition, his frequent identification of incommensurability with incompatibility is unfortunate. Values—for instance, liberty and equality—may be incompatible without being incommensurable. That is, the increased realization of one value may require the decreased realization of the other without its being true that we cannot rank alternative baskets of these values.

45. Berlin, "Alleged Relativism in Eighteenth-Century European Thought," p. 80.

46. Berlin, "The Pursuit of the Ideal," p. 10.

47. *Ibid.,* p. 11.

48. Berlin, "Alleged Relativism in Eighteenth-Century European Thought," p. 80.

49. *Ibid.,* p. 84. The yardstick of a "normal human being" is also crucial within Berlin's arguments for obedience to rules that

> are accepted so widely, and are grounded so deeply in the actual nature of men as they have developed through history, as to be, by now, an essential part of what we mean by being a normal human being. ("Two Concepts of Liberty," p. 165)

Yet the attempt to avoid Platonic timelessness, by way of invoking "history" and "what we mean" leads to the obvious challenge to the generality of Berlin's result, namely, whose history, whose meaning?

50. Berlin, "Alleged Relativism in Eighteenth-Century European Thought," p. 83.

51. Berlin, "The Pursuit of the Ideal," p. 17.

52. *Ibid.,* p. 18.

53. Berlin's pluralism surely excludes any serious hope that "a social structure" might "at most promote active solidarity in the pursuit of common objectives" ("The Apotheosis of the Romantic Will," p. 235).

54. Berlin, "Two Concepts of Liberty," p. 170. This list radically oversimplifies the weighing problem by including only standard liberal-bourgeois values. For other values must also be weighed in the balance—for example, piety, obedience, defiance, honor, and the domination of others.

55. *Ibid.,* p. 164; *ibid.,* p. 165; *ibid.,* p. 166.

56. *Ibid.*, p. 124.
57. F. A. Hayek, *The Fatal Conceit,* ed. W. Bartley (Chicago: University of Chicago Press, 1988), pp. 63–64. Hayek continues: "Hence, the type of liberty made possible by adhering to abstract rules . . . is, as Proudhon once put it, 'the mother, not the daughter of order.' "
58. Berlin, "Two Concepts of Liberty," p. 171.
59. *Ibid.*, p. 169. Similarly, it is because "we are faced with choices between ends equally ultimate . . . the realization of some of which must inevitably involve the sacrifice of others" that "men place such immense value upon their freedom to choose" (p. 168).
60. *Ibid.*, p. 126.
61. *Ibid.*, p. 171. Thus, in ways that cannot possibly be explored here, two of the central themes of Berlin's writings, political liberty and value pluralism, are deeply connected with the third, man's metaphysical freedom. See, e.g., Berlin, "Historical Inevitability," in *Four Essays on Liberty,* pp. 41–117, and "From Hope and Fear Set Free," in *Concepts and Categories,* ed. H. Hardy (New York: Viking Press, 1979), pp. 173–98.
62. Berlin, "The Pursuit of the Ideal," p. 13; emphasis added.
63. Berlin, "Two Concepts of Liberty," p. 127.
64. The long paragraph from pp. 136–38 of "Two Concepts of Liberty," from which the following passages are extracted, is strikingly different in tone from the rest of this section, titled "The Retreat to the Inner Citadel," which treats the attempt to secure "freedom" through eliminating or resisting desire.
65. Berlin, "The Apotheosis of the Romantic Will," p. 237.

Racial Preferences in Admission to Institutions of Higher Education

Lino A. Graglia

"Affirmative action," insofar as it is controversial, is a euphemism for racial discrimination, the advantaging of individuals assigned to certain racial groups and, therefore, the disadvantaging of individuals assigned to other racial groups.[1] Racial discrimination, we were long told—though much less frequently at present—is not only illegal and unconstitutional, but immoral and despicable, among the greatest of sins and never too severely condemned.[2] The result of this teaching was to reduce essentially to one the possible justifications for "affirmative action" by government institutions. Racial discrimination is so great and singular an evil that its practice can be justified only when necessary to combat or counteract other racial discrimination so that the net amount of existing racial discrimination may actually be reduced. Fire sometimes must be fought with fire.[3] It is on this "remedy" rationale that the practice of racially discriminatory "affirmative action" was begun and is still primarily defended. The rationale bears little or no relation to "affirmative action" in practice, however, which has not been limited, or even directed, to providing appropriate remedies to individuals shown to have suffered an injury because of race.

I. From Prohibiting to Requiring Racial Discrimination

The *Brown* decision in 1954,[4] applicable to state law, and a companion case, *Bolling v. Sharpe*,[5] applicable to federal law, prohibited legally required school racial segregation and, it quickly appeared, all racial discrimination by government, state or federal.[6] The power and appeal of the *Brown* nondiscrimination principle proved irresistible and, adopted and ratified by Congress, led to the greatest civil-rights advance in our history, the enactment of the 1964 Civil Rights Act, soon supplemented by the 1965 Voting Rights Act and the 1968 Fair Housing Act. Racial discrimination was at last effectively prohibited, not only in public schools, where segregation by law quickly came to an end,[7] but in all government-supported institutions and activities, and even by private persons and organizations in places of public accommodation and employment.

It is not to be expected, however, that so great and victorious a moral crusade would be permitted to come to an end merely because its objective had been accomplished. On the contrary, total success more easily serves as a spur to still greater accomplishments. There will always be a need of a cause to give meaning to lives in need of meaning and to provide continuing employment to the huge corps of civil-rights professionals that sprung up to fight for the end of racial discrimination. Many people had become accustomed to doing well by doing good. "Affirmative action" is also supported by the belief of activists for "social change" that the "civil-rights revolution" that began with *Brown* must not be permitted to come to an end, that race is the issue through which America may be remade or unmade.

Racial discrimination by government and business had been prohibited and largely ended by the 1960s civil-rights legislation, but equality of condition between blacks and whites obviously would not quickly be the result. It appeared to civil-rights professionals and others committed to social justice, therefore, that the time had come to move to equality of condition by fiat and, there being no more official or public discrimination against blacks still to be prohibited, to begin practicing discrimination against whites. The crucial move was made by the Supreme Court in *Green v. County School Board*[8] in 1968, in which the Court changed the *Brown* prohibition of segregation and all racial discrimination by government into a *requirement* of integration and racial discrimination by government. The move was not made, however, by announcing a departure from or qualification of the *Brown* nondiscrimination principle.

It was not politically feasible in 1968 for the Court candidly to state its new position that although racial discrimination by government was constitutionally prohibited when used to separate the races or disadvantage blacks, it was constitutionally permissible, and indeed sometimes constitutionally required, when used to increase integration or advantage blacks. The Court avoided this by insisting, instead, that although assignment to schools by race to increase integration was indeed now required, it was not required for its own sake, but only as a "remedy" for past unconstitutional segregation, only to overcome the continuing effect of earlier assignment to separate the races.[9] Far from abandoning or qualifying the *Brown* nondiscrimination principle, the Court, we were to understand, was actually enforcing it.

This remedy rationale for a requirement of racial discrimination in the name of enforcing a prohibition of racial discrimination was invalid for two reasons. First, as each new case made increasingly clear, the Court was not in fact requiring school districts merely to overcome the effects of prior segregation; it was requiring them to achieve almost perfect school racial balance even though such balance does not exist even in school districts that never practiced segregation.[10] Second, the remedy rationale, in any event, made little sense: the benefits (if any) and costs of a policy of racial discrimination to increase integration would not seem to depend upon the cause of the lack of integration (racial "imbalance") being "remedied." If compulsory integration is sound social policy in some school districts, it should be sound social policy in all school districts where racial separation exists. What the Court was doing in fact—requiring racial balance for its own sake—bore almost no relation, or an inverse relation, to what it said it was doing—enforcing a prohibition of racial discrimination. Because it is subject to no review, however, and therefore to no requirement that its opinions be factual or logical, the Court could easily weather these deficiencies, especially since only those willing to be perceived as aligning themselves with the former segregationists would be likely to point them out.

Compulsory racial discrimination had to be defended by the Court, it should be noted, not only as consistent with and, indeed, required by the Constitution as interpreted in *Brown*, but also as consistent with Title IV of the 1964 Civil Rights Act. Title IV, requiring the denial of federal funds to school districts that fail to desegregate, defines "desegregation" as the assignment of students to school "without regard to their race" and, redundantly, as *not* the assignment and transportation of students to school "to overcome racial imbalance." In 1971 in *Swann v. Charlotte-Mecklenburg Board of Education,*[11] the first busing case, the Court nonetheless upheld a district court order that required the assignment and transportation of students to school on the basis of race to overcome racial imbalance. This was consistent with the 1964 Act, the Court explained, because it was not requiring racial balance for its own sake, but only to "remedy" earlier racial discrimination.[12] The remedy rationale for racial discrimination was obviously a powerful weapon.

What the Court did to the Constitution and Title IV of the 1964 Civil Rights Act in *Green* and *Swann,* it also did to the Constitution and to other titles of the Act when it encountered the question of "affirmative action" in the contexts of employment and higher education. Title VI of the Act prohibits racial discrimination by institutions that receive federal funds; Title VII prohibits racial discrimination in employment. In *Griggs v. Duke Power Co.*[13] in 1971, the Court, disallowing the defendant company's use of ordinary employment criteria (e.g., high school diploma, literacy) that disproportionately disqualified blacks, held in effect that Title VII required, not that employment decisions be made without regard to race, but that they not be made without taking race into account. In *United Steelworkers v. Weber*[14] in 1979, the Court carried *Griggs* to its logical conclusion by holding that Title VII's prohibition of racial discrimination against "any individual" did not apply to discrimination against whites. The Court completed the picture in 1987 by holding in *United States v. Paradise*[15] that racial discrimination against whites in employment by state institutions did not violate the Constitution.[16]

Turning to the question of "affirmative action" in higher education, the Court held in *Regents of the University of California v. Bakke*[17] in 1978 that Title VI's prohibition of racial discrimination by federally funded institutions, such as the University of California at Davis Medical School, also did not apply to discrimination against whites. Again, racial discrimination was found to be consistent with the Constitution and the 1964 Civil Rights Act when it is used only to "remedy" past discrimination. That the remedy rationale is no more valid in the employment and higher-education contexts than in the grade-school context is demonstrated by the fact that there was no evidence in any of the cases that the preferred blacks had been discriminated against by the employer or educational institution, or that the rejected whites caused or benefited from any such discrimination. The absence of a showing of actual racial injury and racial benefit was simply irrelevant.

II. The Problem: Racial Differences in Academic Qualifications

The remedy rationale for racial discrimination has many more difficulties than its fictional basis. Perhaps the most serious is that the rationale deprives the law of the enormous advantage of a policy of race neutrality, under which all questions of racial characteristics are made legally irrelevant. Whether blacks as a group differ from whites as a group in any regard may be a necessary and useful subject of inquiry in other disciplines, but it is, happily, of no interest to a legal system that deals only with individuals. The remedy rationale for racial preferences, however, makes questions of racial characteristics not only relevant but unavoidable. The basis of the rationale is the assumption that members of all racial groups can be expected to appear in all institutions and activities more or less proportionately to their numbers in the general population. The "under-representation" of any racial group in an institution or activity, it is therefore argued, can be taken as evidence of discrimination against members of that group, and granting them preferences can be justified as a remedy for such discrimination. The argument necessarily invites a search for alternative explanations, and alternative explanations are not difficult to find.

The exceedingly grim facts that are the source of the drive for racial preferences also provide almost certain assurance that their use, at least in granting admission to institutions of higher education, cannot have desirable results. No discussion of "affirmative action" is grounded in reality that does not take cognizance of these facts. The central fact, around which all others revolve, is that there is a very large, long-standing, and apparently unyielding difference between blacks as a group and whites as a group—despite, of course, large areas of over-lap—in academic ability as measured by standard aptitude and achievement tests. Although most knowledgeable and informed people are aware of the existence of this difference, very few are aware—and many apparently have no wish to be aware—of its true extent.

From the beginning of intelligence testing about sixty-five years ago to the present, blacks have consistently averaged about eighteen points lower than whites (about 82 for blacks compared to 100 for whites) on the standard Stanford–Binet IQ test, and a similar gap is shown on other mental aptitude tests.[18] It is a statistical artifact that even small differences in mean scores between two groups—and an eighteen point difference (more than a full standard deviation) is not small—translate into very large differences at the extremes of the bell-shaped curve of normal distribution.[19] One effect is that only 11 percent of blacks have an IQ score above 100, compared to 50 percent, by definition, of the population as a whole.[20] The effect at the low extreme of the distribution curve is that 14.6 percent of blacks have IQ scores of 70 or below, compared to 2.6 percent of whites. More than five times as many blacks as whites (5.6 to 1), that is, fall at or below the score often taken as the boundary in moving from "dull normal" (70–90) to "educable mentally retarded," and the percentage of blacks with IQs at or below 70 is larger than the percentage with IQs above 100.[21]

At the other end (the "right tail") of the IQ spectrum, of most relevance to higher education, 30.9 percent of whites but only 2.32 percent of blacks have scores above 110, 13.4 percent of whites but only

0.32 percent of blacks have scores above 120, and 4.3 percent of whites but only 0.02 percent of blacks have scores over 130.[22] A score of 75 is generally considered necessary for graduation from elementary school, 95 for graduation from high school, 105 for admission to college, and 115 for admission to graduate or professional schools.[23] Because standardized college and graduate and professional school admission tests, such as the Scholastic Aptitude Test (SAT), Law School Admissions Test (LSAT), Medical College Admission Test (MCAT), and Graduate Record Examination, Quantitative (GREQ), have a very large "g" or general intelligence component, which is what IQ tests measure, blacks score as a group relatively poorly on these tests as well.[24] Robert Klitgaard, a former admissions officer at Harvard, reports that in the 1978–79 school year only 143 blacks had GREQ scores above 650, compared to 27,470 whites, and only 50 blacks had scores above 700, compared to 14,540 whites. Among law school entrants in the fall of 1976, the total number of blacks with LSAT scores above 600 (old scale) and with an Undergraduate Grade Point Average (UGPA) above 3.25 (B +) was 39; the number of whites with such scores was 13,151.[25]

Any messenger that brings news this bad will, of course, have to be attacked. In the early days of "affirmative action" (the late 1960s and early 1970s), a principal claim of its proponents was that standard ability and achievement tests were biased against members of racial minorities and therefore not appropriately used in determining their admission to institutions of higher education. If true, the admission of members of such groups with lower scores than are required for whites would not constitute the use of racial preferences but merely an attempt to make prediction more accurate; no "affirmative action" is involved in adjusting measuring devices to measure more accurately. The claim, however, is not true. By test bias is meant, presumably, that the test generally underpredicts the actual performance of members of some group. There is now general agreement that the standard ability and achievement tests used in determining admission to institutions of higher education are not biased by this standard.[26]

Indeed, investigations of test bias have shown that the standard tests very substantially *overpredict* the actual performance of blacks. For reasons that are unclear, blacks do not do as well in college and graduate and professional schools as their scores on admission tests would indicate. Ordinary admissions criteria are so biased in favor of blacks, Klitgaard reports, that making them unbiased would require selective colleges to deduct no fewer than 240 points from the combined SAT verbal and math scores of black applicants (each of the two SAT tests has a score range from 200 to 800). Similarly, to compensate for overprediction, law schools would either have to deduct 50 points from LSAT scores (old scale) made by blacks and four-tenths of a point from their GPAs, or deduct 110 points from the LSAT scores alone.[27] The concern of "affirmative action" proponents that tests be unbiased has not extended to this problem; there have been no suggestions that further predictive accuracy be achieved by making large deductions from blacks' scores.

The very low scores made by blacks on standard admissions tests—even not discounted to account for overprediction—mean, of course, that the number of blacks meeting the ordinary admission criteria for even moderately selective colleges is extremely low and the number for highly selective colleges and graduate and professional schools approaches the vanishing point. For example, if an IQ score of 115 is considered (conservatively) to be the minimum necessary to qualify for medical school—an SAT verbal score of 600, it should be noted, is equivalent to an IQ score of about 125—the number of blacks admitted to medical schools would make up 0.7 percent of the entering class, rather than the 12 percent that would correspond to the proportion of blacks in the American population.[28] The nation's 175 or so accredited law schools may cover a wider range of academic ability than medical schools, but without racially preferential admissions, as small or smaller a percentage of blacks would be admitted to the most selective law schools.[29] Most elite schools of all types, however, now strive to obtain an entering class that is at least 5 to 10 percent black. This is not necessarily a matter of choice, as it is often effectively required by accrediting organizations as a condition of continuing accreditation.[30] To obtain such a high percentage of blacks requires, not that blacks be preferred to whites when all other things are more or less equal—a common understanding of "affirmative action"—or even that the ordinary admission standards be bent or shaded; it requires that ordinary standards be largely abandoned.

In the 1974 entering class of the University of California at Davis Medical School (involved in the famous *Bakke* case), for example, the average science GPA for regularly admitted students was 3.4, compared to 2.4 for preferentially admitted students; the overall GPA component was 3.3 to 2.6; and MCAT scores by percentile were 69 to 34 on the verbal portion, 67 to 30 on the quantitative, 82 to 37 on the science, and 72 to 18 on general information.[31] Only six of the sixteen preferentially admitted students were blacks, however; seven were "Chicanos" and three were Asians, both of which groups have average scores higher than those of blacks.[32] Blacks admitted to the nation's medical schools in 1975–76 had average grades on each of the four MCAT categories that were more than 50 points (on the old SAT-type scale) *lower* than the average scores of whites who were rejected.[33]

At the University of Texas Law School, the average LSAT score for entering students in recent years (1985–1990) has been at about the 92nd percentile for whites and at about the 55th percentile for blacks. An average that high for blacks was made possible only by recruiting blacks on a national basis, despite otherwise very restrictive residential requirements. In addition, blacks are induced to enroll by offers of full scholarships without regard to need, while better-qualified needy whites are denied aid or even admission. Proponents of "affirmative action" justify this as a purely free-market transaction: black law-school applicants with LSAT scores as high as the 55th percentile are a rare and much sought-after commodity, and in free markets such commodities do not come cheaply. A policy so clearly contrary to ordinary notions of fairness and, therefore, productive of racial animosity can only be possible, however, for officials confident that they will not be subject to demands for public justification.

A frequently noted effect of "affirmative action" in admission to institutions of higher education is virtually to guarantee that the preferred students, even those with unusually high scores, are placed in schools for which they are greatly underqualified by the standards applied to others. A black student who meets or comes close to meeting the ordinary entrance requirements at the University of Texas Law School, for example—who has an LSAT score in, say, the 80th or 85th percentile—would likely find himself the subject of intense bidding by Harvard, Stanford, and Yale, where the disparity between his apparent qualifications and those of regularly admitted students (about the 98th percentile) would be significantly greater. On the other hand, black students preferentially admitted to Texas with LSAT scores thirty-five or forty percentile points below those of regularly admitted students could meet or almost meet the ordinary standards at a large number of the less selective schools from which Texas effectively bids them away. The result of this "ripple effect," Klitgaard points out, is that "[b]lack students at each school might be a standard deviation below the white students and therefore might disproportionately occupy positions at the bottom of the class."[34] It is as if professional baseball decided to "advantage" an identifiable group of players at the beginning of their professional careers by placing them in leagues at least one level above the one in which they could be expected to compete effectively.

When a policy of racially preferential admission to institutions of higher education is considered, not in the abstract—with a utopian vision of campuses, classrooms, disciplines, and occupations peopled by members of all racial and ethnic groups neatly in proportion to their share of the American population—but in light of the intractable realities of relative academic competence, it is difficult to see how anyone can consider it a reasonable policy choice.

III. Deception and Denial: Equality by Stealth

The admission of a racially identifiable group of greatly underqualified students to institutions of higher education is virtually a prescription for frustration, resentment, loss of self-esteem, and racial animosity. Forces powerful enough to institute so radical and unpromising a program will, however, be powerful enough to respond to its disastrous consequences with something other than a concession that they have made a terrible mistake. If the racially admitted prove unable to perform competitively, as opponents of the program predicted, that will indicate that the curriculum will have to be changed and new fields of study created. If racial preferences generate racial resentments, it will indicate that whites require specialized instruction in the deplorable history and moral shortcomings of their race. If "affirmative action" is then even more strongly protested, as is to be expected, it will indicate that protest must be disallowed. Once "affirmative action" policies are adopted—always "temporarily"—they acquire a self-perpetuating and ramifying aspect as a symbiosis forms between the specially admitted and those who urged and arranged for their admission.[35]

"Affirmative action" students are almost always convinced, reasonably enough, that they are qualified to compete and expected to succeed at the institutions that have made such great efforts to induce them to enroll. Those who recruited them will have strongly so represented, for few students will knowingly enroll in institutions for which they are not fully qualified. When the specially admitted students discover, as most soon must, that they cannot compete with their classmates, no matter how hard they try, their perception that they have not been helped but used and deceived is well-founded. Finding themselves unable to play the game being played, they will insist, as self-respect requires, that the game be changed. Thus are born demands for black studies and multiculturalism, which perform the twin functions of reducing the need for ordinary academic work and providing support for the view that the academic difficulties of the black students are the result, not of substantially lower qualifications, but of racial antipathy—that the source of the problem is not black but white shortcomings.

When there is no credible response to criticism of a policy that will not be changed, the response will be attempts to suppress the criticism. It is this that explains the current insistence on "political correctness" on the nation's campuses—sanctioned by ostracism, vilification, or worse—and the suddenly discovered need for new restrictions on speech in the form of "anti-harassment" and "hate speech" codes.[36] Nothing is more politically incorrect than to point out that a school's "affirmative action" policy is actually a policy of racially preferential admissions, unless it is to specify the actual disparity in the admission standards being applied to persons from different racial groups. Proponents of anti-harassment codes are correct when they point out that it is extremely humiliating to racially preferred students to have a public discussion of the school's policy of racially preferential admissions. Instead of concluding that the policy is, for this reason alone, very unlikely to prove beneficial, they conclude that such discussions must be banned.

"Affirmative action" is a fungus that can survive only underground in the dark and by intimidating those who would expose it to the light. On the sound principle that what cannot be done openly ought not to be done, "affirmative action" is disqualified as a policy choice. Its proponents operate under the singular encumbrance of being disabled from proclaiming their most significant—that is, their most "affirmative"—actions. On the one hand, "affirmative action" must be defended as a wise and desirable policy choice, while on the other, every effort must be made to conceal, as far as possible, the extent to which it is actually practiced.[37] If "affirmative action" is a morally defensible policy, why are its proponents loath to have it known just how moral they have been? Because, of course, the policy must operate under the encumbrance that no one wants it known that he is, as black Yale law professor Stephen Carter puts it, "an affirmative action baby."[38]

A recent illustration of the deceit inherent in "affirmative action" was provided when Georgetown law student Timothy Maguire disclosed in a student newspaper his discovery that his black classmates were admitted to the school with much lower LSAT scores and GPAs than those required of whites.[39] The result was outraged protest by the black students and indignant disavowal, in effect, of "affirmative action" by those who were most responsible for its adoption. Although known as an ardent proponent of racially preferential admissions, Dean Judith Areen flatly denied that any racially preferential admissions took place at the school she led. Those who mistakenly thought otherwise, she insisted, failed to understand that many factors—for example, a required essay—are considered in determining admission to Georgetown Law School, and that low LSAT scores and GPAs can therefore be outweighed by high scores on the other factors.[40]

We were to understand, apparently, that there is an inverse correlation between high LSAT scores and GPAs and ability to write an essay on why one wants to be a law student at Georgetown. This peculiarity also manifests itself disproportionately or exclusively in the case of black applicants. This explanation made sense to the editorial writers of the *New York Times,* at least, who repeated it in an editorial severely chastising Maguire for his "obsession with numbers" and total misunderstanding of the Georgetown admission process.[41] The news of racially preferential admissions to elite institutions of higher education, practiced almost everywhere for over twenty years, had apparently not yet reached the editorial writers of the *New York Times* as of 1991.[42]

The American Association of Law Schools (AALS), the American Bar Association, Section of Legal Education and Admission to the Bar (ABA), and the Law School Admission Council felt called upon to comment on the well-publicized incident at Georgetown. The result was another example of denial of the use of racial preferences by those who insist upon their use. Like Dean Areen, the highest officials of the legal education establishment answered critics of racially preferential law-school admissions by asserting that the critics failed to understand the complexities of the law-school admission process. "Besides the LSAT and undergraduate GPA," a joint press release they issued explained, "several other considerations are taken into account by law schools for significant portions of their classes." These other considerations include, in addition to "numbers": "personal statements from applicants, letters of recommendation, work experience, and the applicant's prior success in overcoming personal disadvantage."[43] The list included no mention of race. Small wonder that innocent news media, like the *New York Times,* are bewildered as to how strange notions about the use of racial preferences in law-school admissions could possibly have arisen.

To law schools, however, the press release did more than provide a demonstration of lawyerly skill and an example of lawyerly integrity. The AALS and ABA are law-school accrediting institutions. Their stated accreditation standards make clear—and their visiting accreditation committees, usually nicely balanced by race and sex, make even clearer—that a substantial number of black students (probably at least 5 to 10 percent) in entering classes is an accreditation consideration.[44] AALS and ABA officials know, of course, that there is no way that this can be done without discriminating massively in favor of black applicants. That inconvenient fact they would simply bury under a mountain of obfuscation and misrepresentation while proclaiming their commitment to the highest standards of morality.[45]

IV. Race as a Proxy for Disadvantage and Diversity

The various arguments or rationalizations offered for "affirmative action" over the past twenty-some years have grown almost too threadbare with use to stand repetition or require further refutation.[46] By far the most important, that racial preferences can be justified as compensation for past unfair disadvantages—the "remedy" rationale—is obviously invalid because preferences truly meant to compensate for disadvantage would be applied on the basis of disadvantage, not on the basis of race. Persons who have been unfairly disadvantaged or otherwise injured should undoubtedly be made whole to the extent feasible, but race is neither an accurate nor an appropriate proxy for such disadvantage. It is inaccurate because not all and not only blacks have suffered from disadvantage. Indeed, racially preferential admissions to institutions of higher education ordinarily help, not those most in need of help, but middle-class and upper-middle-class blacks who are typically no more and frequently less economically or educationally disadvantaged than the more-qualified whites they replace. The argument from disadvantage has appeal and potency only because, as Glenn Loury has put it: "The suffering of the poorest blacks creates, if you will, a fund of political capital upon which all members of the group can draw when pressing racially-based claims."[47]

Racially preferential admission to institutions of higher education is also an inappropriate means of compensation for educational or cultural disadvantage for several reasons. First, our historic assimilationist national policy has been to insist upon the general irrelevancy of one's membership in a particular racial group—with all of the difficult and distasteful questions involved in determining membership—as a basis for government action. It is inconsistent with that policy, and almost surely unwise in a multiracial society, to emphasize the importance of race by making it the basis of preferential treatment. Second, to admit students substantially less qualified than their fellow students to institutions of higher education is not a means of compensating for lack of qualification whether or not it is the result of unfair educational or social disadvantage. Lack of qualification for a course of study can be rationally addressed only by steps to remove the lack, not by overlooking it and proceeding as if it did not exist.

In any event, if compensation is due to blacks, it should, as Richard Epstein has pointed out, "be paid in cash and not in the currency of places" in colleges and graduate schools, and paid to all blacks, not "only the fortunate admittees" to the schools.[48] Finally, it is plainly unjust, a violation of individual rights as ordinarily understood, that the cost of racially preferential admissions should be largely borne by the particular individuals the racially preferred replace, even though they bear no particular responsibility for the disadvantage for which compensation is supposedly being made.

The newest buzz word for racial discrimination—which after more than two decades of official sanction still may not speak its proper name—is "diversity," a word that is largely replacing the term "affirmative action" (as it becomes less a euphemism than a pejorative) and providing an alternative to the remedy rationale. Lowering admission standards for blacks directly produces (apart from a class with a group of less-qualified students) only a class with more blacks. Just as the remedy argument uses race as a proxy for disadvantage, the diversity argument uses race as a proxy for unusual characteristics relevant to education. Such racial stereotyping—the justification formerly offered for legally compelled segregation—is invalid because individual differences are much greater within than between racial groups.

Just as disadvantage, not race, would be the criterion if the objective were compensation, unusual characteristics or experiences would be the criterion if the objective were educational diversity. In practice, neither rationale is taken seriously, and the only operative criterion is seen to be race. Blacks are preferentially admitted even though they—frequently the children of teachers or other professionals—have a social, economic, and educational background virtually indistinguishable from that of the average middle-class white applicant. "Affirmative action" enforcers do not check schools for diversity of views or experience in the student body any more than they check for disadvantage; they check only for the presence of blacks and—to a much lesser extent—members of other preferred groups.

The diversity argument for racially preferential admissions was made popular by Justice Powell's opinion in the *Bakke* case,[49] the Court's first decision upholding explicit discrimination against whites. Justice Powell was an inveterate seeker of the middle way, which usually meant, as in *Bakke,* his evading the problem by attempting to have it both ways.[50] Expressing views that were his alone, he announced that discrimination against whites is every bit as constitutionally disfavored as discrimination against blacks, to be subjected to the strictest judicial scrutiny and permitted only when found to serve a "compelling interest" that could not be served in any other way. He then held that discrimination against whites in admission to medical school is constitutionally permissible, nonetheless, because it serves the school's interest—protected by the First Amendment, he said—in a student body with a diversity of views. It was not credible, however, that the school's objective was educational diversity rather than simply more blacks—race, as always, was the significant and sufficient criterion for preference—or that the Court would have upheld discrimination against blacks on such a dubious and flimsy ground. Powell's attempt to find a middle way between both protecting and not protecting whites equally with blacks failed, but it made "diversity" a term of art and a rallying cry in the fight for racially preferential admissions.

The diversity argument for racial preferences was accepted by a Supreme Court majority for the first time in *Metro Broadcasting, Inc. v. F.C.C.,*[51] decided in 1990 by a five-to-four vote. The majority opinion was by Justice Brennan, his last opinion for the Court. The Court upheld F.C.C. rules, specifically endorsed by Congress, that granted preferences and exclusive rights to members of specified minority groups (persons of "Black, Hispanic Surnamed, American Eskimo, Aleut, American Indian and Asiatic American extraction") in the awarding of radio and television broadcast licenses. A "congressionally-mandated benign race-conscious program" is constitutionally permissible, the Court held, if it is "substantially related to the achievement of an important governmental interest . . . so long as it does not impose *undue* burdens on nonminorities."[52]

The F.C.C.'s "affirmative action" program met this new race-discrimination standard—less severe than the "strict scrutiny" test—Brennan found, because it was necessary in order to "produce adequate broadcasting diversity." This conclusion did not "rest on an impermissible stereotype," he insisted, because there was evidence of "a strong correlation between minority ownership and diversity of programming."[53] Recent changes in Court personnel—the replacement of Justices Brennan and Marshall with Justices Souter and Thomas—make it doubtful that this permission for racial discrimination on alleged diversity grounds will be extended to nonfederal programs, and the decision may even be overruled. In any event, what the Supreme Court declares constitutional is not necessarily good policy.

V. The Perverse Incentives Created by "Affirmative Action"

Among the defects serious enough to be disqualifying of both the remedy and the diversity rationales for racial preferences is that they create perverse and destructive incentives. The remedy rationale requires insistence, not only upon America's racist past, but even more important, upon the assumption that racism continues largely unabated, although perhaps in more subtle and less overt forms. If blacks disproportionately fail to obtain desirable education and employment positions due to a lack of the usual qualifications, the appropriate remedy, even if the lack is due to past racial discrimination, is to attempt to upgrade their qualifications. If the failure is due to present discrimination, possibly so subtle as to be undetectable, however, the only corrective may be racial preferences and quotas.

Proponents of "affirmative action" must, therefore, continually assert that white Americans are implacably opposed to black advancement and, as a corollary, that recommendations that blacks assume greater responsibility for their progress are essentially futile. One of the most ardent "affirmative action" proponents, Professor Derrick Bell of the Harvard Law School, for example, has devoted a book (widely and favorably reviewed) to such claims as that if a magic pill were discovered to make blacks exceptionally law-abiding, whites would destroy it to prevent that from happening. Black crime, he tells us, apparently in all seriousness, is actually in the interest of whites because much of the country's economic activity—for example, the production of prison uniforms—is dependent upon it.[54]

Despite such claims of white antipathy to blacks, there is every indication that most whites are intensely interested in and supportive of black progress and derive an extra measure of satisfaction from every example of black success. Basketball games and boxing matches seem only to have gained in appeal and marketability as they became increasingly dominated by blacks. The highest incomes in the entertainment industry in recent years have been earned by blacks.[55] The only noticeable expressions of discontent with the fact that Colin Powell is the nation's highest national security officer has been by black proponents of "affirmative action."[56]

No one in academic life can seriously doubt the commitment of the American academic establishment at all levels to finding ways of including more blacks. Professor Bell's claim that elite institutions reject extremely well-qualified blacks in favor of less-qualified whites because of a concern with becoming "too black" is pure fantasy, if only because an excess of highly qualified black applicants for professorships is so rarely a problem.[57] It is paradoxical to claim that institutions that have for over twenty years made extraordinary efforts to help blacks cannot be trusted to treat them fairly under a policy of racial neutrality.

Americans, black and white, undoubtedly seek, like other people, to shield themselves and their families from the effects of poverty and social breakdown which are, unfortunately, associated with the black "underclass." Most also recognize, however, that the country's peace and prosperity require steps to relieve the desperate condition of that class. Most want to believe, if only for self-congratulation, that they live in a just society, and every example of black success is welcomed as corroborating or at least encouraging that belief.

The corollary to insistence by "affirmative action" proponents that whites—or, more ominously, "the white power structure"—are opposed to black advance is the essential futility of hopes for progress by blacks through their own efforts. The only answer to blacks' problems, "affirmative action" teaches, is ever-greater agitation for recognition by whites of their continuing mistreatment of blacks and for additional legislation and practices which set aside a share of all benefits for blacks without requiring that they compete with whites. Black studies are necessary so that blacks may more fully appreciate the extent of their oppression by whites and the fact that their most needed skill is skill at protesting that oppression. Compulsory multiculturalism courses are necessary so that whites may more fully understand the extent to which they are oppressors. Racial preferences and quotas will then be even more urgently demanded by blacks and more readily granted by whites.

The strategy of insisting that white racism is the cause of black problems has been highly successful from the point of view of civil-rights professionals. Black studies are everywhere; compulsory multiculturalism, newer on the scene, has already been widely adopted by colleges and universities;[58] and racial-preference and quota legislation continues to be proposed and enacted in the name of civil rights. President Bush's veto of the 1990 Civil Rights Act, a prescription for racial quotas in employment, was upheld in the Senate by a single vote, after which the President gave up the fight and signed the similar 1991 Civil Rights Act.[59]

"Affirmative action" programs are invariably presented as merely temporary—that they are evil is recognized, but the evil is claimed to be necessary and only to last for a limited time. Instead of being terminated, however, once instituted they are more often expanded and extended to new fields. Thomas Sowell has shown that this has been the worldwide experience wherever they have been tried.[60] A program based on inculcating black resentment and white guilt cannot be the solution to our race-related problems. "Affirmative action's" message that whites are opposed to black success is false, and its corollary that academic success and hard work are pointless for blacks is debilitating, almost certainly the last message that it is in the interest of blacks to hear.

As the remedy rationale for racial preferences requires insistence on pervasive white racism, the diversity rationale requires insistence on the existence of important racial differences. Preference for blacks in admission to institutions of higher education will not produce any significant benefits of diversity unless there are in fact important differences between blacks and whites, and the preferred blacks can be relied upon to manifest them. It is thus in the interest of blacks in general—and perhaps, indeed, the duty of the preferred black in particular—to "act black" as much as possible. In the school context this usually means, unfortunately, displaying an exceptional sensitivity to possible racial slights and an ability to see malignant racism as the explanation of most historical events and social phenomena. The diversity rationale is thus closely tied to and operates to support the remedy rationale: it encourages discovering the racism that the remedy rationale proposes to cure.

Since the black applicant assumed by and required for the diversity rationale is one who holds a certain ideological position, proponents of "affirmative action" easily come to define blacks not by skin color but by their acceptance of that position. The defining characteristic of blackness becomes, specifically, support for racial preferences.[61] As Harvard Professor Derrick Bell put it, "the ends of diversity are not served by people who look black and think white."[62] To admit a student to an institution of higher education as a representative of his race, as "affirmative action" does, is to place an unfair burden upon him—it is difficult enough to have one's acts reflect upon only oneself. To expect in addition that the student will display attitudes and beliefs distinct from those of most of his classmates is to impose an additional burden that cannot aid the student's academic performance or increase interracial understanding.[63]

VI. Why "Affirmative Action"?

The drive for "affirmative action" in admission to institutions of higher education—specifically, for the preferential admission of blacks—is a phenomenon in need of further and more candid explanation than it has so far received. The wide gap, largely ignored in most discussions, between blacks and whites on tests of academic aptitude and achievement means that the admission of more than a very few blacks to selective schools requires the application of much lower admission standards. Blacks must be admitted who are not in the same academic ballpark as the regularly admitted students and who therefore cannot realistically be expected to compete with them academically. Typically, they can be expected to graduate, if at all, only if curriculum requirements and grading standards are generally relaxed—failing grades are almost unknown today in leading professional and graduate schools—

and then only at or near the bottom of the class. The racially preferential admission of substantially underqualified students must lead to demands for special courses, to increased racial separation and tension on campus, and to demands for suppression of the criticism that will result.

How can adoption of a policy that is virtually a formula for the escalating racial consciousness and tension that we are apparently experiencing on our campuses and elsewhere be thought a desirable course of action? It is hard to believe that the remedy and diversity rationales for "affirmative action" can be taken seriously by anyone not strongly committed to it on other grounds. They are certainly not taken seriously in practice, where race and race alone is the criterion for preference.

A more plausible explanation for at least some of the demand for "affirmative action" is that it supports an extensive "civil-rights" bureaucracy that grew up in the long fight to end racial discrimination and that is now prospering and expanding in the movement to reinstate it. Every college and school, if not every department, must now have an "affirmative action" officer and specialists in racial and ethnic group liaison. The more racial tension increases on campus and generally, the more will be the need for their services. Further, although legislation has been enacted prohibiting virtually all racial discrimination, public and private, that it is possible to prohibit, it remains true that a large proportion of blacks live in the desperate social conditions of an "underclass." It is argued by many that improvement of these conditions requires that the issue of race not be permitted to recede from public attention. For better or worse, "affirmative action" serves to keep the issue very much alive.

Racial issues seem also to be for some people part of a larger agenda. There are, particularly in our colleges and universities, earnest seekers of a more just and equal society who find themselves thoroughly alienated from their present society and its institutions. Until the world becomes perfectly just, there will be injustice to combat and satisfaction to be gained by doing so. The worldwide waning of the appeal of socialism has reduced the potential of economic class differences as the basis of hope for "fundamental social change." Race and sex differences are the most likely substitutes, the best candidates for the role of injustices in need of correction. The pursuit of perfect economic equality, it has turned out, may not be such a good idea, but surely no one today can be so insensitive to the demands of justice as to oppose equality in terms of race and sex. Proponents of any proposal advanced in the name of increasing such equality will enjoy a huge advantage over opponents.

The most important basis for the continuing support of "affirmative action," despite its apparent harmful consequences, is indicated perhaps by the arguments made for it by a law professor at a major public university in two debates held about ten years apart. In the first debate, ten or twelve years ago, he supported "affirmative action" with a long list of the then-standard arguments or rationalizations: biased tests, compensation, role models, services to deprived groups, and so on. His enthusiasm for "affirmative action," because of the many good effects he expected it to have, seemed unbounded. Indeed, "affirmative action" was working so well at his school, he pointed out, that the school had decided to drop Japanese Americans from the list of specially preferred groups because substantial numbers of Japanese-American applicants had been found to meet the ordinary standards. He confidently foresaw the day when the same would be true first of Mexican Americans, and then of blacks.

In another debate about two years ago, this professor's enthusiasm was gone and his argument much changed. He still supported "affirmative action," but his reasons had been reduced to a single one: "We simply must have blacks in this institution." The admission of blacks was no longer a means to other ends, but an end in itself. His argument had essentially become simply that his institution had to admit more blacks than the very few who could meet the ordinary admission standards because otherwise political difficulties would be encountered—illustrated by the slogan, popularized after the Los Angeles riots, "No justice, no peace"—and a price might have to be paid. Derek Bok, then President of Harvard University, has made essentially the same argument.[64] The problem is undoubtedly a severe one: if a stable multiracial society requires that all racial groups be more or less proportionately represented in all important institutions and activities, it requires what no multiracial society has ever achieved.[65]

A more promising approach to social stability, surely, is to maintain a system of law, government, and public policy that uniformly insists on the total irrelevance, at least for official or public purposes, of claimed membership in any particular racial group. If the law has no reason to know any individual's race, it will have no reason to know the racial makeup of any institution or activity, and therefore no question as to such makeup can be officially or appropriately entertained. It may be naive idealism to believe that racial peace can be achieved through official inculcation of the view that racial distinctions are odious and pointless, but it is at least an ideal worth pursuing. It was, after all, powerful and attractive enough to produce the great civil-rights movement of the 1960s—the movement that delegitimized all official or public racial discrimination. We can be certain, on the other hand, that racial

peace will not be found through policies that enhance racial consciousness, presume the existence of widespread and near-ineradicable racial
animosity, and insist that racial distinctions are of central importance.

NOTES

1. The term "affirmative action" was perhaps first used ir. Executive Order
   10925, issued by the Kennedy Administration in March 1961, directed to
   eliminating racial discrimination by government contractors. It originally
   meant the taking of positive steps—for example, the widespread advertising
   of job openings—to equalize opportunity for all racial groups. See Herman
   Belz, *Equality Transformed: A Quarter-Century of Affirmative Action* (New
   Brunswick: Transaction, 1991), p. 18. Its current application to the granting
   of racial preferences operates to conceal the fact that it is the practice, not
   the elimination, of racial discrimination that is now involved.
2. As Professors Alexander Bickel and Philip Kurland put it:

   > For at least a generation the lesson of the great decisions of this Court and
   > the lesson of contemporary history have been the same: discrimination
   > on the basis of race is illegal, immoral, unconstitutional, inherently wrong
   > and destructive of democratic society. Now this is to be unlearned and we
   > are told that this is not a matter of fundamental principle but only a
   > matter of whose ox is gored.

   Brief of the Anti-Defamation League of B'nai B'rith *Amicus curiae*, p. 16,
   DeFunis v. Odegaard, 416 U.S. 312 (1974).
3. See Justice Blackmun concurring in *Regents of the University of Califoria v.
   Bakke*, 438 U.S. 265, 407 (1978): "In order to get beyond racism, we must
   first take race into account. There is no other way."
4. *Brown v. Board of Education of Topeka*, 347 U.S. 783 (1954).
5. 347 U.S. 497 (1954).
6. With no explanation other than a citation of *Brown*, the Court disallowed all
   official racial discrimination. See, e.g., *Mayor of Baltimore v. Dawson*, 350
   U.S. 877 (1955) (public beaches and bath houses); *Holmes v. Atlanta*, 350
   U.S. 879 (1955) (municipal golf courses); *Gayle v. Browder*, 352 U.S. 903
   (1956) (buses).
7. All school "desegregation" litigation begun after 1964 involved, not the
   assignment of students to separate schools by race, but demands for compulsory integration. See, e.g., *Green v. New Kent County*, 391 U.S. 430 (1968);
   Raney v. Board of Education, 391 U.S. 443 (1968); *Monroe v. Board of
   Comm'rs*, 391 U.S. 450 (1968).
8. 391 U.S. 430 (1968).
9. In *United States v. Montgomery County Board of Education*, 395 U.S. 225,
   236 (1969), the Court upheld a lower court order that teachers be assigned
   by race to increase faculty racial "balance," but the Court insisted that this
   was required only "as a *remedy* for past racial assignment" and not because
   "racially balanced faculties are constitutionally or legally required" (emphasis in original).

10. See, e.g., *Swann v. Charlotte-Mecklenburg Board of Education,* 402 U.S. 1 (1971).
11. *Ibid.*
12. See Lino A. Graglia, *Disaster by Decree: The Supreme Court Decisions on Race and the Schools* (Ithaca: Cornell University Press, 1976).
13. 401 U.S. 424 (1971).
14. 446 U.S. 193 (1979).
15. 480 U.S. 149 (1987).
16. See, L. Graglia, "The 'Remedy' Rationale for Requiring or Permitting Otherwise Prohibited Discrimination: How the Court Overcame the Constitution and the 1964 Civil Rights Act," *Suffolk University Law Review,* vol. 22 (Fall 1988), p. 569.
17. 438 U.S. 265 (1978).
18. See, e.g., R. A. Gordon, "Thunder from the Left" (book review), *Academic Questions,* vol. 1 (Summer 1988), p. 82:

> The average IQ difference between blacks and whites is a key fact. Conventionally reported as 15 points wide, that figure reflects rounding downward to the nearest whole standard statistical unit when studies are viewed one at a time, and also a bias in favor of stating the difference as it would appear on certain popular tests that, for other reasons, employ slightly larger IQ units, thereby making group differences seem smaller. When all the major studies since the end of World War I are considered together, however, their consistency supports a somewhat higher and more precise figure of 1.1 standard [deviation] units and that is equivalent to 18 IQ points when expressed on the more fundamental Stanford–Binet scale (and to 16.5 IQ points on scales of the Wechsler variety).

See also Alexandra K. Wigdor and Wendell R. Garner, eds., *Ability Testing: Uses, Consequences, and Controversies* (Washington: National Academy Press, 1982), pp. 71–72:

> Many studies have shown that members of some minority groups tend to score lower on a variety of commonly used ability tests than do members of the white majority in this country. The much publicized Coleman study (Coleman et al. 1966) provided comparisons of several racial and ethnic groups for a national sample of 3rd-, 6th-, 9th-, and 12th-grade students on tests of verbal and nonverbal ability, reading comprehension, mathematics achievement, and general information. The largest differences in group averages usually existed between blacks and whites on all five tests and at all grade levels. In terms of the distribution of scores for whites, the average score for blacks was roughly one standard deviation below the average for whites. Differences of approximately this magnitude were found for all five tests at 6th, 9th, and 12th grades. The differences at 3rd grade were somewhat smaller, especially on the verbal and nonverbal general ability tests, but were still about two-thirds of a standard deviation or more. The roughly one-standard-deviation difference in average test scores between black and white students in this country found by Coleman et al. is typical of results of other studies.

19. See Wigdor and Garner, eds., *Ability Testing,* p. 72:

Proportion of People in Two Groups That Would be Selected by Various Cutoffs Assuming Both Groups Have Normally Distributed Scores with Equal Standard Deviations but Means That Differ by One Standard Deviation:

Group with Higher Mean	Group with Lower Mean
.10	.01
.20	.03
.30	.06
.40	.11
.50	.16
.60	.23
.70	.32
.80	.44
.90	.61

20. Linda S. Gottfredson, "Reconsidering Fairness: A Matter of Social and Ethical Priorities," *Journal of Vocational Behavior*, vol. 33, no. 3 (December 1988), pp. 301–2.
21. *Ibid.*, p. 302:

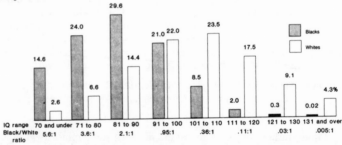

This figure is reprinted with permission from Gottfredson, "Reconsidering Fairness." See also Arthur R. Jensen, *Bias in Mental Testing* (New York: Free Press, 1980), p. 84 (defining IQs below 70 as "mentally retarded").
22. Gottfredson, "Reconsidering Fairness," p. 302.
23. *Ibid.*, p. 303.
24. For discussion of the meaning and nature of "g," see Jensen, *Bias in Mental Testing, supra* n. 21, p. 223.
25. Robert Klitgaard, *Choosing Elites* (New York: Basic Books, 1985), pp. 159–60:

> The region bounded by LSAT at or above 600 and UGPA at or above 3.25 includes 20% of the white and unidentified candidates, but only 1% of the black, 4% of the Chicano, and 11% of the unidentified minority candidates.

(Citing Franklin R. Evans, "Applications and Admissions to ABA Accredited Law Schools," in *Reports of LSAC Sponsored Research: Vol. III, 1975–1977* [Princeton: LSAC, 1979], p. 604.)
26. See, e.g., Wigdor and Garner, eds., *Ability Testing, supra* n. 18, p. 73.

27. Klitgaard, *Choosing Elites,* p. 163.
28. Gordon, "Thunder," *supra* n. 18, p. 82.
29. A 600 LSAT score and 3.25 Undergraduate Grade Point Average (UGPA) were reported as the "minimum needed for effective performance" at "several distinguished law schools." The ratio of whites to blacks meeting this minimum was 337 to 1 in 1976, and 260 to 1 in 1978–79. Klitgaard, *Choosing Elites, supra* n. 25.
30. See J. Segall, "When Academic Quality is Beside the Point," *Wall Street Journal,* October 29, 1990, p. A14; Samuel Weiss, "Accrediting Group Defends Diversity," *New York Times,* August 7, 1991, p. A19.
31. *Regents of the University of California v. Bakke,* 438 U.S. 265, 277–78 n. 7 (1978).
32. *Ibid.,* p. 276 n. 6.
33. Klitgaard, *Choosing Elites, supra* n. 25, at p. 155 n. 4. For more recent data, see also Lloyd G. Humphreys, "Trends in Levels of Academic Achievement of Blacks and Other Minorities," *Intelligence,* vol. 12 (July–September 1988), pp. 231–60: "One can conclude with confidence that minorities applying to graduate schools leave their undergraduate institutions with deficits in subject matter competence that vary from mostly trivial for Asians to very substantial for blacks" (p. 249).
34. Klitgaard, *Choosing Elites,* p. 175.
35. See, generally, Dinesh D'Souza, *Illiberal Education: The Politics of Race and Sex on Campus* (New York: Free Press, 1991).
36. See, for example, *Doe v. University of Michigan,* 721 F.Supp. 852 (E.D. Mich. 1989) (invalidating University of Michigan "hate speech" code).
37. See Harvey C. Mansfield, Jr., *America's Constitutional Soul* (Baltimore: Johns Hopkins, 1991), p. 85:

   Affirmative action is obviously a way of helping people who are considered insufficiently capable of helping themselves. But just as obviously, this fact cannot be admitted. . . . Government and management must therefore give help through affirmative action while denying that they give it, indeed *by* denying that they give it, in order not to hurt the pride of the beneficiaries.

38. Stephen L. Carter, *Reflections of an Affirmative Action Baby* (New York: Basic Books, 1991), p. 50: "[T]he durable and demeaning stereotype of black people as unable to compete is reinforced by advocates of certain forms of affirmative action." See also Thomas Sowell, *Black Education: Myths and Tragedies* (New York: McKay Pub., 1972), p. 292:

   What all the arguments and campaigns for quotas are really saying, loud and clear, is that *black people just don't have it,* and that they will have to be given something in order to have something. . . . Those black people who are already competent . . . will be completely undermined, as black becomes synonymous—in the minds of black and white alike—with incompetence, and black achievement becomes synonymous with charity or payoffs.

39. Michel Marriott, "White Accuses Georgetown Law School of Bias in Admitting Blacks," *New York Times,* April 15, 1991, p. A13; T. Maguire, "My Bout with Affirmative Action," *Commentary,* April 1992, p. 50.

40. "While acknowledging that the law school has a firm affirmative action policy, Dean Areen said there was no dual standard to help foster racial, sex and geographical diversity on campus." Michel Marriott, "Storm at Georgetown Law on Admissions," *New York Times,* April 17, 1991, p. A14.

41. "A Numbers Game at Georgetown Law," editorial, *New York Times,* April 18, 1991, p. A24.

42. Which is to be preferred, one must wonder: that *New York Times* editorial writers believe what they write or that they do not?

43. News Release, June 19, 1991 (copy available from AALS, 1201 Connecticut Ave., NW, Washington, DC 20036).

44. The AALS requires member schools to "seek to have a faculty, staff, and student body which are diverse with respect to race, color, and sex." AALS, *Association Handbook* (1990), p. 22, Bylaw 6–4(c). The ABA requires approved schools to demonstrate, "by concrete action, a commitment to providing full opportunities for the study of law and entry into the profession by qualified members of groups (notably racial and ethnic minorities) which have been victims of discrimination in various forms." *American Bar Association Standards for Approval of Law Schools* (1979), Standard 212.

45. See Lino Graglia, "Race Norming in Law School Admissions," *Journal of Legal Education,* vol. 42 (March 1992), p. 1.

46. See Lino Graglia, "Racially Discriminatory Admission to Public Institutions of Higher Education," *Southwestern University Law Review,* vol. 9, no. 3 (1977), p. 583.

47. Glenn Loury, "The Moral Quandary of the Black Community," *The Public Interest,* no. 79 (Spring 1988), p. 20.

48. Richard Epstein, "Affirmative Action in Law Schools: The Uneasy Truce," *Kansas Journal of Law and Public Policy,* vol. 2 (1992), p. 40.

49. 438 U.S. 265 (1978).

50. For example, he found the use of racial quotas unconstitutional because it violates an excluded applicant's "right to individual consideration without regard to his race" and "involves the use of an explicit racial classification." He then approved of the use of an applicant's ("minority") race as a "plus factor," however, even though it violates the same right and uses the same classification. *Ibid.,* p. 319.

51. 110 S.Ct. 2997 (1990).

52. *Ibid.,* p. 3026.

53. *Ibid.,* pp. 3022, 3016, 3017 n. 31.

54. Derrick Bell, *And We Are Not Saved: The Elusive Quest for Racial Justice* (New York: Basic Books, 1987), p. 143:

> Moreover, the Black Crime Cure drastically undermined the crime industry. Thousands of people lost jobs as police forces were reduced, court schedules cut back, and prisons closed. Manufacturers who provided weapons, uniforms, and equipment of all forms to law enforcement agencies were brought to the brink of bankruptcy. Estimates of the dollar losses ran into the hundreds of millions.

55. See G. Gilder, "Off the Mark," *The American Spectator,* vol. 25 (March 1992), p. 45:

> It is obvious that whites in America desperately want blacks to succeed. From Michael Jordan to Bill Cosby, from Magic Johnson to Eddie

Murphy, from Whitney Houston to Toni Morrison, from O.J. Simpson
to Arsenio Hall, blacks who excel whites in important fields win the most
sincere votes of all: the unimpeachable vote of the marketplace.

56. R. Kennedy, "Taking Powell Seriously," *Reconstruction,* vol. 1 (1990), p.
49. For "blacks on the leftish end of the political spectrum," Kennedy
writes, "Powell's ascendancy provokes a divided set of reactions."
57. Bell, *And We Are Not Saved, supra* n. 54, ch. 6. See L. Graglia, Book
Review, *Constitutional Commentary,* vol. 5 (Summer 1988), p. 436.
58. See Carol Innerst, "College Classes Reflect Multicultural Triumph," *The
Washington Times,* February 17, 1992, p. A1:

More than half the nation's colleges and universities are giving students a
dose of multiculturalism through the curriculum. . . . [M]ore than a third
are forcing students to study issues of race and sex through new multicultural general education requirements. . . .

59. See Lino Graglia, "Racial Preferences, Quotas, and the Civil Rights Act of
1991," *DePaul Law Review,* vol. 41 (1992), p. 117.
60. Thomas Sowell, *Preferential Policies: An International Perspective* (New
York: William Morrow & Co., 1990).
61. See R. Walters, "Critique of Stephen Carter's *Reflections of an Affirmative
Action Baby,*" *Reconstruction,* vol. 1, no. 4 (1992), p. 123: "Are there no
basic cultural and political tenets which form the structure of a black way of
being which should be respected and continued?"
62. Quoted in Carter, *Reflections, supra* n. 38, p. 33.
63. See J. McPherson, "The Black Law Student: A Problem of Fidelities,"
Atlantic, April 1970, p. 99.
64. The elimination of preferences for blacks, he pointed out, would mean "a
severe drop in the number of black students, especially at more selective
colleges and universities." Those who favor such a step must "explain how
universities could suddenly . . . reduce black enrollments to 1.5 percent or
less in scores of selective colleges and professional schools without a devas-
tating effect on the morale and aspirations of blacks. . . ." D. Bok,
"Admitting Success," *New Republic,* vol. 192 (February 4, 1985), p. 14.
65. Sowell, *Preferential Policies, supra* n. 60.

Bad Faith: The Politicization of the University *In Loco Parentis*

Alan Charles Kors

All serious discussion of academic life these days requires, at the least, a description of what people in universities actually are doing, an analysis of what premises or goals nominally motivate such behavior, and the cultivation of a sense of irony. The latter is more important than most observers or critics realize. Whatever the stakes of the current culture wars, the wars themselves are inseparable from the human comedy, and an awareness of that inseparability is essential for the mental health, the morale, and even the wisdom—including the tactical wisdom—of the participants.

The dissonance between people's expressed intellectual or moral commitments and the way they live their lives afflicts us all, of course, and is no argument against those commitments. Noting it, however, is useful far beyond the occasion for *ad hominem* argument and reminds us that behind the claims of the self-anointed righteous ones stands, by and large, the flawed humanity of those often quite less than ordinary souls who claim the high moral ground of our universities. We all know certain species of the academic bestiary: colleagues who denounce the market system as the source of most evil, except for its rational determination of their salaries upon receipt of solicited outside offers; colleagues who declaim against private property, greed, and exploitation, but who talk unendingly about their second homes, the direction of the market, and the difficulty of getting good help; colleagues who deride choice in education while sending their own children to the best of private schools; colleagues who urge upon all others a vision of male-female interaction of which their own marriages or relationships are the antitheses (if not the very practices they would penalize by code or laws). The Universities might well have been wise to divest themselves of companies that did business in South Africa, but there were a lot of academics insisting that they do so who themselves held onto their South African invested CREF or Vanguard retirement accounts rather than shift into what they presumed would be the lower yields of, say, the Calvert Social Responsibility portfolio. One may call such dissonance paradox or hypocrisy, or, simply, bad faith. At some levels, it may well produce outrage; at others, it may simply produce smiles; it probably ought to produce bemused outrage: bemusement that today's ideologues appear so blind to their self-contradictions; outrage that people so blind to their self-contradictions should insist so adamantly upon the moral superiority if not purity of their advocacy and leadership.

Consider, in the bemused mode, perhaps, the "Personals" that dominate the classified advertisements of the February/March 1992 issue of *Lingua Franca,* the new and quite politically correct journal of university life and ambition. The contradictions of contemporary academic personality and culture come vividly to life. I quote directly but discreetly: "Brilliant, stormy historienne. Tall, striking, Italianate woman seeks deeply decent, stable, wealthy, stylish leftist (Gramsci anyone?) for transcendent whatever"—seeks *wealthy* leftist! seeks *stylish* leftist! finds "Gramsci anyone?" a mark of self-deprecatory wit! Welcome to the Antinomian secret life of academe, a "to the pure all things are pure" self-assessment that coexists with the detection of original sin in all others! Or, consider the case of the "Left/Feminist professor, divorced white female . . . attractive, warm, playful, smart, without pretension. Seeks single, secure, progressive man to share talk, critique, laughter, spicy food, film, travel, champagne." No talk of Smith College's denunciation of "lookism" here, and no rejection of the commodification of human qualities: this left feminist is plain-out "attractive"; and it is champagne, not Cribari Zinfandel, that accompanies "critique" for today's oppressed role models. Althusser? Derrida? Foucault? NOT! Or note, again with no self-consciousness about gendered notions of self, the "Female . . . Professor, cultural/social historian . . . slender, attractive, . . . seeks single male counterpart with liberal/Left politics and sense of humor. . . . " What would the professor herself make of an emphasis on "slender" and "attractive" in the culture's discourse apart from her own? Other "Personals" reveal the same dissonance between the ostensible ability to decode the oppression entailed by artificial cultural standards of beauty and the desire to be known as and seen with a looker. Thus, "Post-modern art historian . . . attractive . . . seeks svelte, stylish semiotic soulmate, white female, for mutual iteration and colloquy." Apparently, this postmodernist is no anti-positivistic relativist when it comes to how *he* looks in the mirror or when it comes to the dress and dress size of his "soulmate." No emphasis on "alterity" here! Listen, because this actually is important if one is to address without mystification the future of liberal education: the new ideologues may talk a new language, but they really are still the kids with whom you went to high school. Chances are, however, that the kids with whom you went to high school never heard of *mauvaise foi* and live lives of far better faith than the denizens of academe. The "Personals" of *Lingua Franca*! If you can get a free copy, take a look some time.

I

As in almost all matters human, bad faith with reference to self-regarding behavior or to voluntarily consensual behavior with others, however, is far less troubling and certainly far less dangerous to a free society than bad faith in the exercise of power. In this latter regard, few developments on university campuses have reflected worse faith than the transformation of the Free Speech Movement into the Speech Code Movement. For those of us who lived through the sixties in academic life, and who accepted extraordinary verbal and written abuse as the price to be paid for the fullest possible expansion of First Amendment rights and their equivalents at both public and private universities, it is striking, indeed, to see conservative students convicted, as they were at Dartmouth, of the crime of "vexatious oral exchange" with a professor. Imagine if such a category existed in the period from 1967 to 1973, when *amnesty* was routinely offered to students for terroristic threats, for denying access of students and faculty to classrooms and offices, for destruction of property, and for detaining people against their will. I don't remember the current president of Dartmouth, James Freedman, who taught then at my own university, the University of Pennsylvania, accusing anyone of "vexatious oral exchange" when I sought to teach a class at its appointed hour, and found myself manhandled and obscenely vituperated by students barring access to university buildings. Indeed, when two students were found guilty of physical violence against my person, the sentences, not the students, were suspended, and no reference to their conviction ever was placed on their records or transcripts. At Brown University recently, a student was expelled for shouting demeaning obscenities into the night. His speech was deemed action, although the ACLU of Rhode Island begged the university to treat it as protected speech. There are profound ironies in all this. The president of Brown University, Vartan Gregorian, when he was a faculty member at San Francisco State University, had been willing to serve as campus faculty advisor for the left-militant Students for a Democratic Society (SDS, a group central to the demonstrations, building-takeovers, and violent rhetoric of the late sixties), solely in order to preserve the constitutional rights of this activist student group. In this role, he was, in the name of the fullest possible free speech, nominal advisor to a group that, far from seeing speech as action, insisted that its most disruptive actions should be protected as symbolic speech. How the circle has turned![1]

The further irony, of course, is that the circle still turns before our eyes, depending upon the specific and partisan politics of the speech to be penalized or protected. No more striking example of this exists than in the recent simultaneous defense by academic administrators of both uncensored art at taxpayers' expense, let the chips of being offended by such art fall where they may, and the defense of censorship and speech codes to protect the idealized congeries of the "historically oppressed" from being in any way offended.

Consider, in this light, the behavior of the president of my own university, Sheldon Hackney of the University of Pennsylvania. Dr. Hackney is a distinguished American historian, a sincere and well-intentioned man, and a person who wishes to stand witness to the values he identifies with a free and humane society. In the fall of 1989, he helped to explain to students the harassment policy that he had promulgated, one that included a speech and expression code, and, simultaneously, he became a hero of free expression nationwide by challenging Senator Jesse Helms's efforts to deny taxpayers' funds to the exhibition of the works of Andres Serrano and Robert Mapplethorpe.

Against the advice of libertarians and conservatives, but with the enthusiastic support of the Women's Center, whose director publicly assured President Hackney of the obvious constitutionality of such speech codes, the University of Pennsylvania promulgated in 1987 a harassment policy that replicated the common motifs of free-speech and free-expression prohibitions, common because they reflected the successful "networking" among social-work activists at our universities. Where Penn's sexual harassment code limited itself to behavior (all banned behavior being modified by the clause "unwanted sexual attention that . . ."), Penn's other harassment policies prohibited "any behavior, *verbal* or physical, *that stigmatizes or victimizes individuals on the basis of race, ethnic or national origin,* and that . . . has the purpose *or effect* of *interfering* with an individual's work or performance; and/or*

. . . creates an intimidating or *offensive academic,* living, or work *environment"* (emphases added). (During the debates about harassment policy, initial drafts had sought to include "stereotyping" by race or sex among acts of harassment, but the campus was spared that further prohibition by the successful arguments of diverse "reactionary" faculty. Whether the moral course is to help modify the more wicked into the less wicked or to let the more wicked establish itself on its own terms for purposes of clarifying public debate is a grave issue worth considering!) In addition, in a University Council meeting of such tension that I was thanked personally by high officers of the university and by the chair of the Faculty Senate for not speaking, the university set about to plan what it termed "diversity education," apart from the classroom, for its under-graduates, and decided to incorporate explication of its harassment policy into that program.

Thus, in the same fall of 1989 that saw President Hackney assail Senator Helms for his attempt to purge federally subsidized art of religious and ethnic offense, the University of Pennsylvania offered a Labor Day seminar on Diversity Education to all incoming freshmen that cited explicit "Incidents of Harassment at the University of Pennsyl-vania." Harassment, note well, is an actionable crime at the University of Pennsylvania. The list of harassment incidents included (among some that were presented as having occurred but that the administration later admitted—with public apology—were false or, in some cases, wholly unsubstantiated), two remarkable examples. The first referred to "Gay Jeans Day," an annual event in which various student groups ask members of the university community to wear blue-jeans to show sup-port for gay and lesbian rights. The "Incident of Harassment" described the crime as follows: "During Lesbian, Gay and Bisexual Awareness Week, specifically during Gay Jeans Day (an event designed to heighten awareness of the decisions and risks which gay/lesbian people face pertaining to self-disclosure), several individuals stood near lesbian/gay activists and held out a placard declaring: 'Heterosexual Footwear Day—Wear shoes if you are a heterosexual' and 'Don't bend for a friend.' " The second actionable "Incident of Harassment" was pre-sented thus: "Flyers depicting a stereotypical 'lazy Mexican' were circu-lated around campus to publicize a 'South of the Border' party which was to be held at a fraternity. The same stereotypical image was again used to advertise a different fraternity party in a separate incident." (In the facilitators' manual, by the way, the final agenda item for the part of the day devoted to incidents of harassment was not unrevealing: "Ex-plain that incidents like those just discussed demonstrate the need for a program such as the one being held today. . . .")[2]

Now, here we have a university administration seemingly committed to the notion that when free speech and offense come into conflict, free speech must yield. The problem, however, is that like many major university administrations, it has expressed itself on many occasions in a manner that contradicts the literal meaning of its harassment policies when the offense is taken by what is perceived as groups or individuals right of cultural center.

When the politically correct take on Senator Helms, note well, they do so on general grounds, on the high principles of freedom in general (principles they were less eager to assert when Chicago aldermen forcibly removed a painting of Mayor Harold Washington in a tutu from an art museum several years ago). Among the works of art subsidized by the National Endowment for the Arts (NEA) that so offended Senator Helms and many other Christians was Andres Serrano's "Piss Christ," a crucifix immersed in the artist's own urine. Those who defended Serrano's right not merely to create and display such work (uncontested and uncontestable, I believe), but to do so at taxpayers' expense, were not accused, on their own campuses, of encouraging blasphemy or hatred of Christians. Those who defend the free speech of the politically incorrect, however, are always accused of racism and sexism and homophobia. It is, as noted, a remarkable instance of double standards and bad faith.

Thus, while the university's own "Guidelines on Open Expression" promise content-neutral freedom, and while President Hackney rightfully defended Serrano's freedom to display a crucifix immersed in urine (indeed, and less obviously, his right not to be chilled in his ability to offer such a display by a threat of losing taxpayers' subsidies), President Hackney's administration informed freshmen, in an event in which he himself fully participated, that the sign "Heterosexual Footwear Day" and a drawing that offends Hispanic students constitute not bad taste, or cruelty, or stupidity, but actionable and illegal harassment! The Helms amendment, vying in vagueness and overbreadth with university harassment policies, would have barred *the use of federal funds* for, among other things, "material which denigrates the objects or beliefs of the adherents of a particular religion or nonreligion" and art that "denigrates, debases or reviles a person, group, or class of citizens on the basis of race, creed, sex, handicap, age or national origin." The Mapplethorpe exhibit, which so offended Senator Helms (and countless others), had begun its journey from the Institute for Contemporary Art at the University of Pennsylvania, and many in Congress wanted the ICA to pay for that by a loss of federal funding via the NEA.

Here, from the university's *Almanac* (September 12, 1989), is what President Hackney, who presides over Penn's harassment policy, wrote about Senator Helms's attempt merely to deny federal funds to work that demonstrably offended many Christians at least as deeply as these "incidents of harassment" at Penn had offended some gays and Hispanics:

> Leaving intellectual and cultural life unfettered is clearly a risky thing. Mistakes will be made. Some people or groups will be offended from time to time, but our founding fathers decided long ago that the rewards of freedom were well worth the risks. . . . As for universities, it is clear that it is impossible to fulfill the role as a center of learning, much less pretend to excellence, without a scrupulous respect for freedom of inquiry and freedom of expression. . . . Such freedom creates its problems and poses great risks, but the cost of limiting inquiry and expression is to lose our soul as a university.

In the very same week that he informed Penn's Diversity Education seminars that "offense" of blacks, women, and gays remained a crime at the University of Pennsylvania (not seeing how demeaning it is that we think such individuated, diverse groups each to be singular and incapable of fighting speech with speech), President Hackney, in *The Chronicle of Higher Education* (September 6, 1989), instructed those who were so inadequately appreciative of full freedom as to be tempted by Senator Helms's strictures:

> Given *the impossibly vague and broad language of this proscription,* anyone can easily imagine works that unquestionably should be available to the public that would be denied Federal support. . . . *Social and political satire would be off limits, of course* ["Heterosexual Footwear Day"???]. . . . The issue is not whether Mr. Mapplethorpe's images are pornographic or Mr. Serrano's sacrilegious . . . [but] whether our Government, having decided to support the arts, should be involved in attempting *to suppress certain forms of expression in an attempt to cleanse public discourse of offensive material. . . . The best defense against falsity is not repression but exposure.* . . . We have a positive obligation to protect free expression against threats *from whatever quarter and in whatever form.* . . . [T]he best protection we have found for democracy is *an unregulated market in expression.* (Emphases added.)

Except, of course, at Penn and similar universities! It turns out, alas, that it depends on whose ox is being gored, which is almost the worst sermon of all to preach on freedom. Indeed, it depends on who most efficaciously can wield power, or threaten administrators with disorders that give their administration the appearance of incompetence, which is undoubtedly the worst sermon on *freedom* to preach to those about to move into the corridors of power and advocacy.

Similarly, in April 1988, for example, Louis Farrakhan spoke at the University of Pennsylvania, sponsored by, among other organizations, the Student Activities Committee, the Black Graduate/Professional Students Assembly, the Penn Political Union, the Society of Black Engineers, and the Black Wharton Undergraduate Association. President Hackney and Provost Michael Aiken addressed the University community in the official publication *Almanac* (April 12, 1988). They announced that "many persons" had asked them to prohibit the talk, and that they were not surprised by this, since "[s]ome of his previous remarks are racist and anti-Semitic, and amount to scapegoating." Nonetheless, they rightly and directly reminded the campus: "In an academic community, open expression is the most fundamental value. We can't have free speech only some of the time, for only some people. Either we have it, or we don't. At Penn, we have it." And what of the harassment policy's proscription of verbal behavior that "stigmatizes or victimizes individuals on the basis of race, ethnic or national origin"? And what of the "Heterosexual Footwear Day" poster and the sign that offended Hispanics as "incidents of harassment"?

The same dissonance is apparent throughout the academic world. With no sense of the irony involved, *U. The National College Newspaper,* distributed periodically with many university and college dailies, presented as the two lead stories of its November/December 1990 issue the following: "Colleges Embittered by NEA Controversy. Anti-obscenity clause: 'Communist witch hunt,' " with a photograph of a sophomore gagged, blindfolded, and chained, displaying "her outrage" at censorship; *and* "French teaching program labeled sexist," explaining that "[p]ortions of a French language instruction were eliminated from the curriculum at Amherst College after three female students at Yale U. filed a sexual harassment grievance"; no one was shown bound and gagged protesting *this* censorship, and a senior was quoted as saying: "I had approached the course with a very strong desire to learn the language, but then I started noticing that the camera was lingering on women's bodies." Now, if only Mapplethorpe had filmed the French course, and if only the "Heterosexual Footwear Day" sign had been attached to a cross immersed in urine, everyone would have been protected from "an attempt to cleanse public discourse of offensive material"!

Indeed, in November 1990, Andres Serrano was invited to Penn to give a prestigious lecture at the School of Fine Arts. The board of the Newman Club and the Catholic chaplain were outraged, thinking, perhaps, that the harassment policy might apply to Catholic or, indeed, Christian sensibilities as well. As they wrote to the Dean of the Graduate School of Fine Arts, "we find the subject matter of Mr. Serrano's 'Piss Christ' extremely offensive to Christian sensibilities and the cosponsorship of his lecture by the School of Fine Arts and Institute of Contemporary Art very objectionable. Would you as Dean . . . have approved a lecture equally offensive to the sensitivities of non-Christian religious groups . . . ?" In an interview with the campus newspaper, a student member of the Lecture Committee noted, rightly, that "he was interested in providing a forum for the artist to speak in a place where he would not be restricted by censorship." In short, all offenses are equal, but some offenses are more equal than other offenses!

Thus, in the manner of *Lingua Franca*'s left/feminist postmodernists advertising their slender, attractive selves in search of wealthy, stylish leftists, administrators who position their universities as paragons of the exhilarating risk of pure freedom against the apparent philistine repression of Senator Helms, while criminalizing the free expression of their own undergraduates, leave something to be desired in the way of good-faith consistency. Ashes for the gander and sauce for the goose! The sheer obviousness of the dissonance, however, is precisely the major opening for those of us who wish universities actually to be exhilarating centers of unfettered discourse and expression, and who prefer the public life of such universities to enjoy the same First Amendment protections enjoyed as an inherent right by free citizens in the rest of the society. Public universities now are obliged, in theory, to grant such First Amendment protections, thanks to a suit brought in Michigan by a National Association of Scholars member and the ACLU—a suit that resulted in Federal Judge Avern Cohn's ruling that the University of Michigan's speech code was unconstitutional, both chilling and denying essential First Amendment rights and creating an official state orthodoxy on matters of, among other things, race and gender (*Doe v. Michigan,* 721 F. Supp. 852, 856 [E.D. Mich. 1989]).

Private universities now must do one of two things: either they must grant full First Amendment protections to their students and faculty, or they must admit explicitly that their students and faculty enjoy fewer First Amendment rights than students at city, county, and state colleges or universities. Immediately after Judge Cohn's decision, the office of the General Counsel of the University of Pennsylvania rushed to proclaim that Penn, being a private university, was not bound by this ruling. When I put the question publicly to President Hackney, however—"Do students and faculty at the University of Pennsylvania have fewer rights of free speech and free expression than our peers at Penn State?"—he answered, of course, "No." If an administration answers yes, granting its politically correct thought and expression police the power to suppress offensive speech and expression—far beyond Senator Helms's efforts merely to end federal subsidy of what to him is offensive speech and expression—then, at the least, one might appeal to the laws and ethics of truth in advertising. Let a university, as part of its brochures and catalogues to high-school seniors, explicitly and officially list its protected and unprotected groups, noting that its speech code is *not* meant to protect whites, males, conservative or libertarian blacks, conservative or libertarian gays, evangelicals, Catholics, Zionists, Shiite Muslims, or anti-abortion activists from any offense whatsoever, but is meant to protect all other groups from any offense offered by the unprotected. That, at least, would be a good-faith acknowledgment of how a university discriminated among its members.

II

Of all bad faith afflicting universities these days, however, nothing compares with the restoration of the *in loco parentis* function of offices of student life. Standing in the place of parents, *in loco parentis,* has been one of the roles traditionally assumed by universities in the lives of their undergraduate students. The *in loco parentis* functions of colleges often included strict regulation of visitation rights between the sexes (parietal rules), mandatory chapel attendance, sign-outs and other special protections of women, and, in general, an effort to enforce in the academy some vague consensus about respectable morals derived from educated American society. Rules, regulations, codes, and moral instruction regarding such matters are a part of the folklore of most students who came of age before the cultural revolutions of the late 1960s, although it is a past that quickly seemed remote in the wake of those startling revolutions. For those of us who lived through the sixties and early seventies, when these *in loco parentis* functions were torn down in the name of the adulthood and often moral superiority demanded by and granted to students (if they were old enough to die for their country, etc.; recall, they even acquired the vote), the re-infantilization of students by the generation and heirs of the sixties is nothing less than breathtaking. The generation that, under thirty, trusted no one over thirty, having attained academic power, now trusts no one under thirty. The generation that earned itself the right to vote at eighteen now wishes eighteen- to twenty-two-year-olds to sit at its feet for moral and political instruction. The generation that smoked pot freely on campuses, freed women from monitored early returns to cloistered dormitories, and initiated the sexual revolution, now, from its deep distaste for disinhibited testosterone, bans beer kegs from student functions and, where possible, from parties.

Further, the blatant politicization of the *in loco parentis* role that universities have restored is one of the most under-studied and pernicious influences upon American academic life today. It is not only a generational swindle of epic proportions, but it has made American universities profoundly anti-intellectual and, as academic travelers know, a laughingstock abroad. It is also generally unchallenged by faculty, students, trustees, donors, and the parents who pay a fortune for the services of the Masters of Social Work who now dominate offices of student life. The absence of that challenge is an indication, simultaneously, of the shadows that cover the functioning of this role, of a will to complacency and ignorance, of the moral vacuum of today's universities, and of the fact that few people truly take them seriously as institutions for the cultivation of intellect and spirit.

The speech-code provisions and harassment codes of universities are one instance of this politicized restoration of the university *in loco parentis*. The days when the politically correct supported Free Speech Movements are long gone, except when the threat to free speech is Senator Helms. In Michigan, as noted, the federal court declared the University of Michigan's harassment code unconstitutional, though it was, in fact, a code that was slightly less unreasonable than Penn's at a similar time, modifying "effect" by "reasonably foreseeable," and applicable (unlike Penn's, which held everywhere on campus) merely in "educational and academic centers, such as classroom buildings, libraries, research laboratories, recreation and study centers." Michigan's policy initially prohibited "any behavior, *verbal* or physical, *that stigmatizes or victimizes an individual on the basis of race, ethnicity, religion, sex, sexual orientation, creed, national origin, ancestry, age, marital status, handicap or Vietnam-era veteran status*" (presumably you could call someone who avoided service in World War II a "draft dodger" if you so wished!) "and that has the purpose *or reasonably foreseeable effect of interfering with* an individual's academic efforts, employment, participation in University sponsored extra-curricular activities or personal safety; *or* . . . creates an intimidating, hostile, or *demeaning environment for educational pursuits* . . ." (emphases added).

Although harassment speech codes apply to all members of a university community, let us examine, for a moment, the situation of students. Even for the most devoted advocates of capacious free speech, I suspect, universities always have had a right to protect individual students, defined as "any student" and not merely as "any member of a historically oppressed group," from hateful, personal abuse of power by a professor, exercised in a manner that made it difficult if not impossible for a student to work successfully in a classroom. Surely, professional codes of conduct protected a student from a professor who shouted "Hey, Jew-boy (or 'nigger,' or 'honky'), sit in the back row." Recognizing that diversity of ideas was essential to a free university, however, what free or nonsectarian university ever should *want* to "protect" a Jewish student from a professor who believed that the U.N.'s creation of Israel was a violation of Palestinian rights, or a black student from a professor who believed that a failure of black leadership or family was a primary cause of inner-city decay, or a white student from a professor who believed that all whites benefited from institutionalized racism? The American Association of University Professors (AAUP) code of conduct explicitly recognized that *in the exercise of their scholarly expertise,* professors had academic freedom to speak their minds. Recognizing that free political debate and cultural criticism may involve passionate expression of abuse and denunciation (e.g., the "free-speech" movement of the sixties and the equation of all sorts of people and groups with Nazis, Klan members, and other murderers), what university emerging from the sixties dreamed of "protecting" students from each other's rhetoric and convictions? If the protection of students from direct, intimidating, invidiously discriminatory professorial or administrative abuse or ill manners were all that was at stake (or the protection of members of the university from terroristic threats or defacing and destruction of property), reasonable people could find in the existing explicit or implicit codes of professional conduct and criminal law adequate means of offering students redress against such improbable but possible misconduct. They would *not* need policies of such equivocation as to leave a person incapable of knowing what was or what was not prohibited, with catastrophically chilling effects upon free speech and free expression. Even truth might "offend" and "interfere with" *someone's* ability to work, and, presumably, there are feminist scholars not exquisitely concerned with "stigmatizing" the "phallogocentrism" or "androcentrism" of male students, even if such students are discomfited.

The goal of contemporary harassment policies, however, is precisely political—is precisely, indeed, to protect specific individuals, defined by specific group identities, from, among other things, ideas, expressions, and, we shall see, even private consensual associations that offend; and the way to know that is to consult the terms in which universities began to explain such "harassment" to their students. Thus, at the University of Michigan, the Office of Affirmative Action issued a guide entitled *What Students Should Know about Discrimination and Discriminatory Harassment by Students in the University Environment,* precisely to clarify the nature of prohibited conduct. It cited examples such as: "A male student makes remarks in class like 'Women just aren't as good in this field as men,' thus creating a hostile learning atmosphere for female classmates"; and "Students in a residence hall have a floor party and invite everyone on their floor except one person because they think she might be a lesbian." (Does anyone know a university where claiming that men were not as sensitive as women would constitute "harassment"; or where not inviting the one evangelical "homophobe" to a party would be an actionable offense?) The guide had a section of direct examples under the heading "You are a harasser when . . . ," which was followed by such instances as "You tell jokes about gay men and lesbians," "You display a confederate flag on the door of your room in the residence hall," "You laugh at a joke about someone in your class who stutters," "You comment in a derogatory way about a particular person or group's physical appearance or sexual orientation, or their cultural origins, or religious beliefs." (Again, does anyone know of a student accused of harassment at a university for terming someone a "Jesus Freak," "Moonie," or "born-again bigot," let alone for *laughing* at such?)

Such speech codes notwithstanding, be assured that you may say anything you wish at most American universities about whites, males, heterosexuals, Catholics, Jews as Israelis or Jews as American whites, members of the Unification Church, evangelical Protestants, and, offend them as you will, Episcopalians. On the other hand, you may not offend militant blacks, politicized Hispanics, radical feminists, or activist gays. From the left, you may, on the other hand, call moderate blacks "Oreos" or "Uncle Toms" with impunity (that is social criticism, not harassment!). You may equally abuse anti-feminist women as "barbie dolls," "mall chicks," and "psychological captives" with impunity (that is analysis, not stigmatization that "creates an offensive environment"!). You may tell white students whose parents died fighting for freedom that their mothers and fathers were—depending on contexts—oppressors, racists, sexists, or baby-killers (in Vietnam, though not in abortion clinics!). You may exhibit a cross in urine. If the issue is the sensibilities of white, male heterosexuals, however vulnerable their egos, universities will talk about the perils of freedom, and, indeed, correctly so! If the issue is the sensibilities of politically correct minorities (evangelicals and "Moonies" need not apply), universities will talk about the vulnerability of egos and the absurdity of an ahistorical definition of freedom! Why?

The reason is really quite simple, and profoundly illustrative of the dangers that the politicization of offices and agencies of the administration of student life poses to free and open universities: academic governors of noncurricular student life, to limit my observations to their role, have a political vision and agenda, the fulfillment of which is now one of the central visions of most major universities. This vision and agenda is free to express itself in appropriate classrooms. It is free to appeal to voluntary adherents. It is free to compete for minds by arguments voluntarily heard or read. For its advocates, however, these avenues are not enough. This political vision and agenda have become the very *raison d'être* of a growing number of offices of student life. It is one of the ugliest secrets of American higher education, and citizens concerned with the future of liberal education truly need to be aware of it. Whatever is happening in matters curricular remains open to debate and adjudication through the normal procedures of academic life. In the noncurricular dimension of the university, however, our students and children have been handed over to a group of ideologues who work independently of all the mechanisms of faculty accountability and self-regulation.

Politicized speech-code and harassment policies, thus, are part of a much larger phenomenon of which the academic world and the public quite desperately need to be aware and toward which they must exercise their moral responsibilities: the Orwellian effort to create an official, privileged ideology in noncurricular areas of academic life, to proselytize on behalf of this creed, and to police all areas of student life under its moral and political banners. We see this, above all, in two great "movements" on today's campuses in addition to anti-"harassment" policies: first, "diversity education," either ongoing or limited to orientation or first-year programming; and, second, the effort to guarantee a "humane and decent community" of diverse politically defined groups. These movements seek to justify themselves (and, indeed, often win much sincere support) by appeal to real acts of cruelty or criminality that could be handled by existing law, or by codes of conduct involving behavioral sanctions for explicitly defined behavioral abuses. The essence of these movements, however, is not to penalize criminal or intolerable behavior, but to re-educate those who engage in, who are likely to engage in, or who ever might engage in such behaviors, on the assumption that the view of the world held by most individuals on campuses is the root cause of such behavior. Harassment policies that inhibit speech and expression have come increasingly under attack, aided by the fact that the national ACLU, under Nadine Strossen, at last has developed some consistency in its approach to freedom of speech on the campus. The ACLU, however, advocates "education" to replace such codes. The education people mean when they speak of the reform of people's souls, however, is not the traditional curricular education of scholarly disciplines, but a new moral-political education related to official group identities.

To the extent that such "education" is part of a general model of diverse advocacies on campus, it is, of course, welcome. Why not have a campus in which traditionalist conservatives, evangelicals, Lubavitcher chassidim, Marxists, libertarians, Freudians, Lacanians, Burkeans, radical feminists, Afrocentrists, and Catholic moral theologians, for example, all speak unofficially to voluntary audiences who choose to hear them pronounce upon the evils and means of redemption of the world? In fact, however, universities increasingly mandate official perspectives on the nature and causes of human iniquity and inequity, and assign the tasks of identifying, classifying, and eradicating iniquity and inequity to politicized offices of student life. Such moral reformation follows and advances, almost invariably, a particular ideological agenda: left, politically correct, neo-Gramscian in its analysis of culture and power, and committed to a newly orthodox view of America (if not the whole West) as an inherently and wickedly racist, sexist, and homophobic culture whose products must be deprogrammed and converted to new ideological and moral perspectives if the campus and the world are going to be just and fair.[3]

Among themselves, as I know from a variety of outraged sources on my own campus (I possess almost all of the planning documents for "diversity education" at Penn, and, with their approval, I have tape-recorded interviews with students and others who sought me out to discuss their participation in the programs of the Office of Student Life), the explicit concerns of the social workers, facilitators, and enlighteners of such an undertaking are manifestly ideological. To the public, however, such social engineers present themselves as people engaged in "behavior clarification" and "explanation" of the behavioral codes of a campus. Courses in behavior clarification require bad behavior, and this is always at hand, from the real brutishness of much of human life, from the never-doubted reports of allegedly victimized individuals, from evidence of callousness—racial, sexual, or sexual-preference graffiti, for example—that have a way of occurring when most useful, or, indeed, from instances of bigotry and discrimination by a handful of individuals for which the entire student body, or the entire American culture, is now to be blamed. Anyone wishing to create a crisis requiring "diversity education" on a campus as a solution need only daub a vile slogan here or make a threatening phone call there. Such individual acts will be the Adam's Fall of a university for which all must bear original guilt. They also will be the occasion for countless pronouncements that our universi-

ties—which in fact are not bad places at all for most nonconservatives—
are, to the contrary, centers of unprecedented hatred, cruelty, and
oppression by one set of racial, sexual, and sexual-preference groups
(read whites, males, and heterosexuals) against its marginalized "others" (read all "people of color," women, and gays).

The great barrier to acceptance of such a view is the same great barrier
to all totalitarianisms of the twentieth century: individualism and notions
of individual identity and moral responsibility. To secure a campus in
which students understand oppression and resistance to oppression from
politically correct perspectives, however, students must be made to see
themselves as oppressors qua whites, males, or heterosexuals, and as
victims qua people of color, females, or gays. Offices of student life seize
upon both real and imagined instances of campus racial and sexual
harassment as a pretext for advancing that particular ideological agenda.

Imagine what would occur if, in response to date rape, fraternity
brutishness, or racial violence, nonsectarian universities decided that
their students needed (for sake of argument) a recognition of the need
for Christian grace or a deep grounding in conservative moral theory!
Imagine, further, what would occur if such universities also decided that
they should put into place whatever support services and programs were
necessary both to achieve these as privileged goals and to defeat the
critics of such definitions of our problems and needs. The professoriate
and much of the public would understand and articulate full well the
differences between education and indoctrination, allowable governance of behavioral acts and administrative interference in academic
freedom, open discussion of moral issues from a diversity of perspectives
and the growth of self-serving partisan morality-bureaucracies feigning
to speak for the common interests of all. What an uproar we would hear
about authentic academic liberties!

The response of ever more universities to the sins of humanity,
however, has been the extracurricular institutionalization of a world-
view that is tolerable as one theoretical position open to criticism and
voluntary acceptance or rejection, but intolerable as an official ideology.
It runs as follows: The West, and America in particular, is author of a
sexism, heterosexism, and racism embodied in the culture and institutions from which our undergraduates come; culture and society are not
evolved phenomena conferring survival and life-enhancing benefits
upon the many, open to constant emendation as material conditions and
changes in thinking allow, but means of granting hegemonic dominance
to the few, indeed, to white, "European," heterosexual American males
alone; among the most pernicious effects of such hegemony is the
pervasive harm done to women, blacks, and gays at American universi-

ties; among the worst aspects of this harm is the large number of victims who in false consciousness have internalized the perspectives and values of their oppressors. To deal with this harm, universities increasingly believe, not only the faculty, but, given the ideological un-trustworthiness of much of the faculty, the university *in loco parentis* must explain this view of culture and society to all undergraduates, make them relate to each other from their group identities on the basis of this ideology, and protect the victims of such a society and culture, identified by group, from all forms of abuse that might be visited upon them by their hegemonic oppressors, including the oppressors' freedom of speech and expression. If faculties will not incorporate such perspectives into the requirements of their curriculum (or, indeed, even in many cases if they will), then administrations will hire the appropriate "facilitators," "social workers," "advocates," and "support services" to do the deeper duty of the faculty, and will educate all students about what is owed the victims of American culture and society by universities that understand such things so clearly.

This ideology dominates the administrative offices in the ever-burgeoning "student life" and "support service" areas of our leading universities, with the aid of faculty allies, and with the sincere or cynical approval of central administrations who see it as buying them either justice or peace. Knowing this, one can begin to understand the *Animal Farm/Alice in Wonderland* environment that has emerged unmonitored by most faculty, trustees, donors, and parents of undergraduates.

III

At scores of universities, first-year students, as we say now, have been judged to stand in need of special education in pluralism, generally termed "diversity." The assumption here is that growing up in America leaves one unable to approach the diversity of American society with tolerance and fairness. Diversity, of course, is itself a topic that might be approached diversely, but this is not the case. Where you might think that significant differences include psychological type, religious or secular commitment, politics, taste in art, intellectual styles, fears, longings, and aversions, universities, on the whole, have limited their notions of diversity to race, gender, and sexual preference, occasionally genuflecting to class as well. To achieve a humane community, universities believe, we must overcome prejudices and (a favored term) "raise consciousness" about these essential differences. In 1986, for example, a middle-level administrator at Penn said openly what so many believe:

"We at the University of Pennsylvania have guaranteed students and the community that they can live in a community free of sexism, racism and homophobia" (*Daily Pennsylvanian,* February 14, 1986).

Intimidation aside, how might one create "a community free of sexism, racism and homophobia" as defined by an ideological camp? The answer, at Penn and at a growing number of universities, lies in "diversity education" and "racism/sexism" awareness seminars. They are a force now and a wave of the future! The first such seminars were imposed in 1982 on administrative and support staff in the entire area of "student life." So that this office might understand the reality around it and both explain and change that reality for undergraduates, its members were given an official set of definitions. Thus, "white racism" was defined in the following terms: "Racism and white racism mean the same thing. . . ." The reason for this was explained as follows, for the edification of those about to undertake the moral reformation of undergraduates: "Institutional racism is a necessary condition for individual racism." In brief, then, whites alone, never blacks, whatever their prejudice, can be "racists." Men alone, never women, whatever their prejudice, can be "sexists." One can better understand, then, what Tulane University has in mind when its administration informs undergraduates that "racism and sexism are fundamentally present in all American institutions," and that "[w]e are all the progeny of a racist and sexist society." This is the new official instruction. Afterwards, at Penn, a "Racism Awareness Questionaire [*sic*]" was sent to each participant, who was promised anonymity, but instructed to specify his or her general role and specific department or office in the "University Life Division." There were sixteen questions, most of which will clarify the ideological and political agenda being fostered: "1. Now that you have completed the Racism Awareness Workshop, how much consideration have you given to the subject of American racism?"; "2. How would you rate your awareness of Institutional and Individual American Racism?"; "4. How much are you able to identify the indicators of American racism in a. The University? b. Your department/office?"; "7. How much have you raised issues of American racism in: a. Staff meetings? b. Informal discussions?"; "12. How much do you feel that the training helped build a better sense of trust and teamwork on the problem of American racism in a. The University Life Division? b. Your office/dept.?"; "14. What do you need now to help you further work on the problem of racism in your job? (be specific, use additional pages if needed)." One courageous member of an office wrote to his supervisor that he refused to attend these seminars after the first, stressing that "compulsory awareness seminars," let alone those run by persons "who propound the doctrine that 'all whites are racists,' " intruded upon matters that he deemed to be of "personal conscience," were "counter-productive," and went beyond any institution's rights over his person. He soon after chose to leave the university.[4]

Thus enlightened, the Office of Student Life began offering frequent sensitivity seminars in the dormitories, and, indeed, the university began to sentence people to such seminars for crimes of racism, sexism, and homophobia. In 1984, three years before the promulgation of Penn's harassment codes, one campus columnist at Penn asserted that he ought to be free to hold a conservative Christian view of homosexuality if he respected the rights of individual homosexuals, and objected to having his views officially labeled as "homophobia." Eight administrators and social workers in the Student Life division replied in a letter to the campus newspaper that columns such as his made them proud to have pioneered "increased awareness of the insidious ways in which racism, sexism and homophobia deny the human potential of students and others at the University," and that his "column suggests that we should intensify efforts to counter homophobic attitudes and behavior on the Penn campus" (*Daily Pennsylvanian,* November 14, 1984). So much for intellectual and religious diversity!

In planning for the beginning, in 1989, of Diversity Education for *all* incoming students at Penn, committees reporting to the Vice-Provost for University Life, who oversees the noncurricular sides of undergraduate experience, were charged with focusing on racism, sexism, homophobia, and religious mistrust as the evils which undergraduates should understand and overcome. (Information given to planners for the latter touched a bit on anti-Semitism and Jewish-American princess jokes, but the ordination of women, religion and gays, and religion and abortion loomed even larger in these concerns.) These committees, also, were provided with definitions that have circulated at countless campuses. Penn defined "racism," the most outlawed of all academic crimes, so that it applied not to individuals, but only to members of institutionally privileged groups: "Racial prejudice with institutional power, used to the advantage of one race and the disadvantage of others. The critical differentiation between racism and prejudice is the institutional power to enforce prejudices in a systematic and far-reaching way. Racism is any attitude, action or practice—backed by institutional power—which subordinates people because of their race." Similarly, it defined "sexism," also outlawed, as "[s]ex prejudice with institutional power . . . any attitude, action or practice—backed by institutional power—which subordinates people because of their sex."[5]

Most undergraduates, in this view, enter universities inadequately aware of the effects of American "racism, sexism, and heterosexism" on their psyches, their behavior, and the society and its "victims" around them. Indeed, in this view, most Americans who are black, Asian, or Hispanic, most women, and most gays do not adequately understand the nature and methods of their "oppression," and, indeed, often have internalized the very values by which society oppresses them. The latter phenomenon, "false consciousness," is viewed as a particularly insidious means and product of American oppression. While countless courses in the official curriculum undertake to enlighten students about the unjust ways of their society, this is not enough. The full weight of administrative authority over extracurricular and private life (and thought) must be brought to bear to give politically correct moral enlightenment and inspiration to undergraduates.

Again, it is useful to reflect a moment upon the whole process of such preliminary moral education at our universities. If universities announced that all incoming freshmen should spend a week thinking about the wonder of an America that integrated tens of millions of immigrants from far-flung lands and forged a nation that has defended the option of freedom and civilization upon earth since 1945, for example, few academics would fail to see (or recoil from) the overt political agenda of such preliminary reflection. If universities decided to show all incoming freshmen films on what happens to fetuses during abortion, for example—not, of course, to indoctrinate them, but merely, as the phrase goes, to get them thinking—few academics would fail to see (or ban) such partisan purpose. But set the freshmen class to thinking about racism, sexism, and heterosexism, and that's merely a moral university doing its parental job. After all, they're children, aren't they? They hardly know anything! Who says so? It's the generation that occupied universities and abolished *in loco parentis* authority over its own lives that says so!

Thus, on June 13, 1989, the Board of Regents of Higher Education for the Commonwealth of Massachusetts instituted a "Policy Against Racism and Guidelines for Campus Policies Against Racism," mandating a set of required policies for all public colleges and universities. One naively might expect that such a policy could have been short and sweet: invidious discrimination based on race would be severely punished, and threats, violence, and intimidation against individuals and their property would be prosecuted to the fullest extent of the law. That is not quite what the regents had in mind. For example, one of the "required" policies demanded that all campuses create "[a] program of activities designed to enlighten faculty, administrators, staff and students with regard to . . . ways in which the dominant society manifests and perpetuates racism." This is in fact, of course, a topic on which reasonable people might deeply disagree, and which might well be the subject of formal study in a great diversity of courses and research seminars. Disagreement, however, is not very high on the regents' list of educational objectives. One might imagine American universities that bring together undergraduate populations where Catholics and Protestants, Zionists and anti-Zionists, Afrikaaners and Zulus, Black Muslims and white conservatives, etc., argue passionately, bound only by codes of conduct prohibiting behavioral crimes and improprieties, sometimes understanding and, indeed, sometimes loathing each other (such being, alas, the human condition). In Massachusetts in the 1990s, however, students (and, indeed, faculty) are not to be trusted with such freedom:

> The policy proscribes all conditions and all actions *or omissions* including all acts of *verbal* harassment or abuse which deny *or have the effect of denying* to anyone his or her rights to equality, *dignity,* and security on the basis of his or her race, color, ethnicity, culture or religion. . . . However, diversity alone will not suffice. There must be a unity and cohesion in the diversity which we seek to achieve. . . . Racism in any form, expressed *or implied,* intentional *or inadvertent,* individual or institutional, constitutes an egregious offense to the tenets of human dignity and to the accords of civility guaranteed by law. . . . The Board of Regents and all its institutions bear a responsibility by edict and an obligation by social morality to *eradicate* racism, ethnic and *cultural offenses and religious intolerance.* . . . (Emphases added.)[6]

I wonder what loophole a Salman Rushdie could find in such a policy? Does this really mean, by the way, that the campuses of Massachusetts no longer will abide any derisive criticism of evangelical Christianity, televangelists, WASP culture, Catholic policies on abortion or women as priests, Southern Baptist views of homosexuality, or Zionism? Don't hold your breath! All such policies create a one-way street of "politically correct" repression and indoctrination.

The obvious political intent of these programs bears underlining. The University of South Carolina offers a "University 101" program, conferences and workshops designed to help the nation's administrators and offices of student life to provide appropriate extracurricular freshman-year experiences. The "special focus" for 1990 was on the most politically correct of all current agendas, "cultural diversity." Past conferences have offered administrators ways of overcoming the "greed" of "the Reagan years" and the sins of "American racism." In justifying the imposition of Diversity Education at the University of Pennsylvania, President Hackney opined that it was not from any failure of his administration that human relations at Penn were so bad, but, rather, from his inability to shield students from the consequences of American political choice: the civil-rights setbacks of the Reagan years and the Bush campaign against Dukakis explained why progress at the university had met such barriers.

At the University of Michigan, the Office of Orientation offers a program, "Commitment to Diversity," that identifies for undergraduates the "various types of discrimination" that they needed to address under official auspices: "race, ethnic origin, handicap status, age, gender, sexual orientation, religion, etc." Noting that people bring different definitions of "discrimination" to campus, the planners of "diversity programs" were advised "to establish clear working definitions for your program planning and then to articulate those to participants." At Penn also, "facilitators" of the freshman class's Diversity Education were advised "to define terms" for their young charges, for purposes of clarifying discussion. Penn's program is now considered a model for the country among the "diversity" networkers, so citizens interested in free and tolerant universities should monitor closely the evolution of the campuses they observe. Alas, one should expect the appearance of an official set of definitions as particular and catechistical as the definitions of "faith" and "grace" in any Christian sect.

Thus, for example, "people of color" is defined as "[a] term of solidarity referring to Asians, Blacks, Latinos, Native Americans and Pacific Islanders." (White, presumably, is not a color, and white students are the bloc with reference to whom students "of color" need to feel "solidarity." So much for a campus of individuals!) "Third World" is defined with candid political clarity: "Third world countries have a shared history of economic exploitation and oppression by colonialist powers." (So much for debates among development theorists!) "Heterosexism," again outlawed, is defined as "[a]ttitudes, actions, or institutional practices which subordinate individuals whose sexual orientation is not heterosexual," and it arises from "homophobia," which is "fear or disapproval of attitudes and actions associated with homosexuality and bisexuality."[7] Smith College provided students with a list of "Specific Manifestations of Oppression," defining, among other offenses, "lookism" as "the belief that appearance is an indicator of a person's value" and "ableism" as the "oppression of the differently abled by the temporarily abled."[8] (So much for the "Personals" of *Lingua Franca!*)

IV

One problem that the new *in loco parentis* agenda faces, of course, is that blacks, women, and gays are in fact remarkably diverse and individuated groups on American campuses (and elsewhere)—groups whose members distribute themselves voluntarily across the broad spectrum of political, religious, and moral attitudes and affiliations. Furthermore, blacks, women, and gays see their self-identities in a myriad of individual ways, some placing very little public or political importance on their skin color, sex, or sexual preferences. For many if not most Americans, authentic liberation means the right to define oneself free of imposed stereotypes, to individuate according to the lights of individual conscience, to choose one's affiliations oneself, and to be judged on merit by the quality of one's work and character.

Such individualism, however, as noted, stands directly opposed to the group-think of today's universities. At planning sessions of Penn's Diversity Education programs, for example, one courageous female undergraduate sent a memo to her fellow participants expressing her deep regard for individual rights, identities, and value judgments, and her "desire to protect the freedoms of all members of society." She added:

> The desire of the committee to continually consider the collective before the individual is misconceived. At Penn we should be concerned with the intellect and experience of INDIVIDUALS before we are concerned with the group. Within any group, there are so many diverse and individual experiences that it is impossible to incorporate them into one neat package we might call a group experience. Higher education is the arena in which students develop their critical and analytic skills. It is only these skills, our method of thinking, which can serve to enlighten us. The desire of this subcommittee to dictate what to think regarding groups or individuals does not constitute education; it is merely a process of thought homogenization. Standardization of attitudes destroys intellectual diversity, which is an essential component of education. Higher education may affect an individual's decision to be socially progressive or to be socially conservative; however, education should never be manipulated to achieve one end or the other.

An administrator serving on this committee circled the word "individuals" in this paragraph, and replied to her as follows: "This is a 'RED FLAG' phrase today, which is considered by many to be RACIST. Arguments that champion the individual over the group ultimately privileges [*sic*] the 'individuals' belonging to the largest or dominant group." In a passage of Orwellian double-think, the administrator informed the undergraduate that "in a pluralistic society, individuals are only as significant as their group." Another member of this committee formed to plan the moral introduction of Penn freshmen to university life replied to her argument with the observation that "[f]our-hundred years of educational manipulation by various individuals has indeed retarded social progressiveness." He noted that "[i]f allowing students to pursue their own diversity education would produce an atmosphere of tolerance, Penn would be an ideal campus. Unfortunately, these same individuals have chosen to ignore such social [*sic*] progressive notions." He concluded that "[r]elying on the good-nature of 'intellectually stimulated individuals' doesn't work; we have seen the results." Welcome to the university of the 1990s!

To deal with individuals who depart from the solidarity of group identities and politically correct group agendas, the stand-in parental "facilitators" of today's universities have created the institutions and official ideas requisite to their "progressive" goals. Thus, most major universities have "women's centers" whose radical-feminist directors nominally represent the real interests and needs of "women" per se, but who, in fact, represent some small minority of women. Rising to high salaries and bloated staffs on the basis of their claim to embody the objective interests of women everywhere, they "represent" women in the manner in which Bolsheviks "represented" the real interests of Russian and Eastern European workers. Women's centers certainly do not speak for anti-abortion Catholic women, or orthodox Jewish women, or Republican women, or moderate women, or Islamic women, etc., etc., etc. Thus, most major universities have left-activist black centers or minority centers that have never invited a conservative black to speak on any issue, that promulgate official institutional notions of "racism," and that pretend that "minority culture" forms some political and moral unity on campus. At Penn and most campuses, such centers are given privileged roles in committees, in extracurricular education, and in enforcement of politically defined anti-racist and anti-sexist codes. Imagine if the Maryknoll nuns or anti–Vatican II traditionalists were made the official voices of Catholics on campuses, or if the Lubavitcher Rebbe were given the role of representing all undergraduate Jews, or if Trotskyite sectarians were named the representatives of undergraduates from labor union families. How demeaning! How antithetical to real freedom! How contrary to the goal of free minds in a free society!

Campuses rely desperately on concepts of "false consciousness" and "internalized oppression" to explain away the individuation or lack of militancy of what they see as "historically oppressed groups." In her first interview with the campus newspaper in 1985, the new director of Penn's Women's Center opined that "[w]omen have been socialized into a passive role." Obviously unfamiliar with the women we all teach at Penn, she insisted that "any time there are men in the group, men tend to dominate the discussion." In 1989, the "General Guidelines, Suggested Issues and Resources" report for Penn's "Diversity Follow-Up Programs" alerted facilitators to the issue of "why certain group members continue victim behavior," and warned that "these programs will probably entail medium to high personal/emotional involvement."

In the list of definitions circulated at the planning sessions of Diversity Education, participants were introduced to "Internalized Oppression and Psychological Captivity," defined as "states of mind in which subordinated individuals accept stereotypes and myths of themselves that are perpetuated by dominant society. Acceptance of these prejudiced images and attitudes influence [sic] the behavior of subordinates." Seeking to sensitize women to their "oppression," to less obvious forms of "discrimination" and "harassment," the planning papers of the Penn committees on Diversity Education listed as sexual harassment not only "flirting" on the part of a graduate teaching assistant, but "many explicit sexual jokes," "nude slides in class presentations," and "stupid women jokes." The explanation of "sexual discrimination," which is illegal at Penn, included "seeming invisibility of women," "women's names not remembered/not introduced," "double standards in sexuality and socialization," and (quoting directly from the full entry in the document) "body image: eating disorders, clothes."[9] The "place" of the new "parents" is large indeed.

The lengths to which universities will go to reinforce politically correct group identities rather than individual identities received a kind of *reductio ad absurdum* at the University of Pennsylvania in February 1992, when the Student Health Office organized a set of "Eroticizing Safer Sex Workshops" according to officially designated groups. Thus, in addition to the February 10 "Eroticizing Safer Sex: Workshop for Gay and Bisexual Men," there was a February 11 "Workshop for Lesbian and Bisexual Women," a February 12 "Workshop for Straight Women" and, apart from that, a "Workshop for Men of Color," and, on February 13, a "Workshop for Straight Men" and a "Workshop for Women of Color." Even in the presence of possible death, group identities define being. (If it is any consolation, almost no one attended any of these.)

Not only does this agenda dominate extracurricular "educational" programs at the University of Pennsylvania, but, increasingly, it dominates the adjudication of behavioral infractions as well. In the first instance, Diversity Education programming is required in all first-year dormitories and encouraged in all other residential areas. The mandatory topics are racism, sexism, and heterosexism, but dormitories are free to add, at their discretion, the topics of ageism, ableism, and religious discrimination. A Resource Manual offers a stunningly tendentious definition of problems (e.g., "Racism at Penn"; "Sexism Manifested at Penn in Interactions among Penn's Community Members"; "Sexism/Women's Clergy"; and "Internalized Homophobia") and a breathtakingly narrow and tendentious bibliography of suggested further readings on politically correct topics from politically correct texts. What evangelical or conservative student would apply to be a resident advisor in such a program? In the second instance, the adjudication of behavioral infractions, a growing number of disciplinary cases are resolved by what the university euphemistically calls "educational programming." One student, for example, in a process that is, I fear, increasingly common but largely hidden from public scrutiny, was offered (by the Judicial Inquiry Officer of the University, who reports directly to the Vice-Provost for University Life) the following alternative to going through an actual hearing on the facts of a case:

> Participate in a comprehensive program on sexual harassment, except for the time you are attending classes for which you have registered at the University or are reporting to employment. Said programming shall include weekly assignments which must be performed during each week in which classes are in session through the Spring . . . term. You will be required to present written evidence of completion of assignments and a satisfactory performance must be documented by Ms. Elena DiLapi, Director of the Women's Center, or her representative, before your transcript can be released.[10]

At the University of Beijing, they had a name for all this: thought-reform. In an America committed to free minds and free souls, we once had names for all this: brainwashing and indoctrination. It is the antithesis of education. The politicization of the *in loco parentis* role of American universities has brought into being a vast army of coercive consciousness-raisers and brainwashers, generally in control of the university beyond the classroom (a classroom, note well, from which their presence is not exactly absent). Astonishingly, there is almost no awareness, scrutiny, analysis, and criticism of their role. The revived *in loco parentis* agency at our universities is a partisan abandonment of the freedoms of conscience and expression won by undergraduates in the 1960s. Its goal, under the heirs of the sixties, is the political indoctrination and New Age moral reformation of moderate undergraduates deemed to be the benighted products of a benighted society. Trustees, regents, administrators, faculty, and students who collaborate in this indoctrination should be ashamed of themselves; donors, parents, and undergraduates should look before they leap.

We all should be anguished about this state of affairs, but not wholly discouraged. Recall those "Personals" in *Lingua Franca*. The ideological bullies are in the driver's seat, but they are all too human, and they cannot abolish human nature either in our students or in themselves. Nonetheless, at institutions where students of the most variegated diversities should be invited to participate as free and self-defining individuals in the higher life of the mind, they are, instead, being subjected to external definition by people unworthy of the name of educators. We should not expect the situation to improve spontaneously. The dynamic in place now is self-perpetuating: the very people whose roles and budgets depend upon the belief that our campuses are beset by unparalleled racial, sexual, and sexual-preferential conflicts are the very people charged with assessing the depth of those conflicts; and the more the social workers stress essential group identity, the more likely it will be, alas, that individuals will perceive themselves as separated by essential group differences. When will the nation notice? When will responsible and moral souls respond?

NOTES

1. This is doubly sad, since there are few persons in academic administration with more integrity and tolerance than Vartan Gregorian.
2. "Diversity Education Labor Day Program: Facilitator's Guide," Office of the Vice-Provost for University Life, University of Pennsylvania, pp. 11–13. See also the preliminary "Sexual, Racial, and Ethnic Harassment Policy Resource Manual," Offices of the President, Provost, and Vice-Provost for University Life, University of Pennsylvania, May 1988. All relevant documents pertaining to the University of Pennsylvania (including, in this particular case, the planning documents and committee reports for Diversity Education, the facilitators' manual, and the minutes of relevant meetings of the University Council) are in the author's possession. Throughout, unless otherwise specified, all documents cited are in the author's collection. Authors quoting from these materials may be assured that these documents would be available to them in the case of any *subpoena duces tecum*.
3. The neo-Marxist Italian theoretician and Communist activist Antonio Gramsci offered (among other things) a serious analysis of culture as a complex system for creating and reinforcing the hegemony of certain groups and the submission of others. The ubiquitous neo-Gramscians of today's campuses (often "Gramscian" without having read Gramsci) have vulgarized his analysis of culture into a magical formula for the explanation of why the world makes them angry and unhappy and why it should make all others, once "culture" is demystified, feel the same.

4. "Racial Awareness Workshops [Glossary of Terms]," Spring 1982, and "Memorandum from Janice Somerville to University Life Staff . . . Racism Awareness Training Questionnaire . . . July 6, 1982," Office of the Vice-Provost Janice Somerville, University of Pennsylvania. See also "Initiatives for the Race and Gender Enrichment of Tulane University of Louisiana," Office of the President, Tulane University, June 4, 1990: "Racism and sexism are pervasive in America and are fundamentally present in all American instituituions. . . . It is difficult for us to see and overcome racism and sexism because we are all a product of the problem, i.e. we are all the progeny of a racist and sexist society." The Penn literature, questionnaire and all related documents are in the possession of the author. The same Penn "awareness seminar" drew its definition of "individual vs. institutional racism" from Stokely Carmichael and Charles V. Hamilton, *Black Power: The Politics of Liberation in America* (New York: Random House, 1967). See also, at the University of Pennsylvania's Programming Resource Center, Printed Resource Library Materials, under "African-American Issues— Racism": *A Seminar in Awareness* (University of Pennsylvania); *Syllabus for Facilitators of Racial Awareness* (University of Pennsylvania); and *Racism Awareness Outreach Training Workshop* (University of Pennsylvania). In its 1991 bibliography for resident advisors in charge of "educational" programming, the Programming Resource Center of the University of Pennsylvania offered *one* title under the heading of "African-American Issues— Women and Racism": Angela Y. Davis, *Violence against Women and the Ongoing Challenge to Racism* (Latham, NY: Kitchen Table Press, 1985); there is no doubt that programmers could learn something about violence and challenge from Ms. Davis.
5. "Glossary of Terms . . . ," Office of the Vice-Provost for University Life, University of Pennsylvania, circulated to the Committee on Diversity Education Program, Spring 1989. Subcommittee reports of the committee, also referred to below, are all in the possession of the author.
6. "Policy Against Racism and Guidelines for Campus Policies Against Racism, June 13, 1989," Board of Regents of Higher Education for the Commonwealth of Massachusetts, pp. 2–6.
7. "Glossary of Terms," Committee on Diversity Education, Office of the Vice-Provost for University Life, University of Pennsylvania. The "Oversight Committee on Diversity Education, March 16, 1989 [Minutes]" record that the Penn committee was told the following by Brown University's Assistant Dean of the College, Jean Wu: "Issues are hard to discuss because students have so little vocabulary to use. The experience [of diversity education at Brown] teaches the vocabulary. The facilitators set the tone on how to discuss the issues. . . . Historical data is [*sic*] given to justify the choices [of 'isms']. Fact sheets are distributed that summarize the history of the issue related to university history, U.S. History and the political climate." All documents are in my possession.
8. "Definitions," a handout published by the Office of Student Affairs, Smith College, 1990.
9. "Gender Issues Program Block Outline" [2 pp.], Subcommittee on Diversity Education Follow-Up Programs, Office of the Vice-Provost for University Life, University of Pennsylvania. The document is in my possession.
10. This document is in my possession.

Liberal Intolerance

Joseph Hamburger

I

It is widely believed that persecution originates on the right among defenders of establishments who nervously and shamelessly punish those who undermine the legitimacy of the social order and the existing distribution of privileges. Thus, it is churches that have punished dissenters and atheists, aristocracies that suppressed democratic critics, and bourgeois Babbitts that tried to put down radicals. Looking at the other side of this coin, we can see that liberalism has carried on the struggle for liberty of the press, for toleration and openness. It has provided the martyrs and won the victory for freedom. An even-handed historian might argue that some on the left, for example, radical religious sectarians in the seventeenth century, also were capable of persecution, but, on the whole, in our tradition, this picture is correct. And thus it is all the more startling when we discover a linkage between liberalism and intolerance.

This connection was noticed as early as 1874 by longtime *Economist* editor Walter Bagehot. He had witnessed a greatly increased liberty for the expression of opinion, and being liberal-minded, he was grateful for the change, since things were being said which, only ten years earlier, would have led to disapproval and social penalties. Yet he was surprised to find that "some writers, whose pens are just set at liberty, and who would, not at all long ago, have been turned out of society for the things that they say, are setting themselves to explain the 'weakness' of liberty, and to extol the advantages of persecution."[1]

Bagehot, trying to explain the inclination to persecute, recognized that it could be found on both sides of the political spectrum. Advocates of any opinion might wish to suppress its opposite. It was a matter of temperament. While there were cool, calm, and quiet minds in which the intellectual component of belief predominated, there were also others in which emotion was the largest part, and they were eager, strong, and intense.[2] Such persons, Bagehot wrote,

> wish, above all things, to propagate [their] opinions. They find close at hand what seems an immense engine for that propagation; they find the State, which has often in history interfered for and against opinions,—which has had a great and undeniable influence in helping some and hindering others,—and in their eagerness they can hardly understand why they should not make use of this great engine to crush the errors which they hate, and to replace them with the tenets they approve. So long as there are earnest believers in the world, they will always wish to punish opinions, even if their judgment tells them it is unwise, and their conscience that it is wrong.[3]

The persecutors, Bagehot explained, "not only . . . wish to diffuse doctrinal truth, but also . . . cannot bear to hear the words of a creed different from their own."[4]

This brings us to our own times. We hardly need to be reminded of current manifestations of the persecutory spirit within the academic community. It arises, as Bagehot would have said, from a wish to propagate an opinion; nowadays it is the opinion that our most urgent need is to remove obstacles to equality, especially those connected with race, class, and gender. Those who hold this opinion may not be a majority, yet their beliefs have attained the status of orthodoxy, and those who openly dispute them are execrated as racist, sexist, or elitist—the late-twentieth-century euphemisms for "heretic." The penalties for heresy, of course, have not reached seventeenth-century standards of severity—ears have not been removed, nor tongues cut out, nor has anyone been pilloried (at least, not literally), let alone burned at the stake—but the guilty have been made to suffer consequences, all the same. Classes have been boycotted, employment affected, and those with offensive beliefs have been slandered and ridiculed and made the target of moral outrage.

The persecution has a ripple effect and reaches many who do not openly oppose the orthodoxy. Most university teachers neither openly oppose, nor wholeheartedly subscribe to it, but all the same, many are intimidated, and consequently, the curriculum and research agendas are shaped in response to the powerful moral and social pressures generated by the orthodoxy.[5] If anyone doubts this, they might examine typical course offerings and the topics of papers presented at academic conferences. But the demands for conformity go further, to the way we speak and write, so that now there are guides identifying acceptable and taboo words and modes of expression.[6] The language police have joined forces with ubiquitous invisible censors whose prohibitions make it clear that there are forbidden words, unacceptable thoughts, and dangerous ideas.

It should be noted, though, that not all the censors are invisible. The literary scholar Stanley Fish notoriously asserts, "There's no such thing as free speech and its a good thing, too." The First Amendment, he argues, does not provide an absolute right, for it does not protect speech that has a tendency to incite violence.[7] Moreover, in the traditional theoretical literature bearing on free speech and liberty of the press (e.g., John Milton, William Blackstone), there were assumptions and limitations that allowed for significant denials of freedom to publish. Fish contends that this will always be the case:

> When I say that there is no such thing as free speech, I mean that there is no class of utterances separable from the world of conduct, no "merely" cognitive expressions whose effects can be confined to some prophylactically sealed area of public discourse. And since it is just such expressions that are privileged by the First Amendment (it is expressions free of certain consequences that are to be freely allowed), there is nothing for the amendment to protect, no items in the category "free expression."[8]

Because all speech has implications for conduct, indeed, is conduct, it becomes necessary to evaluate it (and by implication, its publication) in light of its consequences: "speech always matters; because everything we say impinges on the world in ways indistinguishable from the effects of physical action, we must take responsibility for our verbal performances." Fish focuses on university speech codes and concludes that, in view of the dreadful consequences of protecting ugly, hateful, bigoted speech (and who is to say the speech he refers to should not be described in this way?), such codes are desirable.[9] He makes it clear that each case must be decided on its merits, there being no principle that will decide for us, and thus we are left uncertain how far such a policy will carry us and how frequently such judgments will be made. Fish seeks to justify much more than speech codes: he offers a rationale for continuing evaluation of speech and publication and therefore for censorship.

This new censorship is not all that new. Almost thirty years ago, we were treated to an even more candid defense of censorship in the small but notable volume *A Critique of Pure Tolerance*. In it, Herbert

Marcuse, with support from Robert Paul Wolff and Barrington Moore, shamelessly criticized toleration and defended suppression of speech he did not approve. Tolerance, he complained, allows for the expression of views that support the kind of society he found objectionable:

> When tolerance mainly serves the protection and preservation of a repressive society, when it serves to neutralize opposition and to render men immune against other and better forms of life, then tolerance has been perverted.[10]

> Tolerance is extended to policies, conditions, and modes of behavior which should not be tolerated because they are impeding, if not destroying, the chances of creating an existence without fear and misery.[11]

Consequently, suppression is justified. Referring to policies, opinions, and movements, Marcuse, with extraordinary insouciance, said: "Suppression of the regressive ones is a prerequisite for the strengthening of the progressive ones."[12] He left no doubt about the targets and beneficiaries when he added: "Liberating tolerance, then, would mean intolerance against movements from the Right, and toleration of movements from the Left."[13]

These are not isolated passages but are the main burden of Marcuse's argument:

> Tolerance cannot be indiscriminate and equal with respect to the contents of expression, neither in word nor in deed; it cannot protect false words and wrong deeds which demonstrate that they contradict and counteract the possibilities of liberation. . . . Certain things cannot be said, certain ideas cannot be expressed, certain policies cannot be proposed, certain behavior cannot be permitted without making tolerance an instrument for the continuation of servitude.[14]

Although he addressed the question of free expression in society generally, Marcuse proved himself a prophet with respect to universities. With something like a parody of Rousseauian argument, he suggested that the removal of reactionary forces "could conceivably be *enforced* by the students and teachers themselves, and thus be *self-imposed.*"[15] (Italics added.) His actual expectations, however, were not concealed: "[T]he restoration of freedom of thought [take note of the doublespeak] may necessitate new and rigid restrictions on teachings and practices in the educational institutions which, by their very methods and concepts, serve to enclose the mind within the established universe of discourse and behavior—thereby precluding a priori a rational evaluation of the alternatives."[16]

II

It might be suggested that the recent calls for enforcing an orthodoxy are perhaps too idiosyncratic to be taken seriously as a long-term threat. This would be consoling, were it not possible to find a provenance for them in the most respectable of liberal (and in our time, mainstream) authors—John Stuart Mill. Of course, Mill was an advocate of liberty of thought and discussion and of individuality, but, as will be shown, even in *On Liberty* he adopted troubling views which make his support for individual liberty anything but unequivocal. In fact, it will be shown that Mill anticipated what might be called liberal intolerance.

This claim may be greeted with disbelief, for on the surface it appears incompatible with the argument of *On Liberty*. Perhaps it will be seen as worth examining, however, if Mill's description of his purpose is considered. We have a report of a conversation in 1854 with George Grote, a former radical Member of Parliament and a historian of ancient Greece, with whom Mill had been a close friend for the previous thirty-five years. While planning *On Liberty,* Mill told Grote "that he was cogitating an essay to point out what things society forbade that it ought not, and what things it left alone that it ought to control."[17] It is clear that he placed as much emphasis on control as on liberty.

Turning to *On Liberty,* however, the overwhelming impression is that Mill opposes control, whether arising from the state or from public opinion. This is most evident in his defense of liberty of thought and discussion, but the tone, rhetoric, and argument of the book strongly suggest that he would also maximize freedom in the realm of conduct.

It will be recalled that Mill drew a distinction between actions that are self-regarding and others that are other-regarding. That which concerns the interests of others or of society is other-regarding; and that which primarily concerns the individual is self-regarding. "The only part of the conduct of any one, for which he is amenable to society, is that which concerns others. In the part which merely concerns himself, his independence is, of right, absolute. Over himself, over his own body and mind, the individual is sovereign."[18] This distinction is used to determine whether punishment or interference is justified. Mill argues that, if conduct clearly harms others or violates a clearly defined obligation to them or to society, then punishment, either through the instrument of law or through "moral reprobation" (279), is justified. Mill's discussion of this distinction, however, gives the strong impression that the self-regarding realm will be very large and that other-regarding actions that harm others will occur quite infrequently. This impression is created by passages such as the one characterizing other-regarding actions: if a person "is led to violate a distinct and assignable obligation to any other person or persons, the case is taken out of the self-regarding class" (281). Examples of this are the soldier who is drunk while on duty and the man whose self-indulgence leads to a breach of duty to family or creditors. If such consequences do not occur, however, "the interest which society has in him individually . . . is fractional, and altogether indirect" (277). With regard to his own affairs, "[i]ndividuality has its proper field of action" (277).

It turns out, however, that society's interest is anything but fractional. Mill's examples suggest that society has a comprehensive and far-reaching interest in how we behave. He would legally punish persons on welfare if they lived in idleness (295) and parents who neglected the education of their children (301); and he would forbid marriage to those likely to have children without ordinary chances for a desirable existence (304). Going even further—much further—he would use the pressures of public opinion to penalize, as harmful to others, falsehood or duplicity in dealing with them; unfair or ungenerous use of advantages over them; and selfish abstinence from defending them against injury (279).

But Mill goes even beyond this. He takes an extraordinary step and enlarges this sphere to include "not only these acts, but the *dispositions* which lead to them" (279; italics added). These are "properly immoral, and fit subjects of disapprobation which may rise to abhorrence" (279); that is, harsh moral judgments operating through public opinion may be used to punish such dispositions or features of character and personality. It is illuminating to consider Mill's examples of the tendencies of personality that he would punish:

> Cruelty of disposition; malice and ill-nature; that most anti-social and odious of all passions, envy; dissimulation and insincerity; irascibility on insufficient cause, and resentment disproportioned to the provocation; the love of domineering over others; the desire to engross more than one's share of advantages . . . ; the pride which derives gratification from the abasement of others; the egotism which thinks self and its concerns more important than everything else, and decides all doubtful questions in its own favour;—these are moral vices, and constitute a bad and odious moral character. (279)

All of these are subject to the penalty of social disapproval, even though they are only dispositions, vices, manifestations of character, and not actions. I need not emphasize that some of them are commonplace, especially where competition is fierce, and that most of them are more easily included in accusations than proven. Here we have Mill encouraging the expression of "moral reprobation, and in grave cases, of moral retribution and punishment" (279), that is, the application of severe, intrusive, intimidating social pressure. Yet in the same work, in passages that have given his book its reputation as a justification for maximum permissiveness and freedom, he condemned social pressures that denied choice, and he complained that "society has now fairly got the better of individuality; and the danger which threatens human nature is not the excess, but the deficiency, of personal impulses and preferences" (264). Having deplored "a hostile and dreaded censorship" (264), he also advocated using public opinion in ways which, from the point of view of those penalized, would be indistinguishable from censorship. I conclude that whenever any of the dispositions mentioned by Mill appear, liberty would be restricted by him. By making dispositions and character defects punishable, Mill was giving extraordinary discretion to those who set standards and defined what constituted a character defect.

So much for the other-regarding sphere. When we turn to the self-regarding sphere—where the individual is supposed to be sovereign—we find that Mill opens the door to even greater threats to liberty and advocates a surprising reliance on social pressures as a means of exercising control. This self-regarding realm was supposed to be the area in which the individual was free to do as he likes—and presumably also to be what he is—on the assumption that he was not harming others. This was the sphere of action "comprehending all that portion of a person's life and conduct which affects only himself"; it was "the appropriate region of human liberty"; and it included "liberty of tastes and pursuits; of framing the plan of our life to suit our own character; of doing as we like, subject to such consequences as may follow: without impediment from our fellow-creatures, so long as what we do does not harm them, even though they should think our conduct foolish, perverse, or wrong" (225–26). And in another passage, we are told that here "there should be perfect freedom, legal and social, to do the action and stand the consequences" (276).

The consequences, it turns out, will be considerable. In spite of appearances that the self-regarding sphere is a great open space, personal to ourselves, where individuality will flourish, in an inconspicuous passage Mill provided a vast opening for the intrusion of coercive social pressures in this realm. Mill reveals that "the feelings with which a person is regarded by others, ought . . . to be . . . affected by his self-regarding qualities or deficiencies" (277–78).[19] If the person is eminent in qualities conducing to his own good, he will be admired; *but* "if he is grossly deficient in those qualities, a sentiment the opposite of admiration will follow" (278). When we discover what elicits harsh judgments, we find that it is a mixture of conduct and aspects of character—such things as rashness, obstinacy, self-conceit, not living within moderate means, inability to avoid hurtful indulgences, and the pursuit of animal pleasures at the expense of feeling and intellect (278). (It may be asked: Except for the saints among us, who is not at least occasionally guilty of some of these defects?) Without liking the words, Mill describes such persons as having "lowness or depravation of taste" and as "being[s] of an inferior order" (278).

Right-thinking persons, he made it clear, would regard depraved and inferior persons as objects of "distaste, or, in extreme cases, even of contempt." They would avoid the society of such persons, and though he avoids the word ostracism, he tells us that "we have a right, and it may be our duty, to caution others against him, if we think his example or conversation likely to have a pernicious effect on those with whom he associates" (278).

I suggest that conduct or ways of life or even character traits or dispositions that Mill labels depraved and inferior are subject to social pressures from the right-minded that in effect are punishments, and that even in this self-regarding sphere, liberty can be restricted. Mill confirms this: "A person may suffer very severe penalties at the hands of others, for faults which directly concern only himself" (278), that is, for conduct that, by Mill's definition, must be labeled "self-regarding."

Mill wrote a sentence or two indicating that these penalties ought not to be intended as punishments. They were the inevitable, natural consequence of right-thinking persons acting in accord with their individuality. His normative language, however, made it clear that he advocated the making of harsh judgments by the right-minded. Such judgments "ought" to be made. It would be well, he said, if politeness were overcome and this good office were more freely rendered (278).

The penalties for self-regarding deficiencies so far mentioned have been contempt and ostracism—varieties of social pressure. Within this self-regarding sphere, Mill also advocated legislative interference and, therefore, legally sanctioned punishment. He noted that there are "obvious limitations to the maxim, that purely self-regarding misconduct cannot properly be meddled with in the way of prevention or punishment," and that these limitations derived from "the right inherent in society, to ward off crimes against itself by antecedent precautions" (295). In this connection he gave the example of drunkenness in a person previously convicted of violence against another while under the influence of drink. Such a person has committed a crime simply in virtue of becoming drunk again, even if the violent act is not repeated (295).

There is clear evidence, then, that Mill would both legally punish and restrict the persons he labeled depraved and inferior; and, using the pressures of public opinion, he would penalize and intimidate them. In both cases their liberty would be diminished. His willingness to penalize such persons was not a result of careless composition, for Mill said: "There was not a sentence in [*On Liberty*] that was not several times gone over by us [he and his wife] together, turned over in many ways, and laboriously weeded of any imperfection we could discover either in thought or expression."[20] Nor was it an insignificant exception to his argument or an unnoticed inconsistency; nor was he merely recommending the innocuous enforcement of those rules defining decent or civilized conduct which, though restricting choice, do not seriously diminish meaningful liberty. Such explanations fail to take account of evidence that Mill deliberately provided for social controls and that (as will be shown) these social controls were designed to perform an important function in the implementation of his strategy for reform.

The targets of Mill's condemnation become even clearer in other writings of this period, especially *Utilitarianism* and "Utility of Religion," where we also find a more elaborate account of the ways those targeted will be controlled and by whom. In *Utilitarianism,* where Mill describes the truly human, higher pleasures to which all might aspire, he also portrays the contrast—the quest for animal pleasures, selfishness, the want of mental cultivation of the fool, the pig-like person whose condition is that of "a selfish egotist, devoid of every feeling or care but those which centre in his own miserable individuality."[21] This description in *Utilitarianism* is entirely consistent with what appears in *On Liberty,* where the depraved and inferior persons are also characterized by selfishness and the wish for gratification of animal appetites.

We also note that Mill's phrase "miserable individuality" can be juxtaposed with his well-known celebration of individuality in chapter three of *On Liberty.* If we compare the two, it becomes clear that not all manifestations of individuality have his approval, nor will they all be unleashed, nor will all restraints be thrown off in his favored regime.

Mill also makes clear, in writings other than *On Liberty,* how he would use extra-legal methods which can only be described as social controls. In the distant future, when utilitarian morality would be widely shared, control would be achieved through education[22] and conscience,[23] but meanwhile, during the transitional period, he relied heavily on opinion—a device condemned in much of *On Liberty,* though sanctioned in the inconspicuous passages from which I have already quoted. This included the power of praise and blame and favor and disfavor from others, and it was called "a source of strength inherent in any system of moral belief."[24] Mill recognized that through public opinion one could appeal to the love of glory, of praise, of admiration, of respect and deference, and of sympathy. On the other hand, public opinion also had a "deterring force." "The fear of shame, the dread of ill repute, or of being disliked or hated, are the direct and simple forms of its deterring power." These fears and dreads could be manipulated in even harsher ways, however. Worse than knowing one is the object of such sentiments,

> the deterring force of the unfavorable sentiments of mankind . . . includes all the penalties which they can inflict: exclusion from social intercourse and from the innumerable good offices which human beings require from one another; the forfeiture of all that is called success in life; often the great diminution or total loss of means of subsistence; positive ill offices of various kinds sufficient to render life miserable, and reaching in some states of society as far as actual persecution to death.[25]

There is no question that Mill approved the use of some of these sanctions, for he described their use in an imaginary society which he upheld as desirable. In it there would be "a morality grounded on large and wise views of the good of the whole, neither sacrificing the individual to the aggregate nor the aggregate to the individual but giving to duty on the one hand and to freedom and spontaneity on the other their proper province." In this society the inferiors were to be deterred from disapproved conduct by using "the superadded force of shame."[26] This, of course, is a more candid description of what he advocated in *On Liberty,* where he had right-minded persons disapproving those inferior beings who had self-regarding faults.

Why, we might ask, did Mill, the famous advocate of liberty, try to justify penalties, restraints, and control? By answering this question we will discover parallels with intellectuals of the modern left. During the 1850s, Mill fundamentally changed his political agenda and became much more radical than he had been. He developed visionary hopes for the future, but at the same time became aware of deeply entrenched obstacles to fulfilling them—obstacles connected with long cultural traditions and with what seemed to be human nature itself. To overcome them, in view of the morally compelling character of the goal, control became an acceptable means.

During this period, Mill reassessed the reform movement he had been associated with since his youth. It had accomplished a great deal in the way of institutional reform, but the considerable changes that had been made produced fewer benefits than anticipated, for "they had produced very little improvement in that which all real amelioration in the lot of mankind depends on, their intellectual and moral state." Consequently, he shifted his attention away from policies and institutions and towards the "habits of mind" from which all else flowed. Now he looked for change in "the fundamental constitution of . . . modes of thought," and therefore he devoted himself to bringing about nothing less than "a renovation . . . in the basis of . . . belief."[27] This modest undertaking aimed not only at removing existing errors and false beliefs, but also at nothing less than "the reconstruction of the human intellect."[28] Disappointed with the fruits of institutional reform, Mill now looked for nothing less than cultural transformation.

This project was to unfold in two stages. First, it was necessary to clear away the false notions and bad mental habits that prevented the growth of something better. "The old opinions in religion, morals, and politics," although discredited among advanced thinkers (that is, among Mill and his like-minded friends), "have still life enough in them to be a powerful obstacle to the growing up of any better opinions on those subjects." This undergrowth—and he had in mind, mainly, customary morals and religion—had to be cleared away in order to set the stage for a renovation in the basis of belief. Once the old ethos had disintegrated, a new utilitarian ethics was to emerge. After first becoming established by advanced thinkers, it would become part of "some faith, whether religious or merely human."[29] Thus, it would be incorporated into and be reinforced by the "religion of the future."[30] This made him look favorably (in spite of some hesitations) on the idea, derived from the French philosopher Auguste Comte, of "making *le culte de l'humanité* perform the functions and supply the place of a religion."[31]

The old ethos that had to be cleared away was distinguished by a belief that the greatest good could be experienced by individuals regardless of what happened to others. These goods were animal pleasures, and the pursuit of them was reinforced by the assumption that selfishness and egotism were inherently part of human nature. This selfish morality was closely tied to Christianity, which, Mill claimed, also appealed to selfish motives, in its case the selfish wish for salvation.[32] For this among other reasons, Mill wished to extirpate what he called the "poisonous root" of religion, including Christianity.[33]

The new ethos to which he looked forward, in contrast, emphasized an altruism which reflected "the ideal perfection of utilitarian morality." It called for "the happiness, or . . . the interest, of every individual, [being] as nearly as possible in harmony with the interest of the whole."[34] Each person was to consult the welfare of others, and more, he was "to identify his *feelings* . . . with their good."[35] This new ethos would promote "the great purpose of moral culture, the strengthening of the unselfish and weakening of the selfish element in our nature."[36]

This vision and its validation was the work of philosophers, but its implementation ultimately was to come from fundamental changes in education and religion. The new "feeling of unity with our fellow creatures" was to be deeply rooted in our character and in "our own consciousness as completely [as if it were] a part of our nature."[37] Such an ethical outlook, were it to be established, would require a vast cultural transformation, and, understanding this, Mill recognized that only something as compelling as a new religion could bring about the changes in consciousness, motivations, and beliefs that would be necessary. With this in mind, he recommended that the new outlook "be taught as a religion, and the whole force of education, of institutions, and of opinion, [be] directed . . . to make every person grow up from infancy surrounded on all sides both by the profession and by the practice of it." Mill regarded this as entirely feasible and, in spite of uneasiness about some of Comte's proposals, he cited Comte's arguments for such a secular religion as proof of "the possibility of giving to the service of humanity, even without the aid of belief in a Providence, both the psychical power and the social efficacy of a religion; making it take hold of human life, and colour all thought, feeling, and action."[38] Of course, this was the Religion of Humanity, which in writings published during his lifetime, Mill frequently alluded to but almost never mentioned by name.[39]

A question might be raised about the kind and extent of liberty that can exist in a new moral order where all persons are shaped by a secular religion of altruism,[40] but a more immediate threat of control arises during the process of transition to the new arrangements. During this period, in Mill's view, there will be a moral class struggle between those he labeled (with only a modicum of embarrassment) as possessing inferior and superior natures. Whereas the superiors deserved liberty, the inferiors needed to be controlled, for they were (as Mill described them) unthinking, passive, custom-bound, imitative, servile, selfish, vain, egotistical, hedonistic, and pig-like. The superiors, on the other hand, were self-assertive, energetic, choice-making, interesting, eccentric, experimental, unafraid, original, skeptical of Christianity, cultivated, open to change, and modeled on Socrates.[41] This struggle was between those with wholesome individuality and those with miserable individuality; the latter represented the old, selfish ethos, whereas the new altruistic ethos, based on utilitarian morality (as Mill redefined it in *Utilitarianism*), was represented by those few—a kind of vanguard— with the desirable kind of individuality.

The vanguard blazing a path to the new altruistic regime were those with the wholesome individuality eulogized in chapter three of *On*

Liberty. Buried amidst the high-flown liberal rhetoric of this chapter, Mill described the way they would implement his program for reconstruction of the human intellect. They had functions to perform at every stage. They would "point out when what were once truths are true no longer"; that is, they would bring people to recognize that Christianity was a false belief. They would also "discover new truths"; that is, they would contribute to the development of the revised utilitarian ethics which would inform future belief. And finally, they would "commence new practices, and set the example of more enlightened conduct, and better taste and sense in human life"; that is, they would promote the growth of new institutions that would make the new ethics a matter of established habit (267). If successful, the new ethos would become something like a secular religion, and in laying the groundwork for it, Mill was serving as its architect—or, dare it be said?—its prophet.

As I have noted, these passages listing the functions of the persons with individuality appear in chapter three. There was one other function which was introduced—inconspicuously, and with reason—in chapter four. It was to morally discipline the depraved. As those possessing superior natures, those with individuality were to show contempt for, ostracize, and shame the inferiors. In this connection, it should be mentioned that while they were to enjoy tolerance from others, those with individuality were called upon to be judgmental and censorious—the very opposite of tolerant.

With these functions in mind, I suggest that individuality, along with being Mill's ideal of character, was also a carefully crafted description of the kind of character required for a person to serve effectively as part of the vanguard in the cultural and political struggles he wished to promote. Those few that qualified had to be skeptical critics, constructive philosophers, artful founders of a new social order, and moral police.[42] Such varied skills were necessary in view of the magnitude of the task, which included cultural transformation and the reconstituting of our ways of thinking and feeling. Mill contemplated revolutionary change. It was not to come in a sudden explosion, but since it would fundamentally alter values and motivations, it was to be a total revolution. He had in mind a situation in which "the mind of a people [is] stirred up from its foundations," where "the yoke of authority [is] broken," and "an old mental despotism [is] thrown off" (243). The magnitude of the change he looked forward to is indicated by his historical analogies for it—the intellectual fermentation in Germany during the Goethian and Fichtean period; Europe immediately following the Reformation; and the speculative movement at the end of the eighteenth century associated with the philosophes (243).[43] It might be said that such a goal was far-fetched, unreal; but it should be recalled that Mill believed in what he called the "practicability of Utopianism."[44]

III

By recognizing that Mill justified censoriousness as a legitimate way of promoting a new superior moral order, we can discern a link with the defenses of illiberalism that are put forward in our time. Though I am not arguing that Mill is the source of contemporary arguments for intolerance, I am suggesting that he anticipated some of them. I am not claiming that he advocated prohibiting speech and publication, but he did offer encouragement and justification for the vigorous expression of moral disapproval and censure that would have been indistinguishable from the intrusive pressure of public opinion. The mobilization of moral outrage which he advocated would have led to the suppression of the selfish and depraved, just as contemporary intolerance is directed against the bigoted and reactionary. The depraved and the bigoted are not the only targets, however, for inevitably there will be a chilling effect on many others. The campaign unleashed by Stanley Fish and his followers would not only silence bigots but also many others whose inquiries and teaching might suggest the reasonableness of accepting or defending institutions and policies characterized by critics as supporting greed, privilege, prejudice, or inequality. In Mill's case, in spite of his defending liberty of thought and discussion, the moral reprobation which he encouraged would have led to silencing and intimidation and a repressive atmosphere; and it would have been inimical to liberty. Mill's proposals went far beyond gentle encouragements to civility, for he referred to them as penalties which were manifestations of distaste and contempt (282).

This similarity between Mill's way of thinking about reform and the one adopted by some recent theorists suggests the possibility that there may be shared structural features in their arguments that produce the move to intolerance. This possibility invites comparisons, especially with Marcuse, since his extreme position, analytical mind, and forthrightness make him more revealing than many others. In making this comparison, I am not claiming that Mill went as far as Marcuse in advocating repression, nor am I suggesting that they were in all, or even many, respects similar. Unlike Marcuse, Mill was unwilling to encourage or sanction violence; he would not have approved of censorship in the university;[45] he was much more realistic in his expectations; and of course he was much more substantial, morally and intellectually. Yet they were alike in their wish for cultural revolution—for a transformation that went beyond policies and institutions to the ethos, including the character and values, of all the people.

This led to other shared features. Marcuse, like many in the intelligentsia, fundamentally disapproved of capitalistic, bourgeois culture; and he was committed to a morally superior alternative which he wished to bring into existence. Moreover, he had a theory of history which allowed him to assume that radical transformation could take place. These features of his position were the stepping stones to his conclusion that liberty could be restricted: he held that toleration could be withheld from those who by virtue of their attitudes and beliefs were obstacles to the unfolding of the historical process ending in a socialist and just society.

Mill's argument, in spite of all that made him different from Marcuse, included similar characteristics. Mill also was severely critical of existing mores and institutions. An examination of a few of his judgments will indicate how similar he was in this respect to Marcuse. In *On Liberty,* where he described the character that was the polar opposite of the individuality which was his ideal, he provided a portrait of what he regarded as the typical English middle-class person. This person was contemptuously portrayed as passive, slavish to custom, abject, and enervated. He was shaped by Calvinism and had a "narrow theory of life" (265). Such persons thought "that the normal state of human beings is that of struggling to get on; that the trampling, crushing, elbowing, and treading on each other's heels, which form the existing type of social life, are the most desirable lot of human kind."[46] Not surprisingly, he called the English "a remarkably stupid people";[47] and America, by extension, was a place where "the life of the whole of one sex is devoted to dollar-hunting, and of the other to breeding dollar-hunters."[48] To say that Mill was deeply disaffected from his country and its culture would hardly be an exaggeration; nor did Marcuse go further in expressing contempt for middle-class values.

Mill also had a strong conviction that there was a morally superior alternative. It was a completely altruistic society. His condemnation of selfishness in descriptions of English society and in essays about ethics and religion was complemented by the elevation of altruism: "What is wanted is . . . such a state of opinion as may deter the selfish . . . by stamping it as disgraceful."[49] By contrast, each person ought to feel—and ought to be made to feel—"that the good of their country was an object to which all others ought to yield." This he called an "exalted morality" and also a religion, the essence of it being "the strong and earnest direction of the emotions and desires toward an ideal object, recognized as of the highest excellence, and as rightfully paramount over all selfish objects of desire."[50] His revised utilitarianism reflected this judgment, and altruism was the essential feature of his Religion of Humanity. It was not this conviction as such, however, but the certainty with which it was held that laid the groundwork for Mill's approval of restrictive moral and social pressures.

At this stage there is a temptation to suggest that the strength of his conviction was "religious" in character. Of course, Mill notoriously was agnostic and severely critical of Christianity. Yet it is illuminating to consider his ethical beliefs in light of the hypothesis, put forward by Paul Hollander, that many Western intellectuals have put aside the skeptical, critical role and have adopted a quasi-religious perspective. Deeply disaffected from their own societies, they make a "zealous affirmation" with regard to another which is characterized in utopian terms. Of course, Hollander referred to intellectuals' fondness for contemporary "socialist" and totalitarian regimes, whereas Mill's utopia was projected into the future.[51] Apart from this, however, in several ways Hollander's analysis seems applicable to Mill. Like many modern intellectuals, Mill became a spokesman for a secular religion, though, unlike many others, he acknowledged that his beliefs had a religious dimension. In addition to using the phrase "Religion of Humanity," he called it a "religion . . . without a God," and referred to altruistic sentiments as "a real religion."[52] Furthermore, in suggesting that zealous affirmations have filled the ethical void left by the rejection of conventional religion, Hollander offers a plausible explanation for Mill's belief in the necessity of a Religion of Humanity. Moreover, Hollander's description of modern utopias is applicable to Mill's utilitarian morality; they were "purified of individualism, greed, calculation, and the yearning for material and status gain."[53] The "religious" dimension of Mill's thought helps explain his intense moral convictions, which justified restraints and controls.

Like Marcuse, Mill also had a theory of history that confirmed his assumption that a regime based on altruism ultimately could be established. He believed that history moved in a trajectory or progression; and even though he cautiously noted that progress did not necessarily mean improvement, he concluded that "the general tendency is, and will continue to be, saving occasional and temporary exceptions, one of improvement; a tendency towards a better and happier state."[54] This theory was in the main derived from Comte,[55] and it performed a function not unlike Marxism for Marcuse. Mill regarded his own age as transitional—that is, disorganized, marked by conflict, and by disagreements about morality and authority[56]—but he assumed this was not a necessary or permanent condition, and that a stable, harmonious state of society could emerge, one in which there would be agreement about the authority of the morally elevated and intellectually superior. This theory allowed Mill to believe that existing motives, perspectives, and practices, though appearing to be inherently a part of human nature, were in fact changeable. It also allowed him to believe that his vision of the future, though appearing utopian, could be actualized.

The greatest similarity between Mill and Marcuse is to be found in their justifications for restricting liberty. Marcuse had no difficulty in denying toleration to those he characterized as obstacles to the development of a morally superior regime. Thus, the regressive, reactionary right was his target. Mill came close to adopting this position. Those with individuality, the agents of revolutionary cultural change, were to apply morally coercive social pressure to those with "miserable individuality," who in *On Liberty* were inconspicuously described as depraved and inferior (278). They were, in fact, the mediocre mass of selfish, conformist persons whose conduct was shaped by the old, obsolete ethical and religious beliefs. They were distasteful to Mill, but they were additionally objectionable in virtue of their habits of mind, habits which produced stagnation. The English, he complained, of all civilized peoples, were "most wedded to their own customs"; and: "It is remarkable how invariably the instinct of the English people is on the side of the *status quo.*"[57] The achievement of the altruistic society required that such persons change their values, characters, and religion, and until they did, toleration was not to be enjoyed by them.

These parallels remind us that Mill is an early example of what became an identifiable class of intellectuals. Some of the distinctive features of this class are not fully developed in Mill, but some of Mill's attitudes and opinions, though not widely shared in his time, became generic features of the intellectual. Such persons increasingly have become critical of their own societies and have been attracted to proposals for alternative ways of organizing them. Mill appeared early in this evolution, and while disaffected, visionary, and politicized intellectuals are not uncommon today, Mill, whom this description fits, was atypical among his contemporaries.

Intellectuals of this type conceive their function as being concerned with morals and politics, in addition to specifically educational and cultural matters. Their moral function, in this view, consists of serving as custodians of moral standards for society; and from this it is an easy step to assuming responsibility for evaluating society in terms of those standards. Mill had no doubt that there were some—he often called them the "instructed few"—who possessed the highest faculties and the most cultivation, and they were to enjoy the greatest authority in establishing what was best for all.[58] They were also the ones with individuality, who, among other things, were to criticize existing beliefs and point out the many ways in which those beliefs were no longer true. Such persons were the prototypes of the twentieth-century intellectual, who typically is defined as a critic of society.

To criticize and condemn was not enough; alternative beliefs and ways had to be proposed, and this led to intellectuals having a political function as well. For Mill, it will be recalled, those with individuality, in addition to serving as critics, were also to discover new ethical principles and show how they could be put into practice. Although Mill did not use the word "intellectual," he had in mind the tasks that many intellectuals have since taken on themselves, and, like modern intellectuals, he attributed to them a crucial political role in changing society. He was convinced that social progress depended on intellectual activity, which, he said, "is the main determining cause of the social progress." Even more, it was the beliefs propagated by intellectuals that mattered. "The order of human progression in all respects will mainly depend on the order of progression in the intellectual convictions of mankind, that is, on the law of the successive transformations of human opinion."[59] These passages, which reflected Mill's hopes that his own writings could have a decisive influence, anticipate the self-definitions and aspirations of many twentieth-century intellectuals.

Given the belief of some academic intellectuals in their political responsibilities, it is not surprising that they regard politics as more compelling than traditional academic functions. Moreover, the definition of what is political may be greatly expanded, as it was for Mill, by regarding culture—including values and beliefs, literature and history—as being in the realm of politics. On this view, all culture takes on political significance, as defects in it help explain the malfunctions of society; and by purifying it, the intellectual hopes to promote social well-being. Politics is thus brought into the academy, and academic matters are evaluated in political terms. Does a methodology, a research project, an appointee contribute to the eradication of evil? Do they contribute to social progress? Or are they obstacles to it? When such questions guide decision making, the value of traditional academic subjects is depreciated or marginalized; and when the relevance of such questions is challenged, the response is one of moral outrage, censoriousness, and intolerance of the kind that can be witnessed in the university today.

NOTES

1. *The Works and Life of Walter Bagehot,* ed. Mrs. Russell Barrington (London: Longmans, 1915), vol. 6, p. 219.
2. *Ibid.,* pp. 222–23; vol. 5, p. 99.
3. *Ibid.,* vol. 6, p. 220.
4. *Ibid.,* p. 221.
5. Glenn Loury has noted:

   Social pressures and the consequences of engaging in certain kinds of discourse are very severe. Things that can't be talked about on campus today: Are homosexual acts immoral? Can we talk about the extent of differences, overt differences, in academic performance between racial groups? Can we discuss whether or not certain affirmative action practices are effective policy for the university? In other words, there are real restrictions on the scope of debate that can take place.

   And:

   The tolerance that seems to be the mainstay of many of the arguments on the left is not exhibited when people run afoul of certain sacred cows.

   And again:

   The range of considerations that are brought into debate are limited by the self-censorship that attends the strenuous and sometimes irrational response to certain kinds of positions.

   "A Firing Line Debate: 'Resolved: Freedom of Thought is in Danger on American Campuses,' " August 28, 1991 (Columbia, SC: Southern Educational Communications Association, 1991), pp. 9–12. Dinesh D'Souza has referred to "a culture of forbidden questions" and to the moral majority on campuses which, although not a numerical majority, "exercise[s] a kind of moral leverage and [is] very quick to brand any opposition as being tantamount to bigotry" (*ibid.,* pp. 13, 16). See also Eugene D. Genovese, "Heresy, Yes—Sensitivity, No," *The New Republic,* April 15, 1991, pp. 30–35.
6. For example, *The Random House Webster's College Dictionary* (New York: Random House, 1991), which claims to be gender-neutral and includes an appendix titled "Avoiding Sexist Language." See also, Casey Miller and Kate Swift, *Nonsexist Writing,* 2d ed. (New York: Harper, 1988); *Fields' Reference Book of Non-Sexist Words and Phrases* (Raleigh: Fields Enterprises, 1987); and Rosalie Maggio, *The Bias-Free Word Finder: A Dictionary of Nondiscriminatory Language* (Boston: Beacon, 1991), which identifies words prejudicial to women and men as well as those "biased against people because of their race, age, sexual orientation, disability, ethnic origin, *or belief systems*" (italics added).
7. Stanley Fish, "There's No Such Thing as Free Speech and It's a Good Thing, Too," in *Debating P.C.: The Controversy Over Political Correctness on College Campuses,* ed. Paul Berman (New York: Dell, 1992), pp. 235–36.
8. *Ibid.,* pp. 244–45.
9. *Ibid.,* p. 245.
10. Herbert Marcuse, "Repressive Tolerance," in Robert Paul Wolff, Barring-

ton Moore, Jr., and Herbert Marcuse, *A Critique of Pure Tolerance* (Boston: Beacon Press, 1965), p. 111.

11. *Ibid.*, p. 82.
12. *Ibid.*, p. 106.
13. *Ibid.*, p. 109. Marcuse also wrote:

> [T]his means that the ways should not be blocked on which a subversive majority could develop, and if they are blocked by organized repression and indoctrination, their reopening may require apparently undemocratic means. They could include the withdrawal of toleration of speech and assembly from groups and movements which promote aggressive policies, armament, chauvinism, discrimination on the grounds of race and religion, or which oppose the extension of public services, social security, medical care, etc. (*Ibid.*, p. 100)

14. *Ibid.*, p. 88.
15. *Ibid.*, p. 101.
16. *Ibid.*, pp. 100–101. Marcuse's arguments are still used:

> Some of the Left hang onto the view that free speech is sacred. Their argument in favour of speech codes then takes a contorted form: real free speech, they say, can only be had when a tyranny of the repressive speech of whatever target you have in mind has been quieted. Feminists have long argued that pornography silences women, and they must have it silenced to be heard. Some campus liberals argue that if minority students are ever to speak up, they must be protected from the silencing effects of "scientific" racism or homophobia, let alone from real abuse, insult or intimidation.

Alan Ryan, "Princeton Diary," *London Review of Books,* March 26, 1992, p. 21.
17. Alexander Bain, *John Stuart Mill: A Criticism, with Personal Recollections* (London: Longmans, 1882), p. 103. Grote, after repeating this, remarked: "It is all very well for John Mill to stand up for the removal of social restraints, but as to imposing new ones, I feel the greatest apprehensions" (*ibid.*, pp. 103–4).
18. John Stuart Mill, *On Liberty*, in *Collected Works of John Stuart Mill,* ed. John M. Robson (Toronto: University of Toronto Press, 1977), vol. 18, p. 224. There are many variations in Mill's formulations of his distinction; see *ibid.*, pp. 223–24, 260–61, 276, 279–82, and 295. Subsequent references to *On Liberty* will be given in parentheses in the text. *Collected Works* will be cited below as *CW.*
19. This statement is taken from an assertion that uses a double negative. The full statement is: "I do not mean that the feelings with which a person is regarded by others ought not to be in any way affected by his self-regarding qualities or deficiencies."
20. Mill, Early Draft of Autobiography, in *Autobiography and Literary Essays,* in *CW,* vol. 1, pp. 256, 258.
21. Mill, *Utilitarianism,* in *CW,* vol. 10, p. 216; see also, pp. 210–12.
22. Mill, "Utility of Religion," in *CW,* vol. 10, p. 409.
23. Mill, *Utilitarianism,* in *CW,* vol. 10, pp. 228–29.
24. Mill, "Utility of Religion," in *CW,* vol. 10, p. 410. Also: "The principle of

utility either has, or there is no reason why it might not have, all the sanctions which belong to any other system of morals" (*Utilitarianism*, p. 228).

25. Mill, "Utility of Religion," pp. 410–11.

26. *Ibid.*, p. 421.

27. Mill, *Autobiography*, in *CW*, vol. 1, pp. 245, 247.

28. Mill, Diary, February 18, 1854, in *CW*, vol. 27, p. 655.

29. Mill, *Autobiography*, in *CW*, vol. 1, p. 247.

30. Mill to Harriet Mill, February 7, 1854, *Later Letters*, in *CW*, vol. 14, p. 152.

31. Mill, Diary, January 24, 1854, in *CW*, vol. 27, p. 646.

32. Mill, "Utility of Religion," in *CW*, vol. 10, p. 423.

33. Mill, Diary, February 25, 1854, in *CW*, vol. 27, pp. 656–57.

34. Mill, *Utilitarianism*, in *CW*, vol. 10, p. 218.

35. *Ibid.*, p. 231.

36. Mill, "Utility of Religion," in *CW*, vol. 10, p. 422.

37. Mill, *Utilitarianism*, in *CW*, vol. 10, p. 227.

38. *Ibid.*, p. 232.

39. The exception was in *Auguste Comte and Positivism*, in *CW*, vol. 10, pp. 328, 339. Of course, it was mentioned in writings destined for posthumous publication—favorably in "Utility of Religion," in *CW*, vol. 10, pp. 422, 423, and 426, and critically in *Autobiography*, in *CW*, vol. 1, p. 221.

40. This is a question that is not being considered in this paper, though it leads to further concern about Mill's rationale for liberty. Once the Religion of Humanity was in place, the doubts and disagreements of the present transitional era would be greatly reduced, and there would be a "cessation, on one question after another, of serious controversy"; this would be a "consolidation of opinion; a consolidation as salutary in the case of true opinions, as it is dangerous and noxious when the opinions are erroneous" (*On Liberty*, p. 250). Liberty, in other words, is necessary during transitional eras, and when the transitional era ceases, liberty is useful but not required. Mill regarded the transitional era as temporary and not normal; see his *Autobiography*, *CW*, vol. 1, p. 173. In his "Inaugural Address," Mill made an eloquent plea for "free speculation" in the university, but his argument was vitiated by his linking the need for it to the fact that "the specially instructed" were "so divided and scattered that almost any opinion can boast of some high authority," creating a situation in which "no opinion whatever can claim all" ("Inaugural Address Delivered to the University of St. Andrews" [1867], in *CW*, vol. 21, p. 250). Of course, these were the distinguishing characteristics of a transitional era. The argument that Mill's Religion of Humanity and his entire outlook undermine genuine individual liberty has been made in a notable and provocative book by Maurice Cowling: *Mill and Liberalism* (Cambridge: Cambridge University Press, 1963). Although my analysis in this essay is different from Cowling's, my conclusions are compatible with his.

41. Mill, *On Liberty*, ch. 3, *passim*.

42. Of course, Mill used the phrase "moral police" for those intrusions on liberty that were inappropriate (*On Liberty*, pp. 284, 287). I use the phrase for those intrusions on liberty that result from censure by the right-minded—intrusions which Mill approved without acknowledging that the phrase "moral police" was applicable to them as well.

43. See also Mill, *A System of Logic Ratiocinative and Inductive,* in *CW,* vol. 8, pp. 937–40.
44. Mill, "Rationale of Representation," in *CW,* vol. 18, p. 42.
45. Mill, "Inaugural Address," in *CW,* vol. 21, pp. 248–50; yet cf. note 40 above.
46. Mill, *Principles of Political Economy with Some of their Applications to Social Philosophy,* ed. W. J. Ashley (London: Longmans, 1909), p. 748.
47. Mill, Diary, January 10, 1854, in *CW,* vol. 27, p. 641. Mill's close friend Alexander Bain said, "I think his habitual way of speaking of England, the English people, English society, as compared with other nations, was positively unjust, and served no good end." See Bain, *John Stuart Mill,* p. 161.
48. Mill, *Principles of Political Economy,* p. 748 n. 1.
49. Mill, "Newman's Political Economy," in *CW,* vol. 5, p. 449.
50. Mill, "Utility of Religion," in *CW,* vol. 10, pp. 421–22.
51. Paul Hollander, *Political Pilgrims: Travels of Western Intellectuals to the Soviet Union, China, and Cuba 1928–1978* (Lanham: University Press of America, 1990), p. 416 and pp. 416–28 *passim.*
52. Mill, *Auguste Comte and Positivism,* in *CW,* vol. 10, p. 332; "Utility of Religion," in *CW,* vol. 10, p. 422. On Mill's use of the phrase "Religion of Humanity," see note 39 above.
53. Hollander, *Political Pilgrims,* p. 418.
54. Mill, *A System of Logic,* in *CW,* vol. 8, p. 914.
55. Among the ideas derived from Comte were the notion that intellectual activity has a determining influence on progress; the belief that speculation moves through three successive stages; and (though Mill did not accept Comte's formulation, his epistemology, or all his forecasts) the idea that history can be understood in terms of uniformities or laws. See *ibid.,* pp. 916, 928, 912–28 *passim,* and 931–42 *passim*; T. R. Wright, *The Religion of Humanity: The Impact of Comtean Positivism on Victorian Britain* (Cambridge: Cambridge University Press, 1986), pp. 41 and 40–50 *passim*; and Mill, *Autobiography,* in *CW,* vol. 1, p. 219.
56. Mill, *A System of Logic,* in *CW,* vol. 8, p. 922. Of course, the phrase "transitional era" was taken from Comte and St. Simon and was used by Mill in "The Spirit of the Age" [1831], *CW,* vol. 22, pp. 227–34.
57. Mill, Diary, January 26, 1854, and January 17, 1854, in *CW,* vol. 27, pp. 647, 644.
58. Mill, *Utilitarianism,* in *CW,* vol. 10, pp. 211–16.
59. Mill, *A System of Logic,* in *CW,* vol. 8, pp. 926–27; see also pp. 938–39.

The University as Agent of Social Transformation: The Postmodern Argument Considered

Jerry L. Martin

I. The Fundamental Issue

The debate over political correctness has missed the main point. One side claims that the enforcement of politically correct language, attitudes, and behavior is alarmingly widespread. The other side claims that, at most, there are a few isolated, unverified incidents that have been overplayed in the press. In short, the debate has been about whether PC exists.

What this debate overlooks is that there is a very significant body of opinion in academe which holds that, while the term "political correctness" is an epithet to be avoided, the mission of higher education should indeed be political—that the goal should be, not the pursuit of "objective" truth, but nothing less than the fundamental transformation of society.[1] According to this "transformationist" view, education should be, as Miami University professors Henry Giroux and Peter McLaren put it, freed from what Michel Foucault called a "regime of truth" and should become "a form of cultural politics." Teachers should become "engaged and transformative intellectuals" as schools are transformed into "agencies for reconstructing and transforming the dominant status quo culture."[2]

The new view, according to Duke University professor Frank Lentricchia, "seeks not to find the foundation and the conditions of truth but to exercise power for the purpose of social change." The professor's task now becomes helping students "spot, confront, and work against the political horrors of one's time. . . ." As Lentricchia puts it, echoing Marx, "the point is not only to interpret texts, but in so interpreting them, change our society."[3] Wesleyan University English professor Richard Ohmann recommends that faculty "teach politically with revolution as our end. . . ."[4]

Not only teaching but the content of the curriculum itself is to be used for political change. Giroux argues for "the development of curricula that embody a form of cultural politics."[5] Writing about women's studies programs, University of Delaware professor Margaret Andersen explains that "curriculum change is understood as part of the political transformation of women's role in society. . . ."[6]

In order to use institutions of higher education to change society, it is, of course, necessary to control them. Achieving the goal of "human emanicipation, the production of 'better people' through the socialist transformation of society," literary theorist Terry Eagleton points out, will require taking over universities and other cultural institutions. "The democratic control of these ideological apparatuses," he writes, "along with popular alternatives to them, must be high on the agenda of any future socialist programme."[7]

For the transformationist, rebuffing charges of political correctness is only a tactical maneuver; the strategic design is control over the universities themselves. While "the public and well-financed assault on 'political correctness' in the academy needs to be answered strenuously and in an organized fashion by left intellectuals," argues Columbia University professor Jean E. Howard, "that imperative doesn't lessen the need for continued work on transformation *of the academy itself.* While . . . left intellectuals should accept that collectively we have had an impact on changing the educational apparatus and that our real successes have in fact fueled the political correctness attacks, nonetheless, these achievements are not spread evenly across the educational spectrum and are fragile." According to Howard, universities "have been radicalized far too little. To continue that radicalization remains a pressing task. . . ."[8]

It would be a mistake to dismiss the transformationist view lightly, to regard it as either intellectually lightweight or institutionally impotent. It is based on what many regard as the most advanced and sophisticated thinking at elite universities, thinking so dominant that it is declared in a publication of the American Council of Learned Societies (ACLS) to reflect "the consensus of most of the dominant theories" of our time.[9] Going further, a leading literary theorist, J. Hillis Miller, has declared the "universal triumph of theory"—referring not to a single theory, but to the cluster of postmodern views that includes deconstructionist, Marxist, feminist, and related theories of literary and cultural interpretation.[10] While it is not clear how many faculty fully avow the transformationist position, the ideas that legitimate it—such as the critique of truth and objectivity and the emphasis on race, class, and gender—are now commonplaces of academic discussion at colleges and universities across the country. It would also be a mistake to equate the transformationist thesis with older ideas of social reform.[11] There have always been social reformers who wanted to use universities as helpmates of social change. At its least tendentious, the idea that the university should use its human and physical resources for the benefit of the surrounding community is a helpful caution against splendid self-indulgence. If the business school can help small businesses, or the music school improve music education in the schools, that is all to the good. The only danger here is that universities can lose focus and become supermarkets of social services. But the university's contributions to social change do not require a loss of focus. It is entirely consistent with the university's mission, understood as the pursuit of truth and the exchange of ideas, for it to share its expertise and capacity for reflection with the larger community.

Traditionally, even zealous social reformers—such as John Dewey or the "Chicago School" of sociologists in the 1920s—have accepted the principle that the distinctive contribution the university can make to social change is based on the knowledge and thoughtfulness it can bring to the solution of social problems. Consequently, these reformers cherished rather than challenged the idea that the university's first commitment is to the pursuit of truth. A commitment to the pursuit of truth implied that even their own ideas about social reform were open to the test of evidence and reason. And this, in turn, implied that, however fervently the teacher might hope that students would draw progressive conclusions from the evidence, the teacher accepted the obligation to present all sides of disputed questions and to let students decide for themselves.

Traditional social reformers accepted the tension inherent in John Henry Newman's *Idea of the University*. As a Christian, Newman believed that nothing could be more important than the fate of the soul, which, in turn, depends crucially on the acceptance of Christian beliefs and rites. Nevertheless, Newman did not condone every means to that end. According to Newman, the intellectual life has its own integrity and purpose—the pursuit of truth for its own sake—and it is the distinctive mission of the university to foster the life of the mind.

Similarly, even social reformers who felt that nothing was more urgent than progressive social change accepted the idea that the primary mission of the university was not social change but the pursuit of truth. In fact, they believed that the pursuit of truth, particularly the advance of knowledge in the social sciences, would contribute to desirable social change. Hence, social reformers such as Dewey defended academic freedom and the intellectual integrity of the university. Since Dewey's time, the American university's commitment to the pursuit of truth has remained a barrier, sometimes breached but never destroyed, against extraneous activities and partisan, religious, and ideological manipulation.

Traditional social reformers based their ideas for social change on their understanding of truth; the new theorists base their understanding of truth on their ideas for social change. This reversal implies an extraordinary alteration in our conception of education—it turns our intellectual world upside down—and its proponents know it. It is a revolution that they advocate, but not for light and transient causes. They believe that a revolution in thought has taken place that justifies a radical rethinking of the function of higher education. Their revolution is epistemological, and it challenges Newman's first premise: that the aim of the intellect is the pursuit of truth. If the pursuit of truth is a snare and a delusion, as some postmodernists argue, then it cannot and should not be the aim of the intellect or of higher education.

Aspects of this argument echo the Marxist analysis that sees ideas as "superstructure" reflecting and reinforcing relations of power based on modes of production. The Marxist project of uncovering class biases within intellectual and cultural systems remains one strand of postmodern thinking. But, in the end, traditional Marxists were always realists. In fact, they denounced their opponents as "idealists." They did not think that factories and workers and owners were inventions of a theory; they thought they were real, that children really worked fourteen-hour days and miners really died of black-lung disease.[12] These ideas were not idle, rationalizing superstructures; for traditional Marxists, they constituted the palpable, raw facts of life under industrial capitalism.

Marxists tried to have it both ways, of course—"my ideas reflect reality, yours are ideological rationalizations." But their claims—about the rise of capitalism, for example, or class relations in a democracy— were at least asserted to be based on historical and sociological evidence, hence open in principle to challenge by counterevidence. Thoughtful Marxists—Christopher Hill and Eugene Genovese, for example—have welcomed intellectual challenge, and arguments between these Marxists and their critics contributed to the pursuit of truth and hence to the intellectual life proper to a university. In fact, until recently at least, academic Marxist historians, philosophers, and social scientists in this country did not claim the right to silence opposition within the university or to make the university a force for Marxist social change. As a result, it has been possible to subject Marxism to the test of evidence and argument.

The postmodern argument, while it retains strands of Marxism, is both more extreme and more powerful because it directly challenges Newman's premise—that the pursuit of truth is a desirable and even possible goal. Once the pursuit of truth is rejected as a goal, "everything is permitted." Once the pursuit of disinterested truth is debunked, appeals to such commonplaces of liberal learning as objectivity, respect for reason, and academic freedom become question-begging.

It is this postmodern argument for the transformationist view that will be considered here. To evaluate the argument, one must first understand what it is, a task made difficult by the absence of a canonical statement of the argument, end to end. One tends to find separate discussions—here an attack on objectivity, there a discussion of critical pedagogy, perhaps with undeveloped allusions to each other—but no systematic presentation of the argument from beginning to end. But the separate discussions do not form an inchoate mass; they reflect a coherent view that contains an implicit argument. The following is an attempt to articulate that argument, step by step, as a prelude to critical commentary.

II. The Argument

The Transformationist Thesis: The aim of higher education should be, not the pursuit of truth, but social transformation.

Step 1: Perspectives. Metaphysical realism naively assumes that there is a single, definitive description of reality that reason has the power to discern. In the case of literature, it assumes that every text yields a single, definitive reading. But, in fact, there are many interpretations of reality, many readings of every text. Each represents only a perspective: "all thought inevitably derives from particular standpoints, perspectives, and interests. . . ."[13]

Step 2: Relativism.[14] No single perspective on reality can claim to be the exclusive truth. Since "there is no external reality subject to partition and definition, . . . different viewpoints generate different understandings of events. . . ."[15] An interpretation may claim to be "true," but only relative to its own interpretive framework. There is no way we can step outside our perspectives, our interpretive frames, and see whether they fit an external, independently existing reality. Standards of evidence, rationality, and objectivity are themselves relative to the frameworks. Consequently, the pursuit of "objective" truth is a myth and a delusion.

Step 3: Groups. There is no purely individual act of expression. There is no expression or interpretation without language; and language, like all systems of cultural representation, is social. "The literary act is a social act."[16] Hence, texts, interpretations, and other cultural representations reflect the perspectives not merely of individuals but of groups or "interpretive communities."[17] Every act of interpretation or judgment reflects the symbols and norms of one or more social groups.

Step 4: Identity. A person is not an atomistic, autonomous, essential, noumenal self—free to invent its own identity. The self is "socially constructed," constituted by its membership in society or, more precisely, by its membership in particular groups whose interests may be in conflict with dominant social interests.

Step 5: Interests. "[T]here is no possibility of a wholly disinterested statement"—if there were, we would have no interest in making it.[18] In fact, "interests generate thought" and "are *constitutive* of our knowledge, not merely prejudices which imperil it."[19] Every judgment or expression reflects the interests not only of individuals but, more crucially, of the social groups or interpretive communities that constitute the society.

Step 6: Power. Whatever else they may be (or pretend to be), texts and ideas are ways of exercising power. In every communication situation, some people have more power than others by virtue of their membership in different groups. The more powerful are able to use such cultural representations as texts and ideas to shape the thinking, feelings, and behavior of the less powerful. Texts, ideas, and other cultural representations are effective in large part because they mask their purpose and seduce their victims. Marxists, feminists, and others have produced many textual, historical, and social analyses that unmask the latent interests and manipulations behind apparently impartial or high-minded statements and practices. Analyses have shown that institutions of socialization and social control reflect the interests of the dominant groups in a society. High culture in particular represents the ideas and symbols that have allowed the dominant race, class, and gender to maintain hegemony over others.

Step 7: Race, Class, and Gender. The most fundamental interests and power relations are those based on race, class, and gender. The groups suffering the most persistent and intense oppression have been women, minorities, and the poor, both within Western societies and within the reach of the West's global power. The cultural expressions of these groups have been repressed or marginalized by the dominant culture that reflects the interests of Western white male elites.

Step 8: Politics. All cultural expressions and practices reflect, express, and support power relations and are, therefore, political. The question is not whether higher education or some other cultural arena is to be "politicized"—it is political already. The question is whose power is expressed and sustained by a particular institution and whether the current power relationships are to be challenged.

Step 9: Empowerment. It is wrong for some groups to dominate others. The hegemony of one group over another is incompatible with the ideals of equality, liberation, and the full realization of human potential. Hence, Western white male elites should relinquish power over others, and oppressed groups should take power over their own lives.

Step 10: Inclusion. Works reflecting the interests of the dominant class must be unmasked, and their hegemonic biases—patriarchy, racism, and imperialism—revealed. Ideas of what is "central" and "normal" have served the interests of the dominant class, while the traits of oppressed groups have been regarded as "marginal" and "abnormal." These hierarchies and perhaps all hierarchies—perhaps all dualisms—must be challenged.[20] At the same time, work by and for the oppressed must be retrieved and fully appreciated. If these works do not meet traditional academic standards, then the standards should be changed.

Step 11: The Tyranny of Objectivity. Ideals of truth, objectivity, reason, argument, evidence, impartiality, et cetera—elements of a "regime of truth"—are themselves among the instruments of oppression.[21] The "assumed detachment of scientific observers from what they observe," for example, is "made possible through organized hierarchies of science where, for example, women work as bottle washers, research assistants, or computer operators."[22] The vaunted superiority of objectivity over subjectivity, of reason over emotion, of mind over body, of universal over particular, reflects hierarchical or "vertical" traits associated with Western white males, and devalues "horizontal" traits associated with women, minorities, non-Western peoples, and the poor.[23]

Step 12: (Re)vision. The "spurious appeal to objectivity, science, truth, universality" must be replaced by "a politics of truth that defines the true as that which liberates and furthers specific processes of liberation."[24] Ideas and interpretations that support hegemonic structures must be replaced by ideas and interpretations that support the interests and increase the power of women, minorities, and the poor. The test of an idea is not whether it meets traditional canons of evidence and argument, but whether it furthers the political interests of the oppressed, whether it is helpful in "generating the history we want."[25]

Step 13: Political Standards. The regime of truth and the tyranny of objectivity must be replaced by norms more sensitive to the perspectives and interests of oppressed groups, that is, by what its critics call "political correctness." What is said, taught, or published—and who is hired—should be judged, not by hegemonic standards of merit and objectivity, but by whether it advances or hinders the empowerment and liberation of women, minorities, and the poor. New texts should be selected that will help to empower these groups. Traditional texts should be given interpretations that advance the interests of the oppressed. Matters of historical, economic, or scientific interpretation should be included, excluded, or revised in light of this political goal. "Interpretation that shores up things as they are or prevents social change by encouraging resistance to it, by encouraging the view that change is illusion—because action itself, which would produce change, is too problematically beset by unavoidable historical repetition"—should be excluded from the classroom because of its harmful social effects.[26] This does not mean that an "educational" goal is being replaced by a "political" one. Education, like everything else, is already political. It means that a humane and egalitarian politics is replacing an inhumane and oppressive politics.

Step 14: Higher Education. Therefore, the aim of higher education should be, not the pursuit of truth, which is both an illusion and an instrument of oppression, but social transformation—changing ideas, symbols, and institutions from tools of racist, sexist, capitalist, imperialist hegemony to instruments of empowerment for women, minorities, the poor, and the Third World. *Q.E.D.*

Several consequences follow from the transformationist thesis.

Step 15: Critical Pedagogy. If the goal of education were the pursuit of truth, the function of a teacher would be to enable students to see all sides of an issue and to weigh the pros and cons thoughtfully. But this approach to teaching rests on rationalist illusions and supports the status quo by encouraging endless debate. In a transformative university, the aim is not aimless exploration but "changing minds," enabling students to "spot, confront, and work against the political horrors of one's time," helping them become "agents of counterhegemony."[27] One of the main tasks of critical pedagogy is to overcome "patterns of resistance" from students who resist ideas that challenge prevailing norms.[28] Unfortunately, the "tools of rationality alone are inadequate to the task of intellectual change. . . ."[29] Teaching may have to resemble therapy, helping someone overcome resistance to uncomfortable truths long repressed. Critical pedagogy may lead a young woman to see the subtle ways she is oppressed; it may reveal to a young white male his unconscious racism. Teaching that might to a traditionalist seem manipulative—a violation of a student's intellectual freedom—is actually an empowerment, a liberation.

Step 16: Speech Restrictions. Freedom must now be conceived as empowerment for the oppressed and liberation from the hegemonic illusions of the dominant class. The old notion of academic freedom, including the *lehrfreiheit* of the student, rested on the now discredited ideal of disinterested inquiry. "If we abandon a belief in objectivity," writes Betty Jean Craige, "we must redefine the principle of 'academic freedom.' . . ."[30] Since social transformation is the proper function of higher education, freedom of discussion is less important than other values, such as overcoming racism, sexism, capitalism, and imperialism.[31] "To the criticism that they [programs in women's studies, black studies, and Chicano studies] have turned research and teaching into political activism, they may reply that all discourse implies an ideology of some sort. . . . Although their argument raises for many faculty questions of academic freedom and academic propriety, . . . their success in arming students with an ability to analyze texts (albeit with a particular political purpose) cannot be ignored."[32] Except as a tactical expedient, it would be inconsistent to allow racist, sexist, and exploitative ideas to be expressed.[33]

Step 17: Public Denial. The transformationist university is by definition in conflict with the surrounding society. However, it depends on that society for both financial support and whatever degree of autonomy it retains. Transformationists would undermine their base of operations if they were always open and candid about their goals and activities. Therefore, in speaking to the public it will be important to deny that political standards are being enforced and to minimize the extent of curricular and pedagogical change.[34] This may seem deceptive to those who adhere to the ideal of disinterested truth, but for those who understand that the idea of "eternally 'true' theory" must be replaced by "a kind of rhetoric whose value may be measured by its persuasive means and by its ultimate goal," speaking differently to the public than to each other is justifiable.[35]

III. The Argument Considered

Steps 1, 2, and 11: Perspectives, Relativism, and Objectivity

It is not difficult to locate serious arguments about realism, relativism, objectivity, the meaning of truth, and so forth—the history of philosophy from the Greeks to the present abounds in such discussions. But these discussions differ in several ways from the transformationist view. In the past, philosophical critics of such objectivist traditions as realism and rationalism have not tried to derive a new political mission for educational institutions from their critiques. Their philosophical critique has itself been an intellectual project, with intellectual goals and methods, still very much a part of the pursuit of truth. Except for odd characters like Cratylus (who, doubtful about the possibility of making true statements about a changing world, gave up speaking), philosophical skeptics have not thought that their views had practical consequences. Certainly they did not conclude that the impossibility of achieving rationalist or realist standards of objectivity released them from intellectual obligations or made it appropriate for them to indoctrinate their students. Moreover, serious philosophical critiques of objectivity and realism have themselves been presented with clarity, precision, rigor, and a respect for counterarguments, traits regarded by postmodernists as symptoms of the tyranny of objectivity. One literary theorist, Robert Scholes, has pointed out the postmodernist neglect of the referentialist tradition represented by Gottlob Frege, Bertrand Russell, Peter Strawson, and John Searle—a tradition postmodernists nevertheless claim to have refuted.[36] One finds, instead, ritual invocations of Thomas Kuhn and Richard Rorty, unaccompanied by a close reading of their arguments, much less those of their critics. Nevertheless, Kuhn and Rorty are taken to be conclusive and to license anything that can be called a paradigm shift or a conversation—to license, in fact, a politicization of higher education that neither endorses.

Postmodern arguments against objectivity often make the bold and inaccurate assumption that the only forms of objectivism are pristine Cartesian rationalism or empiricist positivism (which, oddly enough, they tend to equate). Since the more extreme forms of Cartesian and positivist thinking are fairly easy to refute (and were indeed refuted long before Jacques Derrida), transformationists end up refuting positions nobody holds—heroically jousting at windmills that have already been knocked down—and declaring an easy triumph over Western rationalism without bothering to examine the more credible and sophisticated forms of objectivism. When they do pay enough attention to recent epistemology to note that most philosophers are neither Cartesian rationalists nor positivists, transformationists sometimes leap to the conclusion that these philosophers must agree with their own relativism. In fact, they often present an argument from authority ("the consensus of most of the dominant theories," says the ACLS report), and thinkers as diverse as Kuhn and Rorty, Hilary Putnam and Donald Davidson, are seen as buttressing this argument.[37] The transformationists seem surprised and puzzled when someone such as Putnam, whose "internal realism" they cannot distinguish from postmodern relativism, attacks their views.

Caricaturing objectivism, transformationists achieve easy triumphs over phantom opponents. Metaphysical realists do not, for example, hold or need to hold that there is a single, definitive description of reality or anything close to it. All they hold or need to hold is that, of the various descriptions of reality, we can say that some are true or more adequate than others, and that reality, and not merely what we say about it, has a role in determining truth and adequacy. Many forms of realism fully acknowledge that mind, language, or conceptual frameworks make a contribution to knowledge. If we did not have the concept of a "key," we could not ask whether one was in the drawer. But, having the concept, we can ask, and the answer will be in the drawer, not in our concepts. There are many ways to analyze the relation between what is in our minds and what is in the world, but none of them is as simpleminded as the simplistic realism attacked by transformationists.

Typical of transformationist reasoning is the argument about "perspectives." It is more metaphor than argument, but the metaphor bears reflection. It is said that, visiting the zoo one day, the British philosopher G. E. Moore and his friend came upon an unusually large elephant. "What a huge elephant!" exclaimed the friend. "From this side at least," added the cautious Moore. The oddity of Moore's comment lies, of course, in the fact that an elephant cannot be huge from merely one side, and points up the fact that, contrary to its use by postmodernists, perspective is a realist, not an anti-realist, metaphor. We can speak quite objectively about lines of perspective—that an object will look larger up close, railroad tracks will merge at the horizon, and so forth. We can arrive at a more adequate understanding of an object or situation if we put perspectives together, allow them to complement and correct each other. In fact, the very concept of a perspective implies that there is something it is a perspective on. The "something" is the difference between a perspective and a hallucination. And it is why it is plausible to think of perspectives, but not hallucinations, as a metaphor for our knowledge of the world.

Another image sometimes presented in transformationist arguments is that of being "inside" our minds, language, conceptual frameworks, or interpretive communities and not being able to get "outside" to see if they are valid or "correspond" to anything. An older use of this image was in the Egocentric Predicament popularized by Bertrand Russell—the solipsistic puzzle that, since all my ideas and experiences are mine, how can I know whether anyone or anything exists outside my own mind? The earnest lady who wrote Russell a letter, saying that, "You and I are the only people who know that solipsism is true," unwittingly showed the impossibility of the view. Like the paradox of the hare that gets closer and closer but never overtakes the tortoise, the Egocentric Predicament may be a challenging, even unsolvable, paradox; but we all know that hares overtake tortoises and that, not only are we not trapped inside our own minds, we are inevitably, inescapably beings-in-the-world. If solipsism were possible, the lone solipsist would exist as the totality of being. But the very ability to pose the question—"Am I the only one?"—shows an understanding of otherness impossible for the solipsist. The totality of being does not ask, "Am I the only one?" What would "I" mean in such a case? To ask the question—to be able to ask it—is to answer it.

What was the argument for solipsism? It was not so much an argument as a powerful image. Think of a person's experience as a collection of ideas and sensations. Then impose the categories "inside/outside." You get an image of a person trapped within his or her own states of consciousness. This image was sometimes called the "box" theory of consciousness. Experiences were seen as images flickering on the interior walls of a box. To update the image, one might imagine a person inside a windowless room, watching the world only on television monitors. There would be no way for the person to know whether the images—of trees, flowers, people—appearing on the monitors corresponded to anything outside the box. A powerful, seductive image. But why accept this image—or the inside/outside dichotomy—as an adequate representation of consciousness? The most obvious characteristic of consciousness is that it is not self-contained; it is intentional, referential, and (except for moments of self-reflection) directed at objects in the world. As the phenomenologists used to say, "consciousness is always consciousness-of"; it is already "outside itself." This may be the defining trait of consciousness. The difference between a mind and a television monitor is that, while the monitor may mirror objects, only a mind can be aware of them. The image of the windowless room is seductive only because it includes a conscious mind that can be aware of the images on the monitor—a mind that can indeed be aware of things, such as the monitors, outside itself. To be consistent, the image would have to be a windowless room with television monitors but no person in it—not a very persuasive representation of consciousness.

The inside/outside image also fails as a representation of knowledge. The most natural thing to say about knowledge is that it is based on evidence, observation, and reasoning. Something is known if it is well-founded; not known if it is not. The most natural account of knowledge does not involve the concepts of inside and outside. To check a belief against the evidence—to look in the drawer to see if you are right that the keys are there—is not to "step outside" your mind or your conceptual system. When you look for your keys, you are using your mind, using your conceptual system, not stepping outside it. It is, however, a commonplace of transformationist argumentation to say that we cannot "step outside" our conceptual frameworks (paradigms, interpretive communities, et cetera)—as if "stepping outside" one's concepts were the best (perhaps the only) way to test one's knowledge. Sometimes we discover that a concept such as "dragon" does not apply to anything (outside fairy tales), or that a concept such as "matter" has to be revised; but we make these discoveries by using concepts, not by stepping outside them.

Far from being the way to test knowledge, it is not clear that "stepping outside our concepts" to see if they "correspond" to reality means anything at all. One tries to imagine hopping outside one's head and then looking at what is in one's head and what is in the world and comparing them. But this is at best a cartoon image. (The character who hopped outside would have to hop outside again to see if his comparison matched, and so on, ad infinitum.) How can something so meaningless be a test of knowledge? Transformationists seem to hold two contradictory views: that the test is meaningful in the sense that it is the correct test of truth (or at least of objectivism), and that it is meaningless (and hence objectivism fails the test). In fact, no objectivist has ever claimed the cartoon-like abilities implied by the test. Most objectivists hold that we understand the world by applying our concepts to the facts of experience. Objectivists understand that there is considerable latitude within a conceptual framework for arranging facts to fit the framework, for positing epicycles on top of epicycles, as the late followers of Ptolemaic astronomy did, to make the theory consistent with the facts. But objectivists also understand, as transformationists seem not to, that sometimes facts finally overwhelm conceptual frameworks. Otherwise there would never be the anomalies that, according to Kuhn, lead to conceptual change. Facts may be theory-dependent, but theories are also fact-dependent.

The transformationist form of solipsism—that we are all trapped within our interpretive communities—is in some ways less persuasive than classic solipsism. It is more logical to apply the inside/outside image to the individual mind than to a group. It is odd to believe that individuals can get outside their own minds but not outside the beliefs of the groups of which they are members: if a person can make one leap, why not the other? Moreover, however powerful group influences may be, it is still true that people challenge their groups' norms, change them, leave one group for another, describe and criticize them with a distance unimaginable if group relativism were right. It has been possible, for example, for people steeped in a culture that regarded African Americans as less than human to have experiences of African Americans that refuted their acculturation. It has been possible for people raised in religious communities to reject religion, and for people raised in secular communities to embrace it. If matters so fundamental as who is a human being and whether there is a God are not determined by cultural membership, then what is left of relativism? The relativist will rush to point out that these experiences themselves (and inferences from them) must be described (and justified) in the language of some group, but so what?[38] The question is whether group membership prescribes ideas and beliefs, and hence circumscribes knowledge and choice, not whether it provides the linguistic apparatus for ideas, belief, knowledge, and choice. Perhaps language is, as Friedrich Waismann said, "open-textured," its rules compatible with open-ended variations; perhaps groups, including whole cultures, are porous, open to new ideas and experiences.[39]

Duke University professor Stanley Fish recognizes that the phenomenon of intellectual and moral change appears to imply that individuals can transcend the norms and symbols of their interpretive communities. His reply is that, like square dancers, they just go from one partner to another, trading one interpretive framework for another. What the individual regards as intellectual progress is only a meaningless do-si-do of changing frameworks. The illusion of progress, says Fish, derives from the fact that, from the point of view of the new framework, it is much better than the old.[40]

Is Fish's account of intellectual and moral change adequate? It would imply that, for any two beliefs, A and B, "progress" could consist equally in going from A to B or from B to A. If A is the belief that African Americans are intellectually inferior, and B is the belief that there are no race-based boundaries to intelligence, then, on Fish's view, the transition from A to B—overcoming racism—is not intrinsically better than going the other way—becoming a racist. Groups supporting racism will see one change as progress; groups opposing racism will see the opposite change as progress. This account of intellectual and moral change presupposes that there is no truth of the matter, no ascertainable way to determine whether the empirical facts support one view and not the other. It also assumes the irrelevance of our understanding of psychological and sociological processes, such as stereotyping and scape-goating, that indicate that racism is driven by powerful irrational urges, not by an alternative reading of the evidence.

The relativist might object that the comparison is unfair because it assumes the truth of one of two beliefs. But why does this make the comparison unfair? To assume that there is no way to tell which view is more accurate would beg the question the other way. The question is which overall view is more plausible—one that holds that racism could be tested against the evidence and that what we know about the dynamics of racism bears upon its credibility, or one that holds simply that racism reflects the views of one group, anti-racism the views of another, and that there is no way to judge between them.

Think of a simpler case. A person who thought that there was only one U.S. president named Adams (perhaps thought the two Adamses were one and the same) learns that there were two. A person who years ago knew there were two Adamses, over the years comes to think there was only one. Is each of these changes equally valid, each justified by its new interpretive framework? To say so is to dispense, not only with a belief that there is an objective fact of the matter, but also with such elemental concepts as learning and forgetting. An account of intellectual change that cannot distinguish between learning new facts and forgetting old ones—an account central not only to Fish's theory of interpretive communities but implicit in other transformationist thinking as well—is hardly the bedrock of an adequate epistemology.

Another argument against objectivity is that, since all knowledge-claims are historically "situated," there is no timeless or eternal truth, and hence no objective truth at all, only rhetoric, politics, and power. Consider the following passage from Lentricchia:

> . . . I am ready to urge (Rorty is not) a materialist view that theory does its representing with a purpose. This sort of theory seeks not to find the foundation and the conditions of truth but to exercise power for the purpose of social change. It says there is no such thing as eternally "true" theory. It says that theories are generated only in history—no theory comes from outside—for the purpose of generating more history in a certain way: generating the history we want. The claims I am making against "true" theories are not themselves grounded on some ultimate "true" theory of purely historical nature. My historical claims make no traditional epistemological demand on my reader; they are points of departure for the work I do. Because I conceive of theory as a type of rhetoric, . . . the kind of Marxist theory that I am urging is itself a kind of rhetoric whose value may be measured by its persuasive means and by its ultimate goal: the formation of genuine community.

> . . . I cannot resist the limited historical claim to truth in Marx's reading of capitalist society, in the limited historical context within which he carried it out. His analysis of the structure of commodity capitalism and the class system and culture it spawns and undergirds, though it fails at some crucial points for our context, yet continues to exert a compelling pressure upon us, and it does so because his context is in some deep sense ours. . . . Again, is Marx's picture "true"? Does it "correspond" to social reality? The answer is that, through an analysis of existing conditions, an analysis penetrated by an astonishingly powerful vision and rhetoric, Marx created a picture which Marxist and many non-Marxist intellectuals today in the West respond to as if it were true, as if in fact this is where we live, what our history at bottom is all about. . . . As a cultural weapon to be deployed in social struggle, Marxist theory is a form of will to power, because what I am calling "culture" is knowledge precisely at the point at which knowledge becomes power, or is on the way to power.[41]

In short, Lentricchia presents as mutually implicative three quite different statements: that "there is no such thing as eternally 'true' theory," that "theories are generated only in history," and that "no theory comes from outside." He then takes these statements to be grounds for not trying to make "ultimate 'true' " claims about history, and hence for regarding theories as mere "rhetoric . . . measured by its persuasive means and by its ultimate goal." He admits that he "cannot resist" the "limited historical claim to truth" in Marx "in the limited historical context within which he carried it out." He concludes that Marx's theory is not "true," does not "correspond" to social reality, but is responded to by some intellectuals "as if it were true, as if in fact this is where we live, what our history at bottom is all about," and hence is effective "rhetoric," a "cultural weapon," and "a form of will to power."

The first step of this argument raises the issue of the "timing" of truth-claims and seems to rest on a confusion. Most philosophers would agree that, while events have dates, truths do not. Julius Caesar crossed the Rubicon in 49 B.C., but the statement that he did so is just as true today, yesterday, and tomorrow as in 49 B.C. Similarly, "a square has four sides" is always true, not true on a particular date or dates. One way to say that truths do not have dates is to say that they are "timeless" or "eternal," but that may be confusing. For some people, these terms suggest that the fact being described persists (like human greed or the ebb and flow of the tides), but of course Caesar is not still crossing the Rubicon, although it is forever true that he did so in 49 B.C. And, for some, these terms may suggest human infallibility, whereas whether truths have dates implies nothing about whether or how we know them to be true. Similarly, whether truths are timeless has nothing to do with whether theories are generated in history. Historicists make a great deal of this fact, and seem to think that the most momentous consequences follow. But the fact that theories are developed at particular times by particular people implies nothing about their truth or knowability. Even the most ardent Platonist knows that Plato developed his theories in fourth-century Athens.

However, wielding the truism, Lentricchia delivers what he takes to be the conclusive blow—that "no theory comes from outside." It is not clear what view Lentricchia is trying to refute here. Has someone held that some theories come from "outside"? Are there people claiming that theories come from divine inspiration? If so, Lentricchia has given them their comeuppance. Some mathematicians hold that mathematical truth is apprehended by reason alone, but even they believe that the undecidability theorem came from Gödel, not from "outside."

Lentricchia seems to think that if theories are generated in history, are not timeless, and do not come from the outside, then they are not worth having at all. But, as we have seen, these arguments rest on confusions and non sequiturs. Whether a theory is generated in history or comes from the outside does not determine whether it is true. Misled by his own argument, Lentricchia finds himself unable to say what he clearly believes, namely, that much of what Marx says is true. Instead, we hear the confessional tone, "I cannot resist" the "limited historical claim to truth" in Marx's analysis. He refuses to say that Marx's picture is, in many respects, "true" and "correspond[s]" to social reality. Instead, he speaks with strained circumlocution—saying that many intellectuals (Lentricchia among them) "respond" to Marx's analysis "as if" it were true, "as if in fact this is where we live, what our history at bottom is all about." One wonders what the difference is, in Lentricchia's epistemology, between responding to something "as if" it were true and believing something to be true? One sometimes senses an epistemological paranoia: he cannot trust any theory that is limited, generated in history, and "subject to revision," not timeless, ultimate, and from outside.[42] He will not trust a fickle theory, though he may act "as if" he trusts it. Interestingly, he does seem to trust his political commitments, which are expressed unreservedly. He never explains whether they might also be limited, generated in history, and subject to revision, not timeless, ultimate, or from outside. He does not speak "as if" there are "political horrors." He does not explain why, if historical interpretation is so unreliable as to dissolve into rhetoric, his political convictions are so unerring that they, rather than evidence, should guide historical interpretation.

Steps 3 through 6: Groups, Identity, Interests, and Power

The transformationist argument posits that the self is socially constructed through membership in various groups, most notably race, class, and gender. One's identity, interests, and power reflect group memberships. Language, ideas, and values, therefore, reflect the interests of groups and provide effective means by which dominant groups can control and shape the self-understanding of less powerful groups. These connections between personal identity, group membership, interests, power, language, and so forth, are sometimes presented a priori, as though they were so interlocking conceptually that they needed no empirical confirmation. Often the connections are simply assumed in interpretations of literary texts, social institutions, and historical events, as if the fact that interesting interpretations could be based on them were sufficient validation—a rather circular proceeding and, in any case, a standard met by every theory with a clever practitioner.

In fact, broken down into individual claims and defined with sufficient precision, some of the transformationist hypotheses should be subject to empirical investigation. The task is not too different from what political scientists do when they study voting behavior. They check empirical evidence to determine how strongly such matters as party affiliation and policy preferences correlate with such traits as race, gender, class, religion, region, and so forth. Transformationists have, however, given little effort to provide empirical support for the correlations they postulate; and the studies that have been made tend to be too weak in their correlations to support the strong theses advanced by the transformationist argument. For example, various efforts have been made to show that women write, think, talk, value, or behave in distinctive ways. The studies are interesting and suggestive, sometimes confirming what we already thought, sometimes surprising us, but they never show that all women write, think, talk, value, or behave differently from men. If some do and some do not, even if most do, such studies provide scant support for transformationist ideas. For example, it has not been possible for even the most discerning readers to deduce the gender of an author from the style alone.[43] Even proponents seem to concede that some women write, et cetera, in "masculine" ways, and that some men write, et cetera, in "feminine" ways. Similarly, efforts by Carol Gilligan and others to show that women value differently—value caring more than justice, for example—have been inconclusive. There are abundant examples of women who care passionately about justice—from the "equal pay for equal work" movement to the advocacy of the right to choose and of ownership over one's own body. Sometimes gender differences are postulated that parallel prefeminist stereotypes. In these cases, however, "feminine" traits once regarded as negative are often reinterpreted in a more positive light. "Feminine" traits that are inescapably negative from a feminist point of view are regarded as reflecting hegemonic social conditioning rather than women's "true" identity.

Even if most women and only some men value caring more than rights, or act cooperatively rather than competitively, or use conversation to establish relationships rather than to assert positions, do the transformationist theses follow? Feminists themselves are not sure how to interpret the results. Are the "feminine" traits inherent in being female or are they social products? The former view, which is sometimes called "essentialism," provides clear support to the idea that gender determines identity and interests, but it is difficult to support in the absence of perfect uniformity among women and it contradicts the transformationist belief in the social construction of the self. But if "feminine" traits are social products, a number of other questions arise. Are they constructions by and in the interest of the dominant class, or by and in the interest of women? Are they stereotypes to be fought—"I have a right to be as competitive as I want to be," says the liberal feminist—or traits to be embraced and asserted—"Not if you want to be true to yourself and women everywhere," replies the radical.[44] If the 'self is socially constructed, and it is only a sexist society that makes men and women different, then why cannot each individual choose his or her own identity? Moreover, if gender traits are all socially constructed, how do you know what the interests of women are anyway? Where a trait is natural, it is easy to identify interests. For example, the need for food is natural; hence, it is in people's interest to have food. Of course, the transformationist rejection of objectivity, as well as the theory of social construction of the self, are incompatible with the idea of natural facts. But, if a trait is cultural, such as wearing lipstick, it is hard to find grounds for saying that it is or is not in the interests of women. It would depend on the preferences of individual women, not on any group interest.

Sometimes transformationists base the thesis that all ideas and cultural expressions are political (exercising power on behalf of group interests) on the claim that no judgment is totally immune from interest, values, or purposes—since otherwise there would be no point even in making the judgment. But this argument rests on a non sequitur. The idea that judgments involve values and purposes does not imply that they are politically loaded or used to give one group power over another. The values could include, after all, such ideals as objectivity and impartiality. Sometimes the non sequitur is masked by an equivocation. A slide is made from "interest" in the broad sense that includes all human values and purposes, including an interest in getting at the truth, to "interest" in the narrow political sense. Consider the following series of steps in an argument presented by Eagleton:

> In chatting to you about the weather I am also signalling that I regard conversation with you as valuable, that I consider you a worthwhile person to talk to, that I am not myself anti-social or about to embark on a detailed critique of your personal appearance.
> In this sense, there is no possibility of a wholly disinterested statement. . . . It is not just as though we have something called factual knowledge which may then be distorted by particular interests and judgments, although this is certainly possible; it is also that without particular interests we would have no knowledge at all, because we would not see the point of bothering to get to know anything. Interests are *constitutive* of our knowledge, not merely prejudices which imperil it. . . .
> The largely concealed structure of values which informs and underlies our factual statements is part of what is meant by "ideology." By "ideology" I mean, roughly, the ways in which what we say and believe connects with the power-structure and power-relations of the society we live in.[45]

In this passage, Eagleton moves from the ways one has an interest or purpose in what one says to the idea that there is no "wholly disinterested" statement. This move plays on a confusion between "disinterested" in the sense of lacking in purpose and "disinterested" in the sense of fair and impartial, lacking in bias. The fact that no statement is without purpose does not imply that none is fair, impartial, or unbiased. The fact that I have a purpose in telling you the date does not mean that my report is biased or unfair.

Eagleton proceeds to play on the equivocation by discounting the idea that factual knowledge may be "distorted by particular interests" (biases) on the grounds that, without "particular interests" (purposes), there would be no "point" in getting to know anything. The conflation is complete when Eagleton says that "interests"—the two senses are now hopelessly entangled—are constitutive of knowledge. Finally, he simply defines the "structure of values which informs and underlies our factual statements" as "ideology" and then defines "ideology" in terms of "power-relations," equating values and power by verbal fiat.

If one keeps the two senses of "interest" distinct, interests pose no challenge to the possibility of objectivity. Interest, in the sense of purpose, is fully compatible with objectivity. If I am interested in knowing what time it is, I look at my watch. Even if I am agitated— afraid I may miss my plane—I look at my watch and it tells me the time. Interest, in this sense, is not only compatible with objectivity; it may actually enhance it, motivating me to be more careful and precise. Interest in the second sense—having a vested interest in a certain outcome—poses no problem for objectivity, because there are always ways to set aside one's vested interests. However much you may wish for a blue sky, you can recognize one that is cloudy and gray. The campaign manager who wants his or her candidate to win, may know that the polling data shows a victory to be unlikely. There are both common-sense and, in scientific contexts for example, highly refined procedures for setting aside interests. Setting aside one's interests is not a heroic act; it is commonplace. Every disappointed expectation represents a cor-rected judgment; every act of kindness, a recognition that someone else's interest may at this moment and in this way be more important than one's own. Human beings could not cope with the world as success-fully as they do without the self-correcting mechanisms that our cogni-tive processes and institutions provide; they could not live together as successfully as they do without self-inhibiting behavior that takes fair-ness and the interests of others into account.

Empirically, it would appear that people quite often set aside or rise above their interests. People do not appear to hold only those beliefs that support their group's interests. It would take very strong arguments to show that we should discount or disbelieve the empirical evidence. Instead, transformationists provide arguments that either rest on equiv-ocation or validly support only weaker claims. They do, of course, present many detailed interpretations that unmask interests lurking within the most apparently disinterested texts and institutions. Even if one credits these interpretations, it is not clear why they are taken as proof that all beliefs are based on interests rather than as steps toward objectivity. If it is discovered, for example, that the generic use of "man" to stand for all human beings suppresses women, the decision to use "persons" instead seems to be a move toward a disinterested fairness and impartiality. The very ability to unmask interests is a tribute to the possibility of disinterested knowledge.

One problem with the transformationist discussion of "interests" is that it is not clear what the term refers to. Sometimes it seems to mean self-interest in the rather straightfoward sense that, for example, a tobacco subsidy is in the interest of tobacco companies. It is in this sense that, say, laws against vagrancy may harm the interests of the homeless, and doing business at male-only clubs may harm the interests of women. In this sense, interest can be said to be empirical in that there are factual methods for investigating whether a certain practice results in benefits to a particular group. One can estimate empirically its impact on such factors as the income, health, personal security, and opportunities of members of the group. One can ask members about their own values and preferences with regard to the practice and its outcomes. In fact, the values and preferences of people are central to the empirical sense of interests. This sense of interest, however, is not congenial to postmodern thinking. To know the real economic consequences of equal pay and not just how the idea of pay has been socially constructed, one might need to believe in an objective reality and objective methods for ascertaining truth about it. Moreover, postmodernist thinking casts doubt on individuals' understanding of their own self-interest. Values and preferences are seen as socially constructed, largely by symbols and institutions that further the interests of the dominant class. Women who want to get married and workers happy to have a home, a camper, and a two-week vacation may be seen as acting under what the Marxists call "false consciousness," oblivious to their "true" interests.

But what determines someone's "true" interests? Some Marxists make a distinction between desires that are real—true needs—and those that are artificial—desires created by such forces as advertising and social conditioning; but such a distinction presupposes that there is such a thing as human nature, an "essentialism" postmodernists reject.

A related question is: Who determines what the interests of a group are? Who speaks for the oppressed? Groups, oppressed and otherwise, are not monolithic. Do they have a single set of interests? How would we find out? If a woman or an African American does not agree with an item on the transformationist agenda, does that (a) disconfirm the view that interests are group-based rather than individual, (b) merely show that this particular agenda is not the one that reflects the group, or (c) show that this individual has false consciousness? The transformationist seems to be committed to the third option, but this option requires some sense of "true" interest incompatible not only with the empirical sense of the term but also with its use in the thesis that belief systems represent group interests. If belief is shaped by group interest, how is it possible for a member of a group to have beliefs that are not in the interest of the group?

Finally, what are the interests of the dominant class? If Shakespeare's portrayal of Prospero supports the power of white, male, European colonialists, does that mean that it supports their interests as well? If so, why is that bad? If the transformationists are right, could it be otherwise? Could there be a Shakespeare who did not support the hegemony of his class? If not, how can there be an anti-hegemonic Lentricchia? He is a white, male, European American—must not his views reflect the interests of white males? But what if his views are identical to those of a radical feminist? If so, does Lentricchia transcend his race and gender?

But, if he can, others can too. Then what was the point of all the talk about identity, groups, and interests?

There are similar—in fact, precisely analogous—problems with the transformationists' use of such terms as "power," "empowerment," and "hegemony." Is power simply the ability to get what one wants, or is there a normative sense of what one should want? When men become feminists, do they lose power or gain it? Or do they lose it in the empirical sense and gain it in the "true" sense? The classic idea that always getting what one wants can be self-destructive, that one can be a slave to one's passions, is grounded in a theory of human nature, of the correct ordering and balancing of the parts of the soul. But this explanation is not open to postmodernists, who reject the idea of human nature. For them, all selves are constructed equal. For them, there is no clear ground for preferring to be one sort of self rather than another, and hence no foundation in human nature for distinguishing between simply getting one's way and a more normative sense of power.

The concept of hegemony is no clearer. When one culture influences another, the influence is often characterized as hegemony. But it is not plausible to regard all cultural influence as hegemonic, if this means that it is coercive or contrary to the interests of the influenced country. As pizza became popular in this country, perhaps Italy became more powerful—but not at our expense. As Levi jeans became popular in Italy, perhaps we became more powerful, but not to their detriment. If power includes the realization of one's values, the spread of Western-style democratic institutions around the world increases the power of the West, but to the benefit, not the detriment, of the new democracies. Denouncing all outside influence that alters indigenous cultures as "cultural hegemony" implies that cultures have nothing to learn from each other. It is an extraordinarily reactionary view, yearning, apparently, for the primordial tribes that dotted the planet five thousand years ago, before any culture bestirred itself to dominate another, the world before cultural hegemony.

Accompanying this yearning, there is a disturbing sense of insularity, of hostility to outside influence, of aggressive self-defense, in transformationist discourse. Cultures should resist the influence of other cultures; groups should assert themselves against other groups; individuals should empower themselves. It is what postmodernists call an "agonistic" tone—we are at war with each other, not in harmony with truth—and the assertion of will against will follows from the postmodern rejection of truth. Replacing the disinterested pursuit of truth with interest-based rhetoric makes, in classic terms, will rather than reason predominant. Marxist theory, correctly understood, says Lentricchia, is "a form of will to power." Similarly, harking back to the Greek Sophists, Fish has emphasized that the goal of rhetoric is simply to prevail, by whatever means are at one's disposal. On this view, argument is a test of wills conducted with verbal weapons, not an exchange of ideas in the pursuit of truth. If there is such a thing as truth, then the person who is open to persuasion, who can give up beliefs that are not well-founded, who is therefore open to the truth, is better off than the willful person who insists on "winning" every argument, a closed soul who can learn nothing. If there is no such thing as truth, then there is nothing but winning—and maybe not even that, since presumably there would also be no truth to the question of who won. Perhaps one could successfully claim to have won. In the absence of a reality-check, one could simply pretend to have won. Is this the goal of human life—to protect oneself from all outside influence? Not if we live in a real world.

Step 7: Race, Class, and Gender

Traditional social reformers tried to create a society in which each individual would be able to fulfill his or her potential. But the group-interest thesis requires that social goals be framed in terms of the power of groups, not the aspirations of individuals. Marx singled out class as the critical category and provided a theory of history to justify this choice. Recent thinkers emphasize race and gender as well. The emphasis on race, class, and gender has less to do with a general theory of social and historical dynamics than with a theory of oppression. In other words, the argument for focusing on race, class, and gender is not so much that they are the moving forces of history as that they identify the most oppressed groups. Occasionally someone mentions that people have also suffered because of their religion or other factors; but, oddly enough, even so persistently persecuted a group as Jews receives scant attention in current debates. No one seems to be proposing that more Jewish texts and topics be added to the curriculum—Maimonides and Spinoza are regarded as just more dead, white, European males. The problem is, of course, that, despite a history of persecution and discrimination, American Jews are rather successful. Sometimes there is hesitation over Asian Americans, some of whom have been successful, while others at this point are less so. There even seems to be a bit of irritation when such groups succeed, refusing merely to be victims, since this success does not fit with the image of a closed, oppressive capitalist society. The emphasis is always on groups that have been oppressed but have not, so far at least, succeeded. Since some members of various groups—some Asian Americans, some Latinos—have been more oppressed or, conversely, more successful than others, the groupings to be favored have to be fine-tuned. Gradations have been established among various Asians and Hispanics, depending on racial background, national origin, and social class. By these criteria, it would be more important for the curriculum to include works by Carlos Fuentes than Miguel de Cervantes, but even more important to include works by Chicana working-class women.

The logic of this position is puzzling. If it is important to focus attention on the precise subgroup that has suffered, then why not go all the way to the individual level? Two individuals may be identical in their group memberships and yet have very different life histories. One may have suffered more hardships or handicaps than the other. If hardships and handicaps are the key to consideration, why not focus on the particular individuals who have suffered the most? The argument for focusing on the group is not clear. Even if it were true that individual identity were formed primarily out of group affiliations, it would not follow that one should treat individuals in terms of their group memberships rather than in terms of their own particular traits and histories. If it is valuable to read the writings of an oppressed person, then one should read the writings of an individual who was in fact oppressed, not the work of an individual who happens to be a member of a group, many or most of whose members were oppressed. Of course, then some members of the white-male-European canon (the slave Epictetus, for example) would count.

Even more doubtful than the focus on the group is the idea that some oppressed people "speak for the oppressed," while others do not. The minority writer who denounces America as hopelessly racist may be seen as speaking for the oppressed, while the minority writer who sees America as an increasingly open society may be seen as a tool of the dominant class. Marx and Sartre may be preferred to Booker T. Washington and Mario Vargas Llosa. In spite of the talk of "other voices," the only voices that count are those who share the general sociopolitical outlook of the transformationists. Besides the problems this view poses for academic freedom and intellectual diversity, it poses a logical problem for the transformationist position. What is the point of all the talk about relativism and group interests if it turns out to be perfectly possible to identify the correct political views regardless of one's race, class, and gender? There is an implicit universalism here that the postmodernist is supposed to reject.

Steps 8, 9, 10, and 12: Politics, Empowerment,
Inclusion, and (Re)vision

Consistent or not, there is an implicit universalism at the heart of the transformationist view as it plays out on American campuses. All the talk of hegemony and domination, inclusion and empowerment, rests on strong normative commitments, a belief in radical egalitarianism and the transformation of people into "better people."[46] Given these strong normative commitments, one might expect to see more discussion of the rich literature on such normative political topics as the different meanings of equality, the ways in which strong values such as freedom and equality can conflict, the epistemological grounding of rights and goods, and so forth. While postmodernists pride themselves on the sophistication of their critical analyses, their normative claims seem to be based on little more than a passion for equality, an anger at what they see as oppression, a shock at "the political horrors of one's time," and a feeling of being "alienated and dispossessed."[47]

When questions about the proper conception of freedom or equality are raised, they are often recast as questions of strategy. What conception of freedom empowers women? What conception of equality undermines capitalism? These discussions do not answer the kinds of objections outsiders would raise, and presumably are not meant to. Individuals who see themselves primarily as members of oppressed groups, and who believe that distinctive insights and perhaps even an exclusive truth follows from that membership, do not necessarily feel the need to answer the objections of outsiders. History is, alas, littered with the remains of groups—some of which have done much harm—that felt no need to justify their beliefs and actions to others. Such an attitude closes rather than opens discussion, protects rather than inhibits irrationality, and encourages the pursuit of power rather than the pursuit of mutual understanding. Epistemologically, no one group has sufficient grounds to claim a privileged status for its beliefs. Institutionally, higher education cannot perform its function—to expand human understanding—if it surrenders to such claims.

Steps 13 through 17: Political Standards and Critical Pedagogy

The mission of a university dedicated to the pursuit of truth is to teach students the modes and methods of inquiry, the major alternative views in each field, and ways to articulate and assess arguments on each side. The university teacher, declares the American Association of University Professors' 1915 Statement of Principles, should set forth justly, without suppression or innuendo, the divergent opinions of other investigators; he should cause his students to become familiar with the best published expressions of the great historic types of doctrine upon the questions at issue; and he should, above all, remember that his business is not to provide his students with ready-made conclusions but to train them to think for themselves, and to provide them access to those materials which they need if they are to think intelligently.[48]

The ethic of teaching that follows from these principles supports the academic freedom of students as well as professors and restricts the right of teachers to use their power over students, which is psychological as well as practical, to push their own agendas.

By contrast, the mission of the transformative university is to produce students who are agents of social transformation. This mission assumes that professors have the right to use the classroom to advance their own political agendas. Teachers should be "transformative intellectuals," says Henry Giroux, "not merely concerned with forms of empowerment that promote individual achievement and traditional forms of academic success" but also with "social engagement and transformation" and with "educating students to take risks and to struggle within ongoing relations of power."[49]

But what right do teachers have, one may ask, to push their own political agendas in the classroom? To justify such a role requires, according to Giroux, a "theory of ethics that provides the referent for teachers to act as engaged and connected intellectuals." Giroux bases this new ethics of teaching on the concept of "emancipatory authority," the idea that "teachers are bearers of critical knowledge, rules, and values" that allow them "to judge, critique, and reject" prevailing social authorities. "In my view," he says, "the most important referent for this particular view of authority rests in a commitment that addresses the many instances of suffering that are both a growing and threatening part of everyday life in America and abroad."[50]

As stated, the argument is not very persuasive. Authority over others cannot plausibly be claimed solely on the basis of one person's "commitment"—since that would imply the logically impossible situation that individuals with opposite commitments would have authority over each other. Perhaps the claim to authority is based, not on the mere fact of commitment, but on the idea that this commitment reflects an accurate diagnosis and prescription for human suffering. Schematically, this argument is of the following form: X is true (and important), hence students should believe X, hence the teachers have the right to ensure that students believe X. This is a plausible argument scheme until one realizes that the first premise should be, not "X is true," but "Giroux believes that X is true." And a second premise would have to be: "Others disagree." From which it follows that students should be taught not one but two points of view. To draw any different conclusion would be to assume a cloak of infallibility. In fact, transformationists sometimes write as if, while there is no truth, political commitments are the one sure guide. "Rather than believe in the absolute truth of what we are writing, we must believe in the moral or political position we are taking with it," conclude University of Pennsylvania professors Ellen Somekawa and Elizabeth A. Smith.[51] Rejecting foundationalism in epistemology, political commitment becomes the new foundation. One would have thought that political commitment—with its complex presuppositions involving economics, social structure, historical causation, human values, and political feasibility—would have been an unlikely candidate for certitude, but it has become the new touchstone for many transformationists.

In any case, political commitment is the touchstone; and hence the goal of critical pedagogy is not open-ended inquiry but the political transformation of the students. This goal presents a pedagogical challenge, since many students do not share the political views of their transformationist professors. This disagreement is not, according to transformationists, a healthy sign, a tribute to the diversity of free minds, a basis for thoughtful dialogue and debate. Instead, it is a problem to be overcome. In fact, this problem—"the problem of resistance" as it is called—is a major theme in transformationist writings on pedagogy. In these writings, student objections are not presented as arguments but as hang-ups, defenses, and emotional blocks, reflective of the repressions of the larger society. Jim Merod writes that "the first resistance any teacher confronts is the student's defense against the threat of change" and places this resistance within the context of "the collective nature of defense structures . . . the cultural and ideological matrix that frames social action." "When the culture at large or the neighborhood that has powerfully informed the precritical intellect becomes an opponent for the somewhat stumped teacher," writes Merod, "such opposition constitutes a defense that dampens the possibilities of bringing distrustful students to the threshold of critical imagination."[52]

Transformationists worry about how to overcome student resistance. Gregory Ulmer recommends "de-programming" students who "still resist the claims of the original surrealists." Drawing on psychoanalysis, he recommends using "transference" to "deal with" their "resistance."[53] A group of feminist seminar leaders complains about the "defensiveness" of some participants—in this case, other faculty in the seminar. In this account, disagreements over points of interpretation—e.g., of Aristotle and of Genesis—were regarded as male resistance. "While attesting to the power of the ideas we sponsored," the seminar leaders write, "this defensiveness was one of the major blocks to acceptance of those ideas." Rather than wrestling with the arguments against their views, they concluded that "the tools of rationality alone are inadequate to the task of intellectual change." So, the next time, they tried "to deal with male resistance by introducing materials that explicitly analyzed it" but found, to their surprise, that this material "elicit[ed] profound levels of hostility." They could not understand why seminar participants felt that "we constituted a kind of 'police force.' "[54]

To their credit, some teachers who share transformationist goals worry about the latent authoritarianism within politicized teaching. While advocating an "anti-hegemonic teaching" that "addresses students as socially and historically inscribed subjects who can be agents of social transformation," University of Connecticut professor Maria-Regina Kecht argues that "instructional methodology should not subordinate the students" but should allow students to "represent their own worlds and perspectives."[55] Similarly, Carnegie Mellon University professor David R. Shumway holds that, "although teaching theory means teaching Marxism, feminism, and other politically motivated discourses, it also means teaching students not to accept uncritically what their teachers tell them." For these teachers, critical pedagogy requires a delicate balance, leading students toward the right conclusions without coercing them. "The best we can do is to create conditions wherein it is possible for students to come to accept the theories we advocate," concludes Shumway. "In spite of our inability to ground or metaphysically support our claims for our theories, we must assume that they will be persuasive to those whose interests they serve."[56]

Far from strengthening the transformationist view, these modest disclaimers further reveal its dilemma. The transformationist proposes to mold students into, among other things, radical egalitarians; but to do so would give teachers authority over students that is incompatible with radical egalitarianism. The dictatorship of the proletariat may have been replaced by the dictatorship of the professoriate, but the dilemma remains the same—how to achieve anti-authoritarian ends by authoritarian means.

In spite of its language of "critical thinking" and "liberation," critical pedagogy limits rather than opens inquiry. It assumes the finality of a single set of political commitments, an assumption that is epistemologically unfounded and untenable. Critical pedagogy also fails ethically because it treats other human beings as less than free and rational agents to be respected. At best, it is paternalistic; at its worst, disingenuous and manipulative.

IV. Conclusion: The Transformationist Vision and Its Consequences

Social reformist and Marxist arguments for harnessing the university to a political agenda always stopped short, in theory at least, of discounting rational inquiry and the need for rational justification. The fact that a view has terrible consequences does not show that it is false, but this is almost the exception that proves the rule. For the consequence in question is the very possibility of subjecting the view to rational scrutiny. The very assertion of the thesis is, as Lentricchia says, "a form of will to power." Although the postmodern critique of objectivity has been put in service of leftist causes, it seems more akin to fascism in its roots. How could the postmodernist resist the following logic:

> In Germany relativism is an exceedingly daring and subversive theoretical construction. . . . In Italy, relativism is simply a fact. . . . Everything I have said and done in these last years is relativism by intuition. . . . If relativism signifies contempt for fixed categories and men who claim to be the bearers of an objective, immortal truth . . . then there is nothing more relativistic than Fascist attitudes and activity. . . . From the fact that all ideologies are of equal value, that all ideologies are mere fictions, the modern relativist infers that everybody has the right to create for himself his own ideology and to attempt to enforce it with all the energy of which he is capable.[57]

The quote is from Benito Mussolini and expresses a central idea of the postmodernists—that, since contending beliefs represent contending interests and there is no rational way to adjudicate between them, the ultimate arbiter is power. For postmodernists, it is primarily verbal power, control over words and images, but power nonetheless.

As Mussolini understood, ideas have consequences. If the great intellectual achievements of civilization are taught solely as instruments of oppression, or are simply thrown out of the curriculum to make room for more "empowering" materials, they will be lost. Older transformationists who themselves received a traditional education think that this is a misplaced fear. They continue to teach—and often to love teaching—Shakespeare even if their love is expressed in clever unmaskings of his patriarchal imperialism. They assume their students will also continue to read Shakespeare and to share their joy. But young African Americans, for example, may not see the point in reading those they have been taught to see as their oppressors. What will the older professor say to persuade them? That they need to know the tradition the better to resist it? Will that be a compelling reason to young people who have already been "empowered"? Why would a woman who has been taught that contemporary science "rapes" nature undertake the study of physics? In fact, many transformationists recommend radical changes in the curriculum. Their goal is not merely to expand the canon but to teach students how to reconceive themselves and to reconstruct their world. Ted Gordon and Wahneema Lubiano, for example, argue that multiculturalism conceived as "exposure to different cultures" is "absolutely meaningless without a reconsideration and restructuring of the ways in which knowledge is organized, disseminated, and used to support inequitable power differentials."[58] Similarly, Jean Howard warns against pluralist multiculturalism: "Equally dangerous, I think, is the threat that the creation of space for the study of difference (ethnic difference, sexual difference, religious difference) will blunt internal dissent by giving various identity-defined groups a 'share' in a pluralist academy." She calls for a "critical concept of difference that would underwrite a left, rather than a liberal pluralist, concept of multiculturalism" and for a way of teaching difference that "aims for the transformation of society and resists the appropriation of the study of difference to the ends of late capitalism. . . ." Students would be "taught to assess how their 'differences' are produced and used in a social system which is unfair and exploitative and which they might challenge."[59] It should not surprise anyone if Dante, Beethoven, and Newton are not parts of this reconstructed education.

But the most serious problem is that the postmodern argument for making the university an agent of social transformation protects itself from criticism, not only theoretically, but institutionally as well. The early steps of the postmodern argument may be questionable, but grant them and the remaining steps—including political correctness, critical pedagogy, speech codes, and denial—follow. Rejecting the principles and procedures of rationality, the view cannot be subjected to rational (as distinct from political) criticism. If the test of a theory is its effectiveness in producing desirable social change, then any critique will be condemned as reactionary. Any counterargument will be seen as oppressive. It is already considered "antifeminist harassment" for male students to pick at flaws in feminist arguments.[60] The door is closed to further debate; the new orthodoxy cannot be questioned. You may freely embrace the transformationist argument; but, having once embraced it, you are never again free to question it. Allow this argument to shape the university, and no one will be free to question it.

Advocates of using the university for social transformation will be unmoved by these considerations. What would be the point of questioning whether racism, sexism, and exploitation are wrong? The very desire to debate the pros and cons of these social evils is seen as part of the problem. Grant that point all of its emotional, moral, and persuasive force; add to it all the arguments and analyses of Foucault, the Marxists, the deconstructionists, et al.; and you still have the question, What if they are wrong? They are not infallible—they could be wrong. Given the limitations of perspective they have themselves emphasized, they may have misread history and misargued epistemology. Racism, sexism, and economic inequality are complex phenomena. It is easy to condemn them but difficult to analyze them correctly, and more difficult still to determine the best solutions. Knowing that the analyses and prescriptions that represent today's most advanced thinking may be tomorrow's debunked myth, would it be wise to stop questioning, to give up the search for truth, to banish competing views from the curriculum, to close off further inquiry, and to substitute for these activities the training of students to become agents of a political ideology? Could a rational person freely choose such a course?

I once knew a woman who was a socialist, a pacifist, and an atheist, as firm in her views as anyone I have ever known. Even so, I was surprised to hear her say one day that, if there were a potion she could give to her young son that would ensure that he would become a socialist, a pacificist, and an atheist, she would do so. Today this same woman, a person of great thoughtfulness about these matters, is neither a socialist, a pacificist, nor an atheist. I do not know whether her son, now grown, still holds to the beliefs he was taught as a child. But I do know that, there being no potion, he is, like his mother, still free to make up his own mind.

NOTES

1. Someone who has not overlooked this point is Lynne V. Cheney. See *Telling the Truth: A Report on the State of the Humanities in Higher Education* (Washington: National Endowment for the Humanities, 1992).
2. Henry A. Giroux and Peter McLaren, eds., *Critical Pedagogy, the State, and Cultural Struggle* (Albany: State University of New York Press, 1989), pp. xxxi, xxi, xxiii, xxvii.
3. Frank Lentricchia, *Criticism and Social Change* (Chicago: University of Chicago Press, 1983), pp. 12, 10.

4. Richard Ohmann, *English in America: A Radical View of the Profession* (New York: Oxford University Press, 1976), p. 335.
5. Giroux, *Critical Pedagogy,* p. 145.
6. Margaret L. Andersen, "Changing the Curriculum in Higher Education," in Elizabeth Minnich, Jean O'Barr, and Rachel Rosenfeld, eds., *Reconstructing the Academy: Women's Education and Women's Studies* (Chicago: University of Chicago Press, 1988), p. 39.
7. Terry Eagleton, *Literary Theory: An Introduction* (Minneapolis: University of Minnesota Press, 1983), pp. 211, 216.
8. Jean E. Howard, "Under Pressure: Political Intervention in the Academy, The Institutional 'Incorporation' of Difference" (paper delivered at the 107th convention of the Modern Language Association, San Francisco, December 28, 1991), pp. 1–2. Emphasis appears in the original.
9. George Levine et al., *Speaking for the Humanities* (New York: American Council of Learned Societies, 1989), p. 10.
10. J. Hillis Miller, "Humanistic Research," in *The Humanities in the University: Strategies for the 1990s* (New York: American Council of Learned Societies, 1988), p. 25.
11. Richard Rorty makes a similar distinction in contrasting his own advocacy of "reform of institutions" with Lentricchia's call for the "transformation of society," which Rorty takes to be "more or less synonymous with 'revolution.' " See Rorty, "Two Cheers for the Cultural Left," in Darryl J. Gless and Barbara Herrnstein Smith, eds., *The Politics of Liberal Education* (Durham: Duke University Press, 1992), p. 235.
12. In an interesting parallel to this point, Daniel Harris has objected that such postmodern gay activists as ACT-UP have hurt progress on AIDS research by regarding it as a "discourse" rather than a disease. Daniel Harris, "AIDS & Theory: Has Academic Theory Turned AIDS into Meta-Death?" *Lingua Franca,* June 1991.
13. Levine, *Speaking,* p. 9.
14. Betty Jean Craige speaks of "the new relativism," but some transformationists avoid the term, which, for some, connotes the total lack of standards. The transformationist view, typically, is not that there are no standards, but that standards are relative in the sense presented in the argument. See Betty Jean Craige, *Reconnection: Dualism to Holism in Literary Study* (Athens: University of Georgia Press, 1988), pp. 8–12.
15. Craige, *Reconnection,* p. 111.
16. Lentricchia, *Criticism,* p. 19.
17. See Stanley Fish, *Doing What Comes Naturally: Change, Rhetoric, and the Practice of Theory in Literary and Legal Studies* (Durham: Duke University Press, 1989), pp. 141–60, and *Is There a Text in This Class? The Authority of Interpretive Communities* (Cambridge: Harvard University Press, 1980), pp. 303–55.
18. Eagleton, *Literary Theory,* p. 13.
19. Levine, *Speaking,* p. 10; Eagleton, *Literary Theory,* p. 14.
20. The need to replace dualism with holism in our thinking and institutional practices is the focus of Craige's *Reconnection.*
21. See Levine, *Speaking,* p. 10; Giroux, *Critical Pedagogy,* p. 127.
22. Andersen, "Changing the Curriculum," p. 61.
23. See Craige, *Reconnection,* p. 11; and Peggy McIntosh, "Seeing Our Way

Clear: Feminist Re-vision of the Academy," in Kathy Loring, ed., *Proceedings of the Eighth Annual Great Lakes Colleges Association Women's Studies Conference* (Ann Arbor: GLCA Women's Studies Program, 1983), p. 6.

24. Giroux, *Critical Pedagogy,* p. 147; Sharon Welch, *Communities of Resistance and Solidarity* (New York: Orbis Press, 1985), p. 31.
25. Lentricchia, *Criticism,* p. 12.
26. *Ibid.,* p. 10.
27. Susan Hardy Aiken et al., "Trying Transformations: Curriculum Integration and the Problem of Resistance," in Minnich, *Reconstructing the Academy,* p. 121; Lentricchia, *Criticism,* p. 12; Giroux, *Critical Pedagogy,* p. xxviii.
28. Aiken, "Trying Transformations," p. 108.
29. *Ibid.,* p. 112.
30. See Craige, *Reconnection,* pp. 123–24.
31. See Stanley Fish, "There's No Such Thing As Free Speech and It's a Good Thing Too," *Boston Review,* February 1992; a slightly different version appears in Paul Berman, ed., *Debating P.C.: The Controversy Over Political Correctness on College Campuses* (New York: Dell, 1992).
32. Craige, *Reconnection,* pp. 128–29.
33. See Herbert Marcuse, "Repressive Tolerance," in Robert Paul Wolff, Barrington Moore, Jr., and Herbert Marcuse, *A Critique of Pure Tolerance* (Boston: Beacon Press, 1965), pp. 81–117.
34. Even Gerald Graff, co-founder of Teachers for a Democratic Culture, an organization dedicated to refuting charges of political correctness, has chided his colleagues for disingenuousness about the changes they propose:

   If they [feminism, Marxism, post-structuralism] continue to spread, they will radically change what it means to "expand the horizons of human knowledge." Since those on the Right recognize this perfectly well, telling them that nothing much has really changed and that it's all been blown out of proportion by the press will only seem to justify their anger and self-righteousness.

   Gerald Graff, letter to the editor, *ACLS Newsletter,* Winter 1991, p. 5.
35. Lentricchia, *Criticism,* pp. 12–13.
36. Robert Scholes, *Textual Power: Literary Theory and the Teaching of English* (New Haven: Yale University Press, 1985), pp. 86–110.
37. Levine, *Speaking,* p. 10.
38. For example, see Fish, *Doing What Comes Naturally,* pp. 142–46.
39. See Friedrich Waismann, "Verifiability," in Antony Flew, ed., *Logic and Language* (Oxford: Basil Blackwell, 1955), pp. 117–44.
40. Fish, *Doing What Comes Naturally,* pp. 141–60.
41. Lentricchia, *Criticism,* pp. 12–14.
42. *Ibid.,* p. 13.
43. See Peter Shaw, "Feminist Literary Criticism: A Report from the Academy," *American Scholar,* Autumn 1988, pp. 495–513.
44. Consider the following statement by Simone de Beauvoir: "No woman should be authorized to stay at home to raise her children. . . . Women should not have that choice, precisely because if there is such a choice, too many women will make that one." See dialogue between Simone de Beauvoir and Betty Friedan in *Saturday Review,* June 14, 1975, p. 18.

45. Eagleton, *Literary Theory,* pp. 13–14.
46. *Ibid.,* p. 211.
47. Lentricchia, *Criticism,* pp. 11, 1.
48. Louis Joughin, ed., "The 1915 Declaration of Principles," in *Academic Freedom and Tenure: A Handbook of the American Association of University Professors* (Madison: University of Wisconsin Press, 1969), p. 169.
49. Giroux, *Critical Pedagogy,* p. 138.
50. *Ibid.,* pp. xxxii, 138, 139.
51. Ellen Somekawa and Elizabeth A. Smith, "Theorizing the Writing of History or, 'I Can't Think Why It Should Be So Dull, For a Great Deal of It Must Be Invention,' " *Journal of Social History,* Fall 1988, p. 154.
52. Jim Merod, "Blues and the Art of Critical Teaching," in Maria-Regina Kecht, ed., *Pedagogy Is Politics: Literary Theory and Critical Teaching* (Urbana: University of Illinois Press, 1992), pp. 153, 161.
53. Gregory L. Ulmer, "Textshop for Psychoanalysis: On De-Programming Freshmen Platonists," *College English,* November 1987, pp. 756, 762–63.
54. Aiken, "Trying Transformations," pp. 112, 115.
55. Maria-Regina Kecht, "The Challenge of Responsibility: An Introduction," in Kecht, ed., *Pedagogy Is Politics,* pp. 11–12, 8.
56. David R. Shumway, "Integrating Theory in the Curriculum as Theorizing— A Postdisciplinary Practice," in Kecht, ed., *Pedagogy Is Politics,* pp. 104–5.
57. Benito Mussolini, *Diuturna,* pp. 374–77, quoted in Henry B. Veatch, *Rational Man: A Modern Interpretation of Aristotelian Ethics* (Bloomington: Indiana University Press, 1962), p. 41.
58. Ted Gordon and Wahneema Lubiano propose a "transformative multiculturalism"—"a transformative, not reformist project"—that focuses on marginalized cultures as "objects of domination." Ted Gordon and Wahneema Lubiano, "The Statement of the Black Faculty Caucus," in Berman, *Debating P.C.* (see note 31 above), pp. 249–50, 253, 255.
59. Howard, "Under Pressure," pp. 3–4.
60. See "New Project on Antifeminist Harassment," *MLA Newsletter,* September 1991, p. 21.

"The Enemy Is Us": Objectivity and Its Philosophical Detractors

Fred Sommers

I. Squaring the Circle

Back in the fifties, when I was a graduate philosophy student at Columbia University, a group of philosophers called the Vienna Circle (the original "logical positivists") was very much in vogue.[1] Some zealous partisans in our philosophical society were concerned to make the Vienna Circle's ideas more available to the general public as an organon for analyzing political questions of the day. This prompted the society to stage a public debate on the feasibility of bringing philosophy to bear on politics. I no longer remember just how the question was formulated, but I remember being chosen to speak against a deliberate effort to make philosophy more relevant to public policy. I remember saying that my opponent was trying to get the Vienna Circle into Union Square. And I added that this attempt would be no more successful than other attempts to square the circle.

All the same, I have always been fascinated by how a philosophical position affects the general culture—by how, say, the doctrine of strict determinism plays in the Presbyterian churches of Peoria or, more seriously perhaps, by how Hegel trickles down through Marx to get people believing and behaving politically as if history moves like an argument to a culminating conclusion. At the time of that debate, we used to say: "Philosophy bakes no bread." In that, we were mostly wrong. It is true that philosophers seldom get to do the baking, but it is undeniable that they supply much of the yeast and flour. What I call "squaring the circle" is the calculated effort on the part of philosophers to effect political change in ways that conform with their theories. Plato tried it unsuccessfully in Syracuse; Lenin and Mao did it more consequentially in Russia and in China; and more recently some French-educated Marxists applied the fruits of their learning to Cambodia. We know that squaring the circle poses grave risks for everyone, especially when the intellectuals who do it are dogmatic or half-baked philosophers with a full contempt for those who oppose them. A little philosophy is a dangerous thing.

Most philosophers remain "purely academic" in what they do and say. There is one area, however, that has always put philosophers in direct contact with practical issues, and that is education. As we all learned from Plato, even the most abstract controversies have their immediate bearing on what to teach and how to teach it. In my day at Columbia, John Dewey's educational theories were even more discussed than his version of pragmatism. But, of course, his philosophy and his educational innovations are intimately related, and today when a popular philosopher like Richard Rorty styles himself as being of the "cultural left" and proclaims himself to be a follower of Dewey, all the old connections are again made to show how the traditional metaphysics and epistemology which Dewey inveighed against are so elitist and stifling to young minds.[2]

As Rorty himself would happily acknowledge, Plato would have considered him a modern-day Sophist. To mention just two points of divergence: where Plato is at pains to distinguish knowledge from opinion and reality from appearance, Rorty, like the Sophists before him, devalues both distinctions, agreeing with Dewey that they are deployed by an intellectual elite. Says Rorty: "Such distinctions conspire to produce the idea that rational inquiry should make visible a realm to which nonintellectuals have little access."[3]

Plato believed that an adequate philosophy of education must be grounded in an account of reality and in a theory of knowledge that explains how we have access to it. Education sheds light on that reality. Plato also held that enlightenment makes one virtuous. For he was convinced that vice has no purchase in one who has knowledge: theoretical understanding guarantees edification of character and practical wisdom. This latter doctrine lost credibility when Christian theologians, and most notably Augustine, persuasively argued that the impulse to evil (which Christians viewed as an urge to defy God and to rebel against His laws) could not be dispelled by merely dispelling ignorance.

The challenge to the former doctrine—that education is enlightenment, that those who are educated apprehend objective truths that transcend them as knowers, that education provides a vision of an objective reality—has been longer in resurfacing, and today there is no Plato to defend these realist ideas from the neosophists who contest them. When a contemporary sophist like Rorty challenges the view that education enlightens the student about an objective reality, we might expect him to be challenged in turn. However, we do not today find the sophistical positions seriously opposed by professional philosophers, not even by those who, by temperament and conviction, would certainly be interested in seeing the objectivist tradition adequately defended.

I shall be commenting on the reasons for this. But however we account for it, the absence of a significant school of realist philosophers has left the learned public without a philosophical counterpoise to the popular philosophy of the insurgent intellectuals who constitute what Rorty calls the "cultural left." This situation may be changing. There are some signs that the insurgent attack on objectivity is beginning to lure some philosophers down from the tower to defend, of all things, "metaphysical realism." So it happened that nonphilosophical readers of the *New York Review of Books* were treated to John Searle's searching critique of the new humanists, a critique that cited Roger Kimball citing Tzvetan Todorov citing George Orwell's character, the torturer O'Brien, who reminds Winston Smith of the price of retaining old-fashioned ideas about objectivity:

> You believe that reality is something objective, external, existing in its own right. . . . But I tell you, Winston, that reality is not external. Reality exists in the human mind and nowhere else.[4]

And Winston Smith learns the hard way that metaphysical realism doesn't pay.

In that review article, Searle discusses a collection of essays called *The Politics of Liberal Education*,[5] originally presented at a conference at the University of North Carolina—a conference that Rorty, who was himself an active participant, described as "a rally of the cultural left." Searle agrees with Rorty that the participants showed "a remarkable consensus in their opposition to the educational tradition"; but, unlike Rorty, whose attitude toward education is conditioned by his rejection of realism, Searle feels the need to defend the traditional universalist ideal of educational enlightenment.

Searle notes that those who oppose traditional education occasionally appeal to Rorty or to Thomas Kuhn to justify their repudiation of the idea that education is engaged in an "objective and disinterested search for truth." According to Searle, Kuhn is misunderstood. Rorty's opposition to objectivity is, however, not open to plausible misconstrual. Searle deals cursorily with Rorty's position by giving a quick "transcendental argument" for "metaphysical realism": in effect, all claims of fact from 'My dog has fleas' to 'Water is made of hydrogen and oxygen' "presuppose for their intelligibility that we are taking metaphysical realism for granted."[6] He says that he hopes to develop his argument for realism in a more professional setting but that, except for one paragraph, he has so far not published anything on the topic. In any case, Searle gives the misleading impression that most analytic philosophers are on the side of a realist, objectivist tradition. But this ignores Rorty's evidence to the contrary.

Rorty's judgment that modern philosophy is a party to undermining objectivity is shared by the University of Chicago historiographer and conceptual historian Peter Novick, in his book on the "objectivity question," *That Noble Dream*. Novick has traced the history of the "noble dream" of historians for an objective account of the past that retrieves it as fact, showing how and why most historians have lost faith in that dream as an ideal for historical scholarship. He argues that disenchanted historians are being persuaded by arguments they find in the work of contemporary philosophers such as Rorty, Kuhn, Nelson Goodman, Hilary Putnam, and Jacques Derrida to conclude, as he himself does, that those who criticize the concept of objectivity are more persuasive than those who defend it. The picture Novick presents is again reminiscent of the heyday of Sophism, except that the current situation lacks balance, since no one is playing the role of Plato.[7]

Thus, we have historians and literary theorists claiming the authority of Anglo-American philosophers like Rorty, Kuhn, Putnam, Norwood Russell Hanson, Willard Quine, and Donald Davidson, and of continental philosophers like Derrida, Jacques Lacan, and Michel Foucault, on the side of their critique of objectivity. And we have Searle discounting the claim by the humanist authors of *Speaking for the Humanities* that "the most powerful modern philosophies and theories have been demonstrating [that] claims of disinterest, objectivity, and universality are not to be trusted. . . ."[8] Searle is right to dismiss that sweeping claim; on the other hand, he underestimates the extent to which much of modern philosophy supports the thesis that truth and objectivity are not "out there" but, in Rorty's Protagorean phrase, "man-made." Searle's unwillingness to acknowledge the complicity of some of the "most powerful" analytic philosophers is partly due to his acute awareness of the political and pedagogical implications of impugning objectivity. It seems it is a distinct embarrassment to him that the philosophers he most respects are being cited by those who are engaged in disparaging reason and objectivity. In effect, Searle's review article leaves the reader with the distinct impression that the literary theorists of the cultural left are just wrong to suggest that many respected Anglo-American analytic philosophers are not metaphysical realists.

Searle is here at odds with Rorty on the facts of recent conceptual history. Rorty has for some time been arguing that modern analytic philosophy is out of sympathy with a realist conception of truth. The issues here are complex, but in the main it is Rorty who is right: Searle is on very poor grounds to suggest that analytic philosophers generally favor a realist position. Speaking myself as an analytic philosopher who has some knowledge and understanding of modern philosophy, and as a realist from the cultural center who is concerned with the way sophistical philosophy is being used by the cultural left, I have come to the conclusion that the intellectual history of our century shows that the enemy impugning realism is, as Pogo would say, "us."

Though I disagree with Rorty on almost every substantive question, I find him and Novick to be reliable guides to the history of the critique of objectivity. When Rorty claims that Dewey, Quine, Goodman, Putnam, and Davidson have been promoting the neosophist doctrine that truth is made rather than found, and when he goes on to show that this puts these thinkers in the same general camp as Foucault and Derrida, I have found him to be credible and insightful. The difference between Rorty and me is not about what has been happening in some of the most important areas of the philosophy of language; it is about whether we should deplore it, as I tend to do, or celebrate it, as he does. I suspect, too, that Rorty would agree with Roger Kimball's characterization of the situation as analogous to that of fifth-century Athens. For now, as then, the fashionable majority of reputable philosophers denies realism and objective knowledge.

In the end, I found that my pleasure in reading Searle's masterful put-down of the cultural left had been not a little spoiled by his unwillingness to grant that many of the confusions about objectivity can be traced to some of the best and most influential Anglo-American philosophers. If Rorty and his cohorts in literary theory are to be cast as the devil, the writings of Quine, Goodman, Kuhn, Putnam, and Davidson are the scriptures they quote. On the whole, Rorty is right to say that these scriptures are aptly quoted.

That the view one takes of the possibilities for objective knowledge will crucially determine one's idea of what to teach, and how to teach it, is clear enough to both sides. Though the debate within educational circles is taking place with a fair and even commendable degree of awareness of the philosophical perspectives that bear on the issues, it is the philosophers who often seem to be indifferent to or incognizant of the pedagogical implications of their theories. Far too few contemporary philosophers who are themselves convinced that truth is "out there" and not "man-made" are alert to the need to defend the objectivity of truth from its sophistical detractors. In some cases, we have philosophers (like Quine) who deplore the radical and left influence on the universities, but whose epistemological and semantic doctrines are being cited in support of the movement to transform the academy on neosophistical lines. Other philosophers, who, like Searle, are consciously realist and aware of the stakes in the realist/anti-realist controversy, seem able to comfort themselves by regarding the pedagogy of neosophism as silly, faddish, and marginal. Searle is able to do this because he has somehow convinced himself that the anti-realist, subjectivist forces are confined to the humanities. He considers this curious:

> One curious feature of the entire debate about what is "hegemonic," "patriarchal," or "exclusionary" is that it is largely about the study of literature. . . . I have not heard any complaints from physics departments that the ideas of Newton, Einstein, Rutherford, Bohr, Schrödinger, etc., were deficient because of the scientists' origins or gender. . . . [M]any members of the cultural left . . . (apparently) accept that in subjects like physics and mathematics there may be objective and socially independent criteria of excellence . . . but where the humanities are concerned they think that the criteria that matter are essentially political.[9]

Searle is right to contrast theoretical physics and literary theory in respect of the *origin* of complaints. Few physicists are deploring the dead-white-European-male (DWEM) origins of their discipline. But he forgets that impugning objectivity often goes hand in hand with explaining the uses of allegedly objective knowledge as an instrument of social control. For example, though physicists are not complaining that their approach to nature is sexist, Searle seems unaware of the common feminist complaints about the "masculinist" nature of the sciences. Admittedly, the critique of the sciences as a "patriarchal construction of knowledge" has so far had little effect on science curricula. It is, however, an important part of the general effort by campus feminists to "transform knowledge" by making it more "women centered." The feminist critique of science is one of the most active areas in feminist philosophy. Feminist philosopher of science Sandra Harding speaks of "the studies of the social construction of what we count as real—both inside and outside the history of science," among which one may count her own works arguing the "androcentric" nature of scientific knowledge and activity. Her argument ties in with the more general thesis that all so-called objective knowledge is social, if only in the minimal sense that reality or matter of fact is not language independent. "Facts cannot be separated from their meanings." Harding finds this to be the deeper significance of Quine's renouncing the distinction between analytic and synthetic truths.[10]

Feminist philosophers consider Descartes to be the archetypical realist rationalist. According to Alison M. Jaggar and Susan R. Bordo, three central Cartesian assumptions are now under a cloud: (1) that "reality has an objective structure unaffected by human understanding"; (2) "that reason is the principal faculty for attaining knowledge of reality"; and (3) that "the faculties of reason and sensation are potentially the same for all human beings regardless of their culture or class, race or sex (universalism). Differences in the situations of human beings are seen as conquerable impediments to a neutral 'objective' view of things."[11] Jaggar and Bordo claim that Nietzsche, Marx, the pragmatists, and, more recently, the deconstructionists in France and Rorty in America have undermined these "Cartesian assumptions." And Jaggar and Bordo point to the feminists' "claim that the Cartesian framework, in addition to other biases, is not gender neutral."[12] It is common to see the use of scare quotes to advertise the suspicion of "what counts as" objectivity. Joyce Trebilcot apprises us of "the apparatuses of 'truth', 'knowledge', 'science', 'revelation', 'faith', etc.," that men use to "project their personalities as reality."[13]

We now find deans and college presidents in the business of admonishing students not to be taken in by claims to objectivity: I cite one of many examples of a new genre of edification from a convocation address delivered by the vice president of academic affairs at the College of Wooster in Ohio. The speaker has since become president of Bates College in Maine.

> [A] major revolution has occurred. . . . Within the last two decades the . . . effort to "objectify" fields of inquiry has been called into question by a challenge to the objectivity of science—the preeminent prototype.

Invoking the names of Norwood Hanson, Thomas Kuhn, Stephen Toulmin, and Sandra Harding, the speaker informed the students that "there is no objectivity even in science." He then confided that "the new view of science, and thereby the new view of any field of intellectual activity is only a whisker away from irrationality and skepticism. But fine lines are important." By this time the students were ready for the uplifting message that "learning and teaching have less to do with truth, reality and objectivity than we had assumed."[14]

At present, classical truth-realism is undeservedly unpopular. There is virtue, therefore, in calling attention to the unpleasant fact that some of the clearest heads in Anglo-American philosophy have been inadvertently complicitous in undermining realism and casting doubt on objectivist ideals and distinctions that are presupposed by the enterprise of an enlightened education. Those of us who, like Searle, are concerned about the pedagogic effects of the assault on objectivity, should not be content with making the point that Kuhn, Quine, Putnam, Goodman, and Davidson are being misunderstood. It is of course easy enough to misunderstand them, but on the question of undermining the ideal of objectivity, they are being understood well enough and in some cases all too well. Nor will it do to say that no one is responsible for the hash the cultural left is making of the anti-realist views of professional philosophers. For in the main, Rorty is right in his interpretation of those views, which place many of our best philosophers within a modern sophistical tradition that subverts realism and the "noble dream." In the end, philosophers like Goodman and Putnam must acknowledge that some of their most cherished positions are being exploited by academic forces who bear a principled animus toward the tradition of educational enlightenment.

I believe, then, that philosophers who belong to the cultural center, and who, like Searle and myself, believe that truth is "out there" and not "man-made," should be focusing attention on the philosophical flank that is providing sophistical aid and protection to the cultural left. I shall be doing that in the remainder of this essay, casting the discussion in terms of the issues dividing realists from sophists and examining some key contemporary sophistical arguments for rejecting realism to reveal their flaws.

The ancient history of the dispute is familiar. In the next section I shall rehearse it as it was first formulated by Protagoras and Plato, then go on to recite some of the positions of the contemporary philosophers that Rorty cites in support of the claim that modern philosophy is mainly on the side of those who deny realism. One must first recognize that the realist conception of truth is indeed in poor repute even among philosophers. Having shown the extent to which "the enemy is us," I will proceed to examine the principal objection of philosophers of language to the traditional thesis that truth is "out there." We shall see that one of the main reasons for the current poor estate of realism is that the nonrealists have placed unreasonable and improper demands on what would count as an adequate realist theory of truth. Because the requirements of adequacy were improperly set up, the defenders of realism were doomed to fail. Once we revise the requirements, we find the way clear for a realist theory of truth. In later sections, I adumbrate a classically realist account of facts in which the relation between what is true and the reality that makes it true is clear and unproblematic. I have included an appendix which shows how such key terms as 'true', 'proposition', 'fact', and 'correspondence' are used in relation to each other.

II. The Neosophists

Framing the issue that divides realists, on the one side, from their sophist and neosophist detractors, on the other, as a dispute over the nature of truth, enables us to usefully focus the discussion in a clear and historically faithful way. The realist friends of objectivity, both ancient and modern, hold that a true proposition corresponds to an objective, nonlinguistic reality—a fact or state of affairs that "makes it true." By contrast, those I call "sophists" reject the postulate that what is true is so in virtue of its correspondence to an objective, language-independent reality. Philosopher of language Donald Davidson is a "neosophist" when he says that correspondence theories "cannot be made intelligible" and that we must "give up facts as entities that make sentences true."[15] Richard Rorty, the contemporary philosopher who is most consciously and openly sophistic, is, of course, happy to accept Davidson's support for the proposal that "the whole idea of truth makers needs to be dropped."[16]

This rather contemporary way of framing the issue is not anachronistic when applied to the older controversy between the Sophists and their objectivist critics. In what immediately follows, I briefly review the classical formulas to remind us that the ancient dispute also turns on the question of whether or not to construe truth as a property conferred on judgments in virtue of their relation to a nonlinguistic, mind-independent reality.

Protagoras, the most famous of the Sophists and the one most respected by Plato, puts the Sophist position in the form of a quasi-definition of truth: "Man is the measure of all things; of things that are that they are, of things that are not that they are not" (Plato, *Theatetus*, 152). Plato wrestled with this celebrated formula in several dialogues, condemning Protagoras's theory for its failure to account for falsehood. He also condemns the theory for its perversion of the idea of education, which Plato conceives as an ascent from ignorance and mere opinion to knowledge. Of Protagoras's proposal he says:

> [It] cannot make someone who previously thought what is false think what
> is true (for it is not possible either to think the thing that is not or to think
> anything but what one experiences, and all experiences are true). (*Ibid.*,
> 167)

Though Plato considered Protagoras hopeless on falsehood and error,
he found that "thinking what is not" presented problems for his own
realist theory of truth. Plato took up the question in the *Sophist*. He
there came up with a solution whose phrasing is strikingly reminiscent of
Protagoras's famous formula, but with two differences. In the first place,
Plato is primarily concerned to characterize falsehood. Second and more
important, for Plato what is true or false is made true or false by reality
and not by man. Thus, Plato, echoing the very words of Protagoras,
characterizes someone who says of Theatetus that he is flying as having
said of what is not, that it is—which is to say, he has said of what is not
flying that it is flying (*Sophist*, 263b).[17] The formula is again repeated in
Aristotle, where we find Plato's definition of falsehood followed by the
corresponding definition of truth:

> To say of what is that it is not, or of what is not that it is, is false, while to
> say of what is that it is, or of what is not that it is not, is true. (Aristotle,
> *Metaphysics*, bk. 4, ch. 7, 1011b25–29)

Thus, the issue dividing the Sophists from their realist critics is truth.
Plato and Aristotle hold to a realist conception of truth; the Sophists
reject it. Medieval philosophers interpreted the realist formulas as
defining truth in terms of "adequation" with or correspondence to
reality: we say what is true if what we say corresponds with reality;
otherwise, what we say is false. Alfred Tarski developed an influential
account of truth in the 1930s—an account he thought of as Aristotelian
in spirit. He, too, reads Aristotle as a truth realist:

> The truth of a sentence consists in its agreement with (or correspondence
> to) reality.[18]

There are difficulties with this as a textual interpretation of the realist
formulas of Plato and Aristotle, but for our purposes, we may count it as
the traditional interpretation. Moving to the current scene, we again find
the crucial issue to be truth. But this time it is the realist theory of truth
that is under fire and in disrepute. In some cases the same philosopher
may move from realism to a sophistical position. Putnam has made this
journey. And Davidson, who, like Tarski, had thought of himself as
holding a version of the correspondence theory, has now come to believe

that all correspondence theories are incoherent. Rejecting correspondence, Davidson claims that realism is a "futile" doctrine:

> The realist view of truth, if it has any content, must be based on the idea of correspondence . . . and such correspondence cannot be made intelligible. . . . [I]t is futile either to reject or to accept the slogan that the real and the true are "independent of our beliefs." The only positive sense we can make of the phrase, the only use that consorts with the intentions of those who prize it, derives from the idea of correspondence, and this is an idea without content.[19]

To deny that true judgments are made true by a mind-independent reality to which they correspond is to regard man, not reality, as the measure of all truth. In my parlance, anyone who rejects truth realism is a "sophist." But the shoe is now on the other foot: today it is the truth realist who is on the defensive. There are complicated reasons for the turnabout, not least among them the strength of a tradition of German idealism that treats much of reality as a "social construction" and that continues to be influential both here and on the continent. Marxism, which has roots in that idealist tradition, and pragmatism are two more-recent philosophies whose critiques of realism have won adherents. But none of these doctrines provides the kind of skeptical arguments that analytic philosophers, temperamentally sympathetic to metaphysical and scientific realism, find compelling.

The truth realist holds that a true proposition corresponds to an "objective, nonlinguistic relatum"—a fact or state of affairs that makes it true. For the contemporary school of Anglo-American philosophers, trained in philosophical logic and philosophy of language, what proved decisive in rejecting realism was the failure to present a coherent account of the "reality" side of the correspondence relation. If the correspondence theory of truth is correct, one should be able to characterize in simple terms the ontological relatum—that which, in or about the world, makes a true statement true. But all efforts to identify things in the world that could serve as the objective relata of correspondence produced no "plausible candidate." As the politicians say: "You can't fight somebody with nobody." If we are looking for a single most important reason for the defection from realism in the powerful school of analytic philosophy, we can find it in the persistent failure of the correspondence theorists to distinguish facts and to specify their nature. Here is Davidson on correspondence theories:

> The real objection is . . . that such theories fail to provide entities to which truth vehicles (whether we take these to be statements, sentences, or utterances) can be said to correspond. If this is right, and I am convinced

it is, we ought also to question the popular assumption that sentences, or their speech tokens, or sentence-like entities or configurations in our brains, can properly be called "representations," since there is nothing for them to represent. [20]

There is, of course, the common use of 'fact' to refer to "true proposition," "true thought" (Frege), or "what a statement, if true, states" (Strawson).[21] But then 'fact' is linguistic; it is what is expressed or stated, and *its* truth needs to be anchored in something "out there" to which it corresponds and which makes it true.

The failure to identify ontological facts was underscored by a famous debate some thirty-five years ago between Peter Strawson and John Austin in which Strawson criticized Austin's version of the correspondence theory, persuasively showing that none of Austin's suggestions for the ontological relatum made any sense. Strawson argued that statements are not like names or descriptive expressions; those parts of the statement direct us to things in the world, but the statement as a whole does not:

> That (person, thing, etc.) to which the referring part of the statement refers, and which the describing part of the statement fits or fails to fit, is that which the statement is *about*. It is evident that there is nothing else in the world for the statement itself to be related to. . . . The only plausible candidate for (what in the world) makes statements true is the fact it states; but the fact it states is not something in the world. . . . Roughly, the thing referred to is the material correlate of the statement. . . . [T]he fact to which the statement "corresponds" is the pseudo-material correlate of the statement as a whole.[22]

If Strawson is right, truth realism cannot come up with the ontological facts it needs for correspondence. For the truth realist holds that the statement as a whole corresponds to a fact, an objective relatum that makes it true. Strawson concludes that "the demand that there should be such a relatum . . . is logically absurd."[23]

In "The Structure and Content of Truth" (given as the Dewey Lectures in 1989), Donald Davidson disavows correspondence. He commends C. I. Lewis for having "challenged the correspondence theorist to locate the fact, or part of reality, or of the world, to which a true statement corresponds" and quotes with approval Strawson's verdict that the idea of "truth-making facts" is logically absurd. Davidson, too, comes to the conclusion that correspondence theories are "incomprehensible" and not "merely false."[24]

Note that both Davidson and Strawson believe that the truth realist's failure to meet C. I. Lewis's challenge is due to the essential *unintelligibility* of the idea of a nonlinguistic correlate to truth. This strong doctrine—that the very idea of ontological "truth-making" facts is incoherent—should have aroused more suspicion: one must wonder about the cogency of a challenge to produce X followed by the communiqué that X is not the sort of thing that could *possibly* be produced. And indeed, when one looks into the matter, one finds that the challenge to truth realism was made in such a way as to doom the search for the ontological relatum to failure. We shall see that the Lewis-Strawson-Davidson requirement to locate something in the world that makes a true statement true, and the subsequent declaration that the failure to locate it is fatal to correspondence theory, betray confusion about the nature of existence.

III. Truth-Making Facts

What follows is less anecdotal and more closely argued. My hope is that nonphilosophers, bemused by the facility with which the cultural left makes use of arcane philosophical arguments in its own pursuit of cultural hegemony, will not mind taking the trouble to read my argument (though, indeed, some parts are only there for the record and may safely be skimmed or skipped). After all, the campus insurgents, looking for ways to license their assault on traditional education, certainly do spend some of their nights making what sense they can of Lacan or Derrida or Rorty. Fortunately, the realist antidotal position is by its nature not a mystifying doctrine, and its central principles can be made accessible to any cultivated person. Or so I hope the reader will find.

The assault on objectivity is an assault on the idea that a proper education delivers to us the facts that make our true statements true. One way of subverting objectivity is to deny the very idea of truth-making facts. Accordingly, *defending* the ideal of objective truth—and with it the classical ideal of a nonsophistical education—requires us to clarify the notion of a truth-making fact. It requires much more, but that much is basic.

What a fact is cannot be made clear before we get clear about existence and nonexistence. For it is plain, on *any* account of truth, that the existence of elks is the fact responsible for the truth of 'There are elks' and that the nonexistence of elves is the fact responsible for the truth of 'There are no elves'. Since these are good specimens of "truth-making" facts, the genuinely challenging question concerning facts ought to have been: What do such referring phrases as 'the existence of elks' and 'the nonexistence of elves' refer to? The clearest answer puts one in a good position to see that those who announced the demise of correspondence were overly hasty. More to the point, since statements like 'Elks exist but elves do not exist' are nontrivial truths, it is plain that existence and nonexistence (of elks, of elves, etc.) are real, nontrivial properties, admirably suited for the truth-making role played by the objective, nonlinguistic correlates of a classical correspondence theory of truth.

In what follows I outline a defense of a realist conception of truth that (1) shows how to meet the main objection to the idea of a nonlinguistic relatum for correspondence, and (2) offers a conception of facts in the full spirit of a realist or correspondence theory of truth.

A realist conception of truth

We come first, then, to the therapeutic task of dealing with the arguments of the sophistical detractors of truth realism and correspondence. Our aim here is not to prove metaphysical realism but to give a proper version of it that is not subject to the Strawson-Davidson indictment that realist conceptions of truth are incoherent and that correspondence to fact is "an idea without content."

The clue to a proper understanding of truth realism is to be found by attending to such simple truth-making facts as the existence of elks and the nonexistence of elves. The existence of elks is a positive fact; the nonexistence of elves is a negative fact. Since these facts are nontrivial, it must be that the existence of elks and the nonexistence of elves are *nontrivial properties*. But this puts any student of philosophy on immediate alert. For Immanuel Kant has warned us never to think of existence as a property of the things that exist. The temptation to think of existence as a property on a par with other properties is hard to resist. We may call it Anselm's Apple. St. Anselm (1033–1109) argued that God must exist since he is by definition a perfect being and so must have all the properties of a perfect being. Were it true that God did not exist, we should have the contradiction that a perfect being lacked one of the attributes that a perfect being must have, since an all-powerful, all-knowing, etc. being that lacked existence, would hardly be perfect. Anselm's argument for the existence of God has been known as the "ontological argument." Many a philosopher has been tempted to bite into Anselm's Apple, following him into fallacy by treating existence as an attribute or property of that which is said to exist.

Kant refuted Anselm's "ontological proof" by showing that we should never think of existence as a property of what exists. Suppose, argued Kant, I think of a dollar bill, and then think of it as crumpled. My concept of a crumpled dollar bill is now more determinate and rich: I have added BEING CRUMPLED to my original idea of the thing. But now suppose I wish to enrich my original thought by thinking of the dollar bill as *existent*. That, says Kant, adds nothing: my idea of an existing dollar bill adds nothing to my idea of a dollar bill; the concept of a dollar bill and the concept of a dollar bill that exists are one and the same concept.

We may put Kant's point in several ways:

(1) While 'is a crumpled dollar bill' is a richer, more determinate predicate than 'is a dollar bill', 'is an existent dollar bill' is no richer than 'is a dollar bill'.

(2) "Existence is not a real predicate." That is, it does not signify a property of a thing that contributes to our idea of its character. For example, 'is a perfect being that exists' does not add to our concept of a PERFECT BEING.

(3) "By however many predicates we may think a thing . . . we do not make the least addition to the thing when we further declare that the thing *is*. . . . When, therefore, I think of a being as a supreme reality, without any defect, the question still remains whether it exists or not." (Kant, *Critique of Pure Reason,* A598–B630)

Consider a hungry elk. It is hungry and it exists. Being hungry is a property or state of the elk but existing is not. Since Kant, philosophers have learned to avoid the temptation to say that the existence of elks characterizes them. This is even more clear when we consider nonexistence. Elves do *not* exist. But we are not tempted to say that the nonexistence of elves is a property or characteristic of elves. So, too, must we refrain from thinking of existence as a property of elks.

That elks exist and that elves do not exist are nontrivial truths made true by the existence of elks and the nonexistence of elves. So the first thing to say of existence and nonexistence is that they are nontrivial properties but *not of the things that are said to exist or not to exist.* Just as the nonexistence of elves is not a property of elves, so the existence of elks is not a property of elks. What, then, are they properties of? To this question the realist has a plain answer: (the fact of) elk-existence and (the fact of) elf-nonexistence are properties of the real world. According to this view, facts of existence and nonexistence characterize the world.

We normally make our judgments with respect to the real world or some spatiotemporal region. Any world (or world region) is a totality characterized by the presence of certain things and by the absence of certain things. For example, the contemporary world is positively characterized by the presence of elks, of snow, of oceans, of salinity, of happiness, of misery, of animal life, of Boston, of President Clinton, etc. It is negatively characterized by the absence of elves, of Winston Churchill, of Atlantis, etc. Any truth claim is a positive or negative existential judgment of presence or absence with respect to a world under consideration. The "world" which is the domain of the claim may be quite limited. Thus, I may look into a drawer and say 'There are no scissors', thereby claiming that the little region of reality consisting of the objects in the drawer is characterized by the nonexistence of scissors. Quite often the domain of the claim (the DC) is the whole world. To say that some boy admires every astronaut is to claim that the world is characterized by the presence of a boy who admires every astronaut. The DC need not be a real world. For example, we make truth claims about the realm of Greek mythology (an unreal world, characterized by the existence of flying horses and the nonexistence of flying kangaroos), or about works of fiction, as when we say 'Sherlock Holmes was not poor'. When I say 'There no longer are any saber-toothed tigers', I claim that the contemporary world is characterized by the nonexistence of saber-toothed tigers. The DC is a past world when I make a historical claim that saber-toothed tigers roamed North America tens of thousands of years ago. Anything in the world under consideration is a thing, a mere "existent," in the trivial, uninformative sense that Kant derided. In the *informative* sense, to exist or to fail to exist is to characterize the world by *specified* presence or absence. The existence of elks and the nonexistence of elves are properties of the real world, a world characterized by the presence of elks and the absence of elves. Nontrivial existence as an attribute of the world is always specified presence (for example, *elk*-existence); nontrivial nonexistence is specified absence (for example, *elf*-nonexistence).

Let 'Q' be a proper name or descriptive term. Call a world that has (one or more) Q (things) in it, "{Q}ish." Call it "un{Q}ish" if none of its constituents is (a) Q (thing). Consider my office. In it there is a gray desk, books, a computer. There is no copier in my office, no cat, no stove, and so on. Let O be the "world" under consideration (the office). Then O is {gray desk}ish, {Sommers}ish, un{cat}ish, and un{Quine}ish. The wider contemporary world is {elk}ish, {Quine}ish, un{immortal man}ish, and un{elf}ish. {Elk}ishness—the existence of elks—and {Quine}ishness—the existence of Quine—are positive attributes of the world. Un{elf}ishness—the nonexistence of elves—and un{Santa Claus}ishness—the nonexistence of Santa Claus—are negative attributes of the world. The world's {Quine}ishness makes 'Quine exists' true, while 'There is no Santa Claus' is made true by the world's un{Santa Claus}ishness.

The besetting temptation to attribute existence to things that exist comes from a use of 'to be' that Aristotle called 'being *haplos*', which has been variously rendered 'being without qualification', 'being *tout court*', and 'being *simpliciter*'. Thus, I might understand 'Tame tigers are' to say 'Being characterizes tame tigers', thereby taking a bite from Anselm's Apple by attributing existence to tame tigers. The "mondial" conception of existence (existence as a property of the world) prohibits all talk of existence (nonexistence) *tout court* or *simpliciter*. Instead, we understand 'Tame tigers are' or 'Tame tigers exist' to say that something is a tame tiger. 'Something is a Q' signifies, not existence *tout court,* but the existence of a Q (something being a Q). Here we use 'being' as 'being-so-and-so' (what the Scholastics called 'being *secundum quid*').[25] Abjuring all talk of existence *tout court*, while allowing talk of the existence (nonexistence), in the mondial sense, of {Q}ishness or un{Q}ishness, interdicts the attribution of mere existence ('being *haplos*') to *things*. For we are now confined to talk of Q-existence and Q-nonexistence as mondial attributes, attributes possessed by a world characterized by the presence or absence of (a) Q.

Thus, facts like the existence of elks ({elk}ishness) and the nonexistence of elves (un{elf}ishness) are characteristics of the world. Such facts are not *in* the world but existential states *of* the world. Holding fast to this doctrine delivers us from temptation: we have got free of the thought that facts are something we might find "in the world." The search for such "facts" is indeed futile. Quine's presence is a fact, but while Quine himself is present in the world, Quine's *presence* is not present in the world—any more so than Santa's absence. Quine's properties (e.g., his acumen, his pertinacity, his repute, etc.) may be thought of as being in the world, but to think of Quine's presence or any other fact as being in the world is to take another bite from Anselm's Apple by thinking of Quine's existence as just another property of Quine.

We can now see why the Lewis-Strawson-Davidson challenge to the correspondence theorists to locate the facts that make true statements true was an improper challenge that could not possibly have been met by the truth realists. Consider the existence of mangy cats. This is the fact that makes 'Some cats are mangy' true. Strawson asserts that such facts are "pseudo entities," entities that could never be "found in the world." With this the truth realists agree: there are mangy cats in the world, but there is nothing in the world like "their existence." Strawson's arguments against Austin's correspondence theory were well directed against the latter's misguided attempt to identify facts with "historic situations" in the world. Strawson showed that Austin's *in-world correspondence theory* was indeed untenable. Unfortunately, Strawson and Davidson believed that in putting paid to in-world theories they had put paid to all theories that postulate "objective nonlinguistic" truth-making facts, leaving us, as Davidson says, with "nothing interesting or instructive to which true statements might correspond."[26] But that is a profound error.

Both Strawson and Davidson have failed to see that facts are objective properties *of* (not *in*) the world and that the original demand on correspondence theories to "locate facts" imposed an impossible adequacy-condition on correspondence theories of truth. They were thus led to the strong verdict that correspondence theories are "unintelligible," "logically absurd," and "without content."

Note that Strawson's and Davidson's verdict that the idea of an objective fact in the world was without content is very much like Kant's verdict against the idea of existence as a property of things on a par with other properties of things in the world. And, indeed, Davidson and Strawson have in effect rediscovered that the facts—the existence and nonexistence of things—cannot logically be thought of as being in the world. Unfortunately, because they remained unaware that their negative judgment about facts *was* tantamount to a rediscovery of Kant's healthy skepticism concerning existence as a property of things in the world, they failed to see that philosophy still faced the challenge of specifying a sense for the existence and nonexistence of things that serve as truth-making facts.[27] Lacking, as they thought, any plausible candidates for the ontological side of correspondence, Strawson and Davidson prematurely concluded that correspondence-to-fact was a mystifying, futile doctrine that needed to be abandoned. The idea that the facts of existence and nonexistence are truth-making, nontrivial properties, not of things *in* the world but of the world itself, seems to have escaped them altogether.

A word about "representations"

Like Strawson, Davidson jettisons truth-making facts. He then goes on to recommend that mental representations of facts be jettisoned as well:

> If we give up facts as entities that make sentences true, we ought to give up representations at the same time, for the legitimacy of each depends on the legitimacy of the other.[28]

The truth realist will point out that nothing has been given up, since the whole idea of a "mirror" to the facts is a mistake of those who have not got free of the idea that objective facts, if such there be, must be in the world. Both Davidson and Rorty tie the fate of "representations" to the fate of truth-making facts. Both therefore announce a double victory over the truth realist. Not only does he lose facts, he also loses "representations" of them. But a classical correspondence theory tied to existence and nonexistence as nontrivial mondial attributes is unaffected on both counts. We picture, represent, or mirror things that are in the world. Elks are in the world, but their presence is not. (We represent elks; we do not represent their presence. Nor, a fortiori, do we represent the absence of elves.) Elk-presence and elf-absence are objective truth-making mondial attributes. The philosopher with a clear notion of fact as presence and absence is the last one to be tempted to think of propositional content as "representing" the ontological correlate to which it "corresponds." Rorty's and Davidson's objections to a "mirror" semantics thus miss their primary target.

IV. How We Experience Facts

Apperception

Commonly, the domain of a claim is not the whole world but the region of reality in one's immediate vicinity. Looking for matches in my kitchen fixes the domain as the totality of objects in my kitchen. If I fail to find any, my claim 'There are no matches' would be made true by the fact that the totality of things in the region under consideration is characterized by the nonexistence of matches. If I come upon some matches, I have two kinds of experiences:

(1) I see the matches.

(2) I see that there are some matches.

In both cases my experience is "objective." But we distinguish between perceiving something in the region as a match (object perception) and "apperceiving" the region itself as {match}ish (mondial or propositional perception). If I find no matches, I may conclude there are none. In that case I apperceive the world under consideration as un{match}ish.

In apperception, I take the world as {Q}ish or as un{Q}ish. Apperception is epistemically as fundamental as the perception of objects; it is not necessarily dependent on object perception. The experience of *absence* illuminates the independence. Not finding matches, I (rightly or wrongly) apperceive my little world as un{match}ish. Looking for Pierre in the restaurant, Sartre keenly experiences his not being there; he apperceives the "world" as un{Pierre}ish. Neglect of apperception as a special but fundamental kind of objective experience leaves us without an empirically grounded conception of the facts that make true statements true. The effect on modern philosophy has been to discredit correspondence, undermining realism and giving preference to nonrealist conceptions of truth. Inattention to apperception also obscures the nature of belief.

To apperceive the world as un{Pierre}ish just is to believe that Pierre is not there. So understood, belief is a mondial attitude; it is how we "take" the world to be. Explaining belief in terms of "taking" and "mistaking" treats "taking" as epistemically primitive. Taking something to be so and so ([ap]perceiving it as so and so) is primitive in the sense that it is the sort of thing any sentient creature does to objects in its environment and to the environment itself. It is what the gosling does when it takes Konrad Lorenz for its mother (perceiving him as its mother). It is what an anguished abandoned kitten does when it experiences its suddenly desolate world as un{mother}ish (apperceiving its world as un{mother}ish).

The object of belief

The credulous child takes the world to be {Santa}ish. But the belief in Santa Claus is commonly construed as a "propositional attitude" to what 'There is a Santa Claus' expresses. In the first way of describing the belief, the attitude is toward the world. In the second way of thinking about the belief, the attitude is toward a propositional content—THE EXISTENCE OF SANTA CLAUS (THAT THERE IS A SANTA CLAUS)—a propositional *characterization* of the world. My own preference is for thinking of belief as an attitude toward the world (taking or mistaking it for a {Santa}ish world). To view belief as an attitude toward a characterization of the world (taking the characterization to be veridical) is perhaps not wrong, but, for the present at least, philosophers are not notably clear about what entertaining a proposition consists of and what it means to have an attitude toward one. (This situation in the philosophy of mind is not improved by philosophers given to doing Speculative Neurology and talking about propositions as mental representations.)

Moreover, treating belief as an attitude toward a proposition may arbitrarily rule out allowing for animals having such beliefs. There seems to be no inconsistency in holding that a barking dog (apperceiving its environment as {intruder}ish) believes there is someone at the door, while denying that the dog entertains and has attitudes toward propositions. Propositional attitudes are problematic; attitudes toward the world are less so. The world is always with us, ready to be "taken" one way or another.

V. Why Modern Philosophy Erred on *Existence*

The neosophists reject truth-making facts. But of course they do not reject facts. The progenitor of modern philosophy of language, Gottlob Frege, explained how one may speak of facts while not admitting them as truth makers. Frege rejected correspondence; for him a "fact" was nothing but a true proposition (true thought). That influential doctrine played a determining role in licensing the "linguistic turn" away from truth realism. Oblivious to apperception and to truth-making facts, modern philosophers of language face the question posed by Davidson: the question of "how, given that we cannot get outside our beliefs and our language so as to find some test other than coherence, we can have knowledge and talk about an objective public world which is not of our making."[29] His latest answer, which applies Bayesian decision theory to a theory of linguistic interpretation, is to be found at the conclusion of "The Structure and Content of Truth." Putnam also rejects a classical correspondence truth-realism, characterizing a true sentence as one that the members of a linguistic community are justified in asserting. This gives us "a fact of the matter as to what the verdict would be if the conditions were sufficiently good, a verdict to which people would converge if we were reasonable." Eschewing the term "anti-realism," Putnam calls his view "a *human* kind of realism, a belief that there is a fact of the matter as to what is rightly assertible for us, as opposed to what is rightly assertible from the God's eye point of view so dear to the classical metaphysical realist."[30] Other philosophers are not so squeamish: Michael Dummett, for example, takes his own rejection of correspondence seriously, calling himself an "anti-realist."

Why has modern philosophy been so inattentive to the positive conception of existence and nonexistence as nontrivial mondial properties? I noted that Frege initiated a vogue of linguistically sublimating facts. All the same, I think that the ontological conception of facts as truth makers would have come to the fore had Frege not presented a distracting alternative account of nontrivial existence. Frege's proposal is that existence, like number, is a property of concepts. According to this, when I say there are no elves I attribute a property to the concept of being an elf: the property of having nothing falling under it.

> [E]xistence is analogous to number. Affirmation of existence is in fact nothing but the denial of the number naught. Because existence is a property of concepts the ontological argument for the existence of God breaks down.[31]

This passage shows how much, for better or for worse, modern philosophy of language owes to the circumstance that its origins lie in Frege's philosophy of mathematics. Construing existence and nonexistence as properties of concepts has kept analytic philosophy well away from a clear conception of facts as existential world attributes. The problem facing Frege was the same as the problem facing the post-Kantian truth realist. The existence of elks makes 'There are elks' true. But "existence is not a property." It is evident from Frege's remark about the ontological argument that he, too, was consciously addressing himself to the question posed by Kant's warning against attributing existence to things that exist: Of what, then, *do* we predicate existence nontrivially? Of the world, say the realists. Of concepts, says Frege. While not every philosopher of language accepted Frege's idea that existence was a property of concepts, this distracting doctrine diverted modern analytic philosophy from the path leading to a clear conception of existence that could serve for a classically realist account of truth.[32] Frege's doctrine that existence is a property of concepts will lead one to say of a newly discovered black hole that its existence does not characterize the world but the concept of a black hole—a neosophistical doctrine that offends against a sense of reality (a sense that is no longer as robust among philosophers as it once was).

VI. Existence and Reality

There is the world and there are the things that exist "in" it. What of the world itself? Should we speak of it, too, as existing? We need not do so. But if we do, we would be understood to say that a domain of worlds (some of which are {elf}ish, etc.) is characterized by the existence of our "actual" world with *its* peculiar properties ({elk}ishness, un{elf}ishness, etc.). As David Lewis recognized, one must then democratically allow for the existence of these other, "nonactual" worlds, all of which exist within the encompassing domain of worlds. On the other hand, we may abjure possible worlds and still think of the world as existing in a "singleton" domain of worlds. Saying that the world exists would then be understood as saying that the singleton domain of worlds contains it. Since that domain contains no *other* worlds, we should not have committed ourselves to a Lewis domain of many (possible) worlds, all of which exist alongside our actual world.

We do, of course, speak of the *real* or actual world, opposing it to fictional, mock, or nonactual domains. Mock domains (e.g., fantasy author J. R. R. Tolkien's world, or the fauna of Greek mythology) are expressive systems that exist as intensional human products *within* the world, in much the way a proposition or a symphonic composition does (see the appendix below). For the one-world actualist, any nonactual world is a human fabrication and as such exists in the real world as a cultural artifact.

As for the facts that make what we say true, we have seen that it is a profound mistake to think of *them* as constituents of the world. (Facts are *of* the world, not *in* it.) Nevertheless, as attributes of the real world, facts constitute a real domain in their own right. Our realist ontology has three different kinds of reality: the world, the things in it, and the facts of existence and nonexistence that characterize it. It is with respect to the totality of things that constitute the world that we say 'There is no such thing (in it) as an elf'. It is with respect to the facts that characterize the world that we say things like 'There is no such thing—no such fact—as the existence of elves'.

VII. Conclusion

The classical idea of an education that aims to introduce the student to a realm of objective knowledge is everywhere under fire. One expects critiques of objectivity from idealists, from Marxists, and from French intellectuals of almost any doctrinal coloring. But one does not expect an assault on objectivity to be grounded in doctrines of the analytical wing of modern Anglo-American philosophy. Yet that is what we are getting, and the champions of truth realism have yet to get their bearings. My aim in this essay was modest enough: polemically, to face the enemy that is us by confronting and rendering harmless the main sophistical charge that truth realism is incomprehensible and untenable; constructively, to sketch a realist theory that grounds truth in the facts of existence and nonexistence, providing an ideal of objectivity that is the aim of a traditional education. I argued for two kinds of objectivity. There is the reality of the things in the world and the reality of the world itself. These two realities are *experienced* in different ways. We perceive things in certain ways, and we apperceive the world in certain ways: we see and we believe.

The essay was limited in its purpose. It presented no arguments in favor of realism but confined itself to clearing away some obstacles to the acceptance of realism. It left a host of other questions untouched.[33]

The linguistic sublimation of objectivity has been accompanied by an equally fashionable assault on "rationality" and "logic" as socially constructed instruments of hegemonic control. The status one accords to rationality is intimately tied to the status of realism, but the essay was confined to the latter topic. Another question, avoided but not evaded, was whether it is possible to observe or to think of objects in the world in a way unmediated by theory. In my terms this is the question (deserving separate attention) of the extent to which apperception qualifies perception. (The thesis that perception is thoroughly "theory-laden" need not necessarily bear negatively on the central thesis of this essay. If, as Norwood Russell Hanson argued, the pre-Copernican sees a different sunset than the post-Copernican, this does not affect the realist doctrine that 'The sun is setting' is made true by the presence of a setting sun.)

The whole question of *moral* realism was not touched—though, here again, the topics are adjacent, since opening the way to a coherent realism of existential fact may clear a path for a realist conception of moral truths, thereby undercutting popular arguments for value relativity.

It is regrettable that coping with so large a theme in so a small a space made it inevitable to be telegraphic in dealing with complicated and subtle nonrealist doctrines. Unlike their classical precursors, the neo-sophist philosophers have well-wrought positions; for example, none is vulnerable to Plato's charge of not having an account of error. But it was no part of my present aim to compare realism to the various nonrealists' systems. I had first to present the plausible candidate that the nonrealists had said could not be there. Modern philosophers are fondest of calling their opponents' positions incoherent or "futile" rather than false. I have shown that truth realism is coherent; to my mind, the burden of argument has always rested with those who would claim it is false. In any case, before comparisons can be made, one must first establish a cogent theory of facts for the realist side.

I still believe that philosophers do their best work in ivory towers. But that is because I believe that even from a political standpoint some of the most consequential confrontations are "air battles," taking place far above the madding crowd. Philosophers who are concerned to influence education or public culture should look critically at the philosophical allies of the opposition. For when we find a rival philosophy providing sophisticated weapons to political opponents, we are alerted to what may be wrong with that philosophy, and we may be moved to subject it to professional scrutiny. It is in this spirit that one may be motivated to examine the new sophism whose philosophical proponents have inadvertently become party to undermining the learned public's faith in objective and disinterested inquiry and scholarship.

I am convinced that neosophism is a very harmful doctrine, and equally convinced that the harm is mainly inadvertent. A real gulf separates Nietzsche from the racist fascists who made use of some of his more extreme ideas. Very probably Nietzsche would have been appalled by his posthumous "disciples." All the same, one cannot help regretting that he did not express himself in ways that did not quite so readily lend his thought to abuse and misconstrual. There is even less doubt that philosophers like Quine and Kuhn are unhappy to find their views welcomed and cited by intellectual insurgents intent on "transforming knowledge" by unmasking a "capitalist, patriarchal hegemony" that is at the basis of traditional science and scholarship. But political tendentiousness has always been the nature of the sophist beast. Philosophers who keep supplying grist for the mills of academics who "do not view knowledge as a matter of getting reality right but rather a matter of acquiring habits of action for coping with reality"[34] cannot complain when they find themselves with an unwanted lay constituency.

Having always been a convinced realist myself, my primary motivations for criticizing the neosophists have not been political but philosophical. Even so, it pleases me in many ways to find the neosophist critique of realism as flawed as I suspected it to be.

Appendix

The text of this essay made use of a number of interrelated terms, among them 'proposition', 'true', 'corresponds', 'fact', 'expresses', 'signifies'—in such phrases as 'expresses a true proposition', 'signifies a fact', and 'corresponds to a fact'. In lieu of a glossary, I thought it best to explicate these terms discursively. This section appears as an appendix since the main argument is, I trust, accessible to the reader without it and since its inclusion in the body of the essay would be distracting.

Characterizations and characteristics

A statement is an asserted sentence, which is to say, it is a sentence uttered as a claim about the world. A true statement signifies a fact, the positive or negative existential world *characteristic* that makes it true. A false statement is vacuous with respect to signification: it fails to signify a fact. But any statement expresses a proposition that purports to characterize the domain under consideration. The proposition expressed is an existential *characterization* that may or may not be true of the world (may or may not "correspond to" a mondial *characteristic*). Propositions are human products. Saying something for the first time is like whistling a tune never before heard or thought of. The tune does not exist prior to the act of whistling it. Thereafter, it exists and may be whistled again. Similarly, the proposition expressed does not exist except as the product of an initial speech act, such as asserting a declarative sentence. But thereafter, like the tune, the expressed proposition is part of the world's (intensional) furniture. Having been expressed, it is there for anyone to repeat it.

Characterizations are "linguistic." Characteristics are "objective." Expressions denoting characteristics will be written here in lower-case letters. Expressions denoting characterizations will be written in upper-case letters. For example, 'There are elks' expresses the proposition THAT THERE ARE ELKS (THE EXISTENCE OF ELKS, THERE BEING ELKS, {ELK}ISHNESS). This proposition is a *characterization* that correctly characterizes ("is true of") the world. By contrast, the existence of elks (that there are elks, {elk}ishness) is a *characteristic,* a property that the world possesses. In the case of 'There are elks', the characterization expressed—{ELK}ISHNESS—*corresponds* to a (world) characteristic—{elk}ishness. In the case of 'There are elves', the false proposition THERE BEING ELVES does not correspond to any existential characteristic of the world.

Strawson pointed out that the terms of a statement connect up with reality, and he challenged Austin to show how the statement as a whole could do that. Here Strawson touched on an important feature of realist truth theory. For the classical truth-realist does treat statements as he treats terms. Both are thought of as characterizing expressions. But they characterize different aspects of reality: what nonvacuous terms characterize are *in* the world; true statements characterize the world.

A nonvacuous term, Q, expresses the characterization BEING Q; it signifies the characteristic of Q-ness; and it denotes one or more Q-things. For example, 'billionaire' expresses the characterization BEING A BILLIONAIRE; it signifies the characteristic of being a billionaire; and it denotes one or more things having the characteristic signified. Analogously, the true statement 'Someone is a billionaire' expresses the characterization SOMEONE BEING A BILLIONAIRE; it signifies the fact of someone being a billionaire; and it denotes one or more things having the characteristic signified.

Terms come in contrary pairs. 'Wise' and 'billionaire' express positive characterizations; 'unwise' and 'nonbillionaire' express negative characterizations. Statements come in contradictory pairs. 'Someone is a billionaire' expresses a positive (propositional) characterization; 'No one is a billionaire' expresses a negative characterization. The statement 'Some Swede is poor' signifies the fact of someone being a poor Swede. The realist construes this fact to be the existence of a poor Swede. Similarly, the statement 'No Swede is a trillionaire' signifies 'no Swede being a trillionaire', which is just the fact of the nonexistence of Swedish trillionaires. Thus, just as 'poor Swede' signifies the characteristic of being a poor Swede, denoting whatever has this characteristic, so does 'Some Swede is poor' signify the characteristic of being {poor Swede}ish, denoting whatever has that characteristic. Since {poor Swede}ishness characterizes the world, the truth realist holds that 'Some Swede is poor' *denotes the world*. But so too do 'Some Texan is a billionaire' and 'No Texan is a trillionaire'—since these statements also signify existential characteristics of the world. In general, different true statements signify different facts, but all true statements denote the world.

FACTS and facts

'Some Texans are billionaires' expresses the true proposition THAT SOME TEXANS ARE BILLIONAIRES. Adhering to our upper-case convention, we may speak of this as a FACT. FACTS are true propositions, *expressed* or *stated* by true sentences. According to the truth realist, FACTS correspond to and are made true by facts.

FACTS correspond to facts. This gives us two ways of stating the truth conditions for a statement, 'S':

'S' is true if and only if 'S' expresses a FACT.

'S' is true if and only if 'S' signifies a fact.

Any statement makes a claim about a domain. Just as a nonvacuous term, K, signifies a characteristic (being K) and denotes a thing that has the characteristic in question (a K-thing), so a true statement, which expresses a true characterization and signifies a fact or world characteristic, denotes the world so characterized. This gives us a *third* way of stating the truth conditions of a statement:

'S' is true if and only if 'S' denotes its domain.

True statements denote the world. False statements are vacuous; they fail to denote the world.

Different true statements, like different nonvacuous terms, signify different characteristics. In 'An Athenian philosopher who influenced Plato was snubnosed', the nonvacuous terms 'Athenian philosopher' and '(someone) who influenced Plato' signify different characteristics, but both denote Socrates. So too, true statements like 'There are elks' and 'There are no elves' signify different (existential world) characteristics, different facts ({elk}ishness, un{elf}ishness), but both statements denote one and the same world.

The key elements in the above account of statement meaning and realist truth conditions are:

'S'   (a statement or asserted sentence)
[S]   (the proposition THAT S; the proposition expressed by 'S')
<s>   (the fact, if any, that s)
W   (the world)

In the favorable case, these elements are related as follows:

[S] characterizes W (is true of W, "obtains," is a FACT or true proposition)
<s> is a characteristic of W (is a fact)
[S] corresponds to <s>
'S' signifies <s>
'S' denotes W
'S' is true

NOTES

1. Logical positivism is a branch of analytic philosophy that criticizes traditional philosophy for allowing itself to be occupied with "meaningless" questions to which no verified answer can be given. For example, some positivists held that questions concerning the existence of God or the reality of an afterlife are pseudo-questions unworthy of being discussed, since they are practically unverifiable and, therefore, to all intents and purposes, meaningless. The logical positivists, who also called themselves "logical empiricists," prided themselves on their rigorous use of logic and on their critical methods. Though the positivists' theory of meaning is no longer accepted, their careful analytic techniques and their attention to language and meaning have become a feature of Anglo-American philosophy.
2. Richard Rorty's most accessible book is *Contingency, Irony, and Solidarity* (Cambridge: Cambridge University Press, 1989).

3. Richard Rorty, *Objectivity, Relativism, and Truth* (Cambridge: Cambridge University Press, 1991), p. 22.

4. John Searle, "The Storm Over the University," *New York Review of Books,* December 6, 1990, p. 40.

5. *The Politics of Liberal Education,* ed. Darryl J. Gless and Barbara Herrnstein Smith (Durham: Duke University Press, 1992).

6. Searle, "The Storm Over the University," p. 40.

7. Thomas Kuhn's major work, *The Structure of Scientific Revolutions,* 2d ed. (Chicago: University of Chicago Press, 1970), argued that scientific progress was not so much a march to objective truth about nature as a series of revolutions highly conditioned by paradigmatic and often revolutionary ways of viewing the world. Norwood Russell Hanson, most notably in his *Patterns of Discovery* (Cambridge: Cambridge University Press, 1958), had earlier criticized the traditional view that scientific theories are confirmed by the observation of facts. According to Hanson and Kuhn, observations bearing on a theory are never neutral, since the facts themselves are not given independently of the theory they are meant to confirm. The views of Kuhn and Hanson are often cited by those who would deny the objective authority of science. Cf. Peter Novick, *That Noble Dream: The "Objectivity Question" and the American Historical Profession* (Cambridge: Cambridge University Press, 1988), ch. 15.

8. Searle, "The Storm Over the University," p. 39; quoting from George Levine et al., *Speaking for the Humanities* (New York: American Council of Learned Societies, 1989).

9. Searle, "The Storm Over the University," p. 36.

10. Sandra Harding, *The Science Question in Feminism* (Ithaca and London: Cornell University Press, 1986), p. 183.

11. Alison M. Jaggar and Susan R. Bordo, eds., *Gender/Body/Knowledge: Feminist Reconstructions of Being and Knowing* (New Brunswick: Rutgers University Press, 1989), pp. 3–4.

12. *Ibid.*

13. Joyce Trebilcot, "Dyke Methods," *Hypatia,* vol. 3, no. 2 (Summer 1988), p. 3.

14. Donald W. Harward, "Resisting Authority," *Wooster, A Quarterly Magazine for Alumni and Friends of the College of Wooster,* vol. 101, no. 2 (Fall 1986).

15. Donald Davidson, "The Structure and Content of Truth," *Journal of Philosophy,* vol. 87, no. 6 (June 1990), p. 305.

16. Rorty, *Objectivity, Relativism, and Truth,* p. 31n.

17. See also Plato, *Euthydemus,* 283e, and *Cratylus,* 385b, for similar formulations of truth.

18. Alfred Tarski, "The Semantic Conception of Truth," *Philosophy and Phenomenological Research,* vol. 4 (1944), p. 342. Tarski also speaks of sentences "describing" "states of affairs" (*ibid.,* p. 345).

19. Davidson, "The Structure and Content of Truth," p. 304.

20. *Ibid.,* p. 303.

21. Gottlob Frege, "The Thought: A Logical Inquiry," *Mind,* vol. 65 (1956), pp. 289–311; P. F. Strawson, "Truth," in *Logico-Linguistic Papers* (London: Methuen, 1971).

22. Strawson, "Truth," pp. 194–95.

23. *Ibid.*, p. 194.
24. Davidson, "The Structure and Content of Truth," p. 309.
25. For an account of the Scholastic distinction between 'being *simpliciter*' and 'being *secundum quid*', see C. J. F. Williams, *What is Existence?* (Oxford: Clarendon Press, 1981), p. 4.
26. Davidson, "The Structure and Content of Truth," p. 306.
27. Frege saw the need for a positive account of existence, and his solution was to treat attributions of existence as he treated attributions of number. See note 31.
28. Davidson, "The Structure and Content of Truth," p. 304.
29. Donald Davidson, "A Coherence Theory of Truth and Knowledge," in *Truth and Interpretation: Perspectives on the Philosophy of Donald Davidson,* ed. Ernest LePore (Oxford: Blackwell, 1986), p. 310.
30. Hilary Putnam, *Realism and Reason, Philosophical Papers,* vol. 3 (New York: Cambridge University Press, 1983), p. xviii.
31. G. Frege, *Die Grundlagen der Arithmetik,* published with English translation by J. L. Austin *en face* as *The Foundations of Arithmetic* (Oxford: Basil Blackwell, 1952).
32. For an excellent sympathetic discussion of the doctrine that existence is an attribute of concepts, see Williams, *What Is Existence?*, ch. 2.
33. In particular, I did not consider any of the objections to realism and correspondence that derive from such Quinian doctrines as the indeterminacy of reference and translation, truth holism, or the rejection of the analytic/synthetic distinction—doctrines that cast doubt on the possibility that any sentence, taken individually, can be said to denote or correspond to something "out there." See W. V. Quine, "On What There Is," in Quine, *From a Logical Point of View,* 2d ed. (Cambridge: Harvard University Press, 1961); and Quine, *Ontological Relativity and Other Essays* (New York: Columbia University Press, 1969).
34. Rorty, *Objectivity, Relativism, and Truth,* p. 1.

Contributors

Howard Dickman is a Senior Staff Editor at *Reader's Digest*. He received his Ph.D. in History from the University of Michigan in 1977, and has written numerous articles and reviews for magazines and scholarly journals. He is also the author of *Industrial Democracy in America: Ideological Origins of National Labor Relations Policy* (1987), and the co-editor of *Liberty, Property, and the Foundations of the American Constitution* (1989), *Liberty, Property, and Government: Constitutional Interpretation before the New Deal* (1989), and *Liberty, Property, and the Future of Constitutional Development* (1990).

Daniel Bonevac is Professor and Chair of the Department of Philosophy at the University of Texas at Austin. He received his Ph.D. from the University of Pittsburgh in 1980. He is the author of *Reduction in the Abstract Sciences* (1982), *Deduction* (1987), and *The Art and Science of Logic* (1990), the editor of *Today's Moral Issues* (1992), and a co-editor (with William Boon and Stephen Phillips) of *Beyond the Western Tradition* (1992). He has published articles on Kant, metaphysics, semantics, and philosophical logic.

Stanley Rothman is Mary Huggins Gamble Professor of Government at Smith College and Director of the Center for the Study of Social and Political Change. He received his Ph.D. in Government from Harvard University. He is the author of *European Society and Politics* (1970), and the coauthor of *Soviet Politics and Society* (1977) and *Roots of Radicalism* (1982). His most recent books include *The Media Elite* (1986), *The IQ Question, The Media and Public Policy* (1988), *Watching America: What Television Tells Us about Our Lives* (1991), and *The Mass Media in Liberal Democratic Societies* (1992). He is also the author or coauthor of over 120 articles in professional journals, and has written reviews and articles for such magazines as *Commentary, The New Leader,* and *The Columbia Journalism Review.*

Seymour Martin Lipset is Hazel Professor of Public Policy at George Mason University and Senior Fellow of the Hoover Institution at Stanford University. He has held endowed chairs at Stanford (1975–1992) and Harvard (1965–1975). He has been President of both the American Sociological Association and the American Political Science Association, and has been elected to honorific societies in the United States and abroad: the National Academy of Sciences, the American Philosophical Society, the National Academy of Education, and the American Academy of Arts and Sciences. He has received honorary degrees from various American and foreign universities, including the Hebrew University of Jerusalem, the University of Buenos Aires, and the University of Brussels. He is the author or coauthor of twenty-one books or monographs and has edited twenty-four others.

Eric Mack is Professor of Philosophy at Tulane University and a faculty member of Tulane's Murphy Institute of Political Economy. He has published numerous articles in moral, political, and legal philosophy, especially on such topics as the foundation of natural rights, property rights and economic justice, contractual rights, anarchism, the moral status of bad samaritans, and the morality of killing innocents in the course of self-defense. His essays have appeared in such journals as *Ethics, Philosophical Studies, Philosophy & Public Affairs,* and *The Monist,* and in many scholarly anthologies.

Lino A. Graglia is A. Dalton Cross Professor of Law at the University of Texas School of Law, where he teaches constitutional law, civil rights, and antitrust. He is a graduate of Columbia Law School (L.L.B. 1954), where he was an editor of the law review, and of City College of New York (B.A. 1952). Upon graduation from law school, he served as an attorney in the Department of Justice in Washington, D.C., for three years, and then was in private practice in Washington and New York City for nine years. He has taught at Texas since 1966. His books include *Disaster by Decree: The Supreme Court Decisions on Race and the Schools* (1976), a critical analysis of Supreme Court decision making and of the decisions that led to busing for school racial balance. He speaks and writes on issues of judicial review, constitutional interpretation, racial discrimination, and antitrust.

Alan Charles Kors is Professor of History at the University of Pennsylvania, where he teaches seventeenth- and eighteenth-century European intellectual history. He is the author and editor of several works in that field, the most recent of which is *Atheism in France, 1650–1729: The Orthodox Sources of Disbelief* (1990). He has received two awards for distinguished college teaching, and he co-founded the residential college-house system at the University of Pennsylvania. In July 1991, he was confirmed by the United States Senate to the National Council on the Humanities.

Joseph Hamburger is Peletiah Perit Professor of Political and Social Science, Emeritus, at Yale University. He is currently a Fellow at the Woodrow Wilson International Center for Scholars in Washington, D.C. He is the author of *James Mill and the Art of Revolution* (1963), *Intellectuals in Politics: John Stuart Mill and the Philosophic Radicals* (1965), and *Macaulay and the Whig Tradition* (1976), and coauthor (with Lotte Hamburger) of *Troubled Lives: John and Sarah Austin* (1985) and *Contemplating Adultery: The Secret Life of a Victorian Woman* (1991). His current work focuses on J. S. Mill's argument for liberty in relation to his views about religion.

Jerry L. Martin has been at the National Endowment for the Humanities since 1987 and currently serves as Acting Chairman. He received his Ph.D. in Philosophy from Northwestern University in 1970. A faculty member at the University of Colorado at Boulder from 1967 to 1982, he served as chairman of the Philosophy Department and as founding director of the University's Center for the Study of Values and Social Policy. From 1982 to 1987, he served as a Mellon Congressional Fellow and as a legislative assistant to then–Congressman Hank Brown of Colorado. He has written and lectured on topics in epistemology, the philosophy of mind, ethics, political philosophy, and public policy. His articles have appeared in *The Philosophical Forum, Man and World,* and *Philosophy: The Journal of the Royal Institute of Philosophy*.

Fred Sommers is Harry A. Wolfson Professor of Philosophy at Brandeis University. He is the author of numerous articles on metaphysics, logic, and philosophy of language. His book *The Logic of Natural Language* was published by Oxford University Press in 1982.

Index